Revisioning Duras

Film, Race, Sex

Revisioning Duras

Film, Race, Sex

edited by
James S. Williams

with the assistance
of Janet Sayers

LIVERPOOL UNIVERSITY PRESS

First published 2000 by
LIVERPOOL UNIVERSITY PRESS
Liverpool L69 7ZU

British Library Cataloguing-in-Publication Data
A British Library CIP Record is available

ISBN 0-85323-546-5 (hardback)
0-85323-556-2 (paperback)
Typeset in Minion
by BBR, Sheffield
Printed by Redwood Books, Trowbridge

Contents

Part III: Sex

Acknowledgements

We would like to thank the following for their generous support of this project: the French Institute, London; the School of European Culture and Languages, University of Kent; the Social Sciences Faculty, University of Kent, and the *Journal of European Studies*. Chapter 7 is a shorter and modified version of a chapter in Martin Crowley's *Duras, Writing, and the Ethical* (Oxford University Press, 2000), and we are grateful to the publisher for granting us permission to use this material. Chapter 10 is a significantly revised version of a chapter in Alex Hughes's *Heterographies: sexual difference in French autobiography* (Berg, 2000), and we would like to thank the publisher for allowing us to publish this material. Finally, stills from the films of Marguerite Duras are reproduced by kind permission of Jean Mascolo.

Contributors

James Creech Professor of French, Miami University, Ohio

Martin Crowley Lecturer in French, University of Cambridge

Wendy Everett Senior Lecturer in French and Film Studies, University of Bath

Renate Günther Lecturer in French, University of Sheffield

Marie-Paule Ha Associate Professor of Comparative Literature, University of Hong Kong

Owen Heathcote Senior Lecturer in French, University of Bradford

Gill Houghton PhD student in Visual Arts, Goldsmith's College, University of London

Alex Hughes Professor of French Studies, University of Birmingham

Kate Ince Lecturer in French Studies, University of Birmingham

Catherine Rodgers Senior Lecturer in French, University of Wales Swansea

James S. Williams Senior Lecturer in French, University of Kent at Canterbury

INTRODUCTION

Revisioning Duras

James S. Williams

> Je dis simplement: il faut la [Duras] lire. Encore. Et l'aimer encore davantage. Il suffit de la lire pour être aimé d'elle. (Y. Andréa)

Few women writers or intellectuals of the postwar period have provoked such extremes of response as Marguerite Duras. During her lifetime, when she became the most widely read living French author, she was the object both of adulation and denigration in France. On the one hand, she enjoyed the loyal and public support of friends, critics and exegetes such as Michelle Porte, Michèle Manceaux, Christiane Blot-Labarrère and Madeleine Borgomano.[1] She was also championed, almost obsessively, by Alain Vircondelet, who wrote the first major study of her work in 1972.[2] His subsequent hagiographical *Marguerite Duras: vérité et légendes*, complete with photographs selected by Duras's son Jean Mascolo, is very much the official version of the Duras story in which he upbraids her detractors.[3] Such empathy and even collusion with the word of Duras is matched in *La fiction d'Emmedée*, a highly fictional portrayal of Duras by Jean-Pierre Ceton, a younger writer whom she had promoted during the 1980s along with Denis Belloc.[4] On the other hand, however, many critics have taken the view of the writer and journalist Angelo Rinaldi that Duras became a sorry casualty of the French literary star system which simply indulged and exacerbated her narcissism. Her apparent self-absorption and overexposure during the 1980s was put under a harsh microscope by Frédérique Lebelley in *Duras ou le poids d'une plume*, which Duras tried to prevent from being published.[5] In France her literary style has been comprehensively pastiched and parodied, or simply dismissed, by Philippe Sollers among others, as symptomatic of a late twentieth-century writer.[6]

Certainly, the reception of Duras's work in France has run along familiar political lines. Margaret Sankey has shown how, after the publication in 1984 of the autobiographical novel *L'amant*, winner of the Prix Goncourt and a world bestseller, the media focus on Duras's life led to her progressive rejection as an icon of the Mitterrand Left (her belittling, for example, in *Le Nouvel Observateur* and *Le Canard Enchaîné*), at the same time as her recuperation by the Right as both the 'great woman writer' and 'éternal rebel' (*Le Figaro*) on account of her tendency for ill-considered remarks on topics ranging from politics to drugs and football, remarks which served effectively to strengthen the status quo. Sankey argues convincingly that the Left really failed to understand Duras's relation to politics: 'To expect Duras ... to adhere to any given political line is to misunderstand her focus, and this would explain the rather exasperated, impatient nature of some of the comments made about her in the more left-wing newspapers'.[7] It is precisely the hyperbolic tone and singular lack of compromise in Duras's media performances which the feminist critic Marcelle Marini, for one, has celebrated. Referring in particular to Duras's controversial intervention in the 'Petit Grégory' affair, an article in *Libération* in 1985 entitled 'Sublime, forcément sublime Christine V.',[8] where Duras proposed Villemin as the killer of her own son even though the case was still sub judice, Marini writes that Duras is the only female writer in the French tradition to have dared to present herself as a '*monstre sacré*', allying, often through osmosis, the grotesque with the sublime.[9]

How can we account for such a major polarization in attitudes towards Duras? Three years before Duras's death in 1996, Marilyn Schuster 'revisited' Duras's work from a specifically American perspective and produced a useful summary of contrasts between Durasophiles and Durasophobes:

> To revisit Marguerite Duras in the last decade of the twentieth century is to revisit the contradictory and impassioned feelings about women that mark western culture. Durasophobes find her offensive because she goes too far, because she transgresses the boundaries of the feminine. Or, she doesn't go far enough, she reconfirms a masculine, masochistic, and misogynist future of woman. Durasophiles find her fascinating because she intently explores from within the 'dark content of female sexuality' that has shaped our culture. Or, because she unsettles and remaps female subjectivity and sexuality. Durasophobes parody the incessant repetition that marks her texts. Durasophiles are caught up in the hypnotic spell of a repetition that is never quite the same, and seem bound to reproduce it in their own texts.[10]

Schuster's own assessment of Duras's radicalism reflects some of these basic ambivalences, in particular regarding sexuality, race, Judaism and colonial identity. In her opinion, while Duras may destabilize the hegemonic figure of woman, she also exhibits a kind of fatalism that reconfirms the conservative, dominant order. One of the many paradoxes Schuster outlines is the fact that

Duras's texts display a gendered orientalism spoken from the margins by a subjectivity that cannot imagine a space for language or desire beyond the margins. This conclusion may be compared to the findings of oppositional Duras critics like Trista Selous, who argues that she is ultimately a conventional and 'monolithic' portrayer of masochistically-inclined *femmes fatales*.[11] According to Selous, the Duras reader, faced with a seamless discourse of unexplained narrative lacunae, or 'Blanks', is obliged to accept a masculine-encoded position and fantasize possible explanations for the 'other' desire of the female protagonists according to the clichéd rules of romantic fiction. In my own work, I have similarly contested Duras's wish to have it both ways, that is, to claim to be committed to the Other and the Outside while producing work that often performs in the opposite direction due to a compulsive rhetorical practice of appropriation, recuperation and sublimation.[12] Schuster ended her discussion, however, with the important and vital hope that 'in the long run Durasophobes and Durasophiles will draw back from their passions, from their own stakes in this figure of femininity, to recognize the power of her language and the caution of her tales'.[13] Is this now beginning to happen?

The special Duras issue of *La Nouvelle Revue Française* in March 1998 is emblematic of the level of personal reminiscence about Duras recorded over the last five years.[14] In a sense, however, this process simply extends and intensifies Duras's own consistent self-invention and self-mythologizing in later works like *L'amant*, where she knowingly and tantalizingly fused and confused her life and legend (a childhood brought up in the jungles of what was once French Indochina, a mother battling in vain against the tide of the Pacific Ocean, her experience in the French Resistance alongside Mitterrand, her period as a political radical and militant (including an appearance on the barricades in Paris during May 1968), a nearly fatal coma lasting five months in 1988–89, etc.). One could perhaps argue that this creative use of legend constitutes what Susan Cohen has claimed in Duras as a radical feminist strategy.[15] Yet it becomes increasingly hard to sustain such an approach following the pivotal publication by Gallimard in 1998 of Laure Adler's comprehensive biography entitled *Marguerite Duras*, which sheds further light on the making of the Duras legend and prevents any simple enshrining of Duras as a national literary icon. Drawing on the unedited material of eighteen boxes of documents transferred with Duras's own authorization to the Institut de la Mémoire de l'Edition Contemporaine (IMEC), Adler pieces together and confirms with minimum fuss what was already more or less generally known: that prior to joining the Resistance in September 1943 Duras worked for the collaborationist Vichy administration on the Commission for the Control of Printing Paper; that she had an affair with a German officer (Charles Delval) who had arrested her husband Robert Antelme (an event only half explored in *La douleur*); that, unbeknownst to Duras, her partner at the time, Dionys Mascolo, fell madly in love with Madame Delval with whom he had a child. Other less sensational and not unexpected facts are relayed by Adler, for instance, that Duras was actually highly meticulous in her revision of manuscripts, in direct contradiction of the final, manifesto-style statement in *Emily L.* that one should write in a single, continuous sweep and leave the results untouched.

It is not my intention here to judge the historical worth of Adler's biography which is already the object of much scrutiny and debate.[16] Of more immediate interest is the problem that Adler cannot help raise but which equally she does not resolve, namely, the particular link between Duras's life and her work. For a reactionary critic like Vircondelet, the life and work fit smoothly together, an approach that has led to misreadings and misunderstandings. For instance, in his 1991 biography of Duras, Duras's work is mined as a source of biographical information and a means of proving that she is both a lay mystic in the tradition of Pascal and a champion of the exploited.[17] In the introduction to his recent collection entitled *Duras, Dieu et l'écrit*, he even writes that Duras had loved and respected all the contributors—as if Duras's approval were a *sine qua non*.[18] Vircondelet's conformist and positivist approach is most evident, however, in *Marguerite à Duras* (1998), a rapidly produced account of Duras's early family links with the region of Duras in the Lot-et-Garonne from which she took her name. He writes with satisfaction that the area represents the missing piece of the jigsaw which Duras had so carefully constructed, particularly on account of the information it provides about the absent father.[19] Yet even in some of the other recently published and more theoretically sophisticated work on Duras, the biographical figure of Duras hovers inexorably and precariously. For example, in her introduction to a wide-ranging selection of previously published essays on Duras, Bettina Knapp ends up presenting Duras's work in largely personal terms.[20] Commenting, for instance, on Duras's unique style of displacements and blanks, Knapp writes: 'The voids existing in Duras's writing style, as noted by so many critics, paralleled a gaping abyss in her own life. She herself made mention of alcohol's corrosive effect on her writing style. During her periods of detoxification she actually experienced the blanks or blackouts her protagonists know.'[21] As if fully justified by Duras's own authorial statements, Knapp provides a short review of Duras's childhood and background in order to argue that this 'subversive provoker, always in search of the inaccessible—her past—remained, no matter her age, the archetypal *puella*'.[22]

This close identification of body with the literary corpus has been justified on the grounds that it operates whenever Duras talks about herself as a writer.

In fact, the theme is stretched to breaking point in Duras's last single-authored text, the slender yet searingly beautiful *C'est tout* which was virtually ignored when it first appeared and which concluded on a genuinely terrifying note: 'It's done, I think. My life is over./ I am nothing now./ I have become absolutely frightful./ I no longer hold together./ Come quick./ I have no mouth left, no face.'[23] If the dimensions of the absolute, of all or nothing, subtend most of Duras's work, there are no textual strategies left in *C'est tout* to mediate and offset their traumatic effect. The temptation would thus be to view the Duras corpus now as a 'dead body' and thereby to execute what Vircondelet blithely recommends (with the words of Duras's *L'été 80* in mind): 'all that is left to do is to write over, write on this "dead body" of Duras, her work, her life, her places'.[24] In her long afterword to the expanded and bilingual version of *C'est tout*, an eloquent and at times awestruck account of the text through reference to Duras's later life and work, Blot-Labarrère takes this logic to its inevitable conclusion. She states:

> This death in a book consorts with a death by the book: is it not the book which on 19 February 1996 demands in its turn the death of its author, Duras? Extravagant demand! Delirium? Perhaps, but what a symbol! The departure of the writing and of the writer for a higher level or nowhere, far from dividing them, links them, as in life, to a single and unique destiny. While the fires of death dance in the night, the chiaroscuro of the mind has more to say than any learned commentary, there is no more Duras because there is nothing more to write. The work has devoured the life which puts an end to the work in a perfect coincidence.[25]

This method of collapsing Duras's work and life into a totality, and thus making one a phantom echo of the other, perhaps explains how Duras the resourceful and enterprising cook can now be found on the bookstore shelf alongside Duras the writer.[26] Olivier Todd concluded a double review of *C'est tout* and Adler's biography with the condescending comment: 'It still leaves me sceptical about MD's place in twentieth-century French literature. She was, however, a superb cook. Having lived through the Occupation, she was able to concoct exquisite dishes out of almost anything. Her *queues de porc* will certainly survive.'[27]

For all its sexism, Todd's review does, however, raise an important point that needs to be addressed: the central role and status of Yann Andréa, her partner for the last sixteen years of her life and with whom she engaged in a complex erotic form of cross-gender, intertextual collaboration, resulting in texts, films and interviews for, with, and about each other.[28] It was around the figure of Andréa (or 'Y.A., homosexual', as she sometimes called him) that the overlapping of life and work, reality and fantasy, was most fully realized by Duras. It even led one reviewer recently to refer to Andréa, without any trace of irony, as 'Yann Andréa Steiner', the title of Duras's 1992 book where 'vous'—identified as Andréa—is reincarnated as Jewish.[29] In a short confessional interview he gave to *Libération* just days after Duras's death, Andréa took a cool and matter-of-fact view of his involvement with her, downplaying his role to that merely of 'assistant'.[30] This self-deflating, anticlimactic stance, coming as it did after the agonizing *C'est tout*, was clearly intended as a signal that Duras's life should now be left in peace and that her work be viewed properly in its entirety and without distraction, i.e. without media interference and distinct from the accumulated, secondary discourse of interviews, commentaries, special notes and directions (including, in the case of *Les yeux bleux cheveux noirs*, even her own *prière d'insérer*). In the same interview, as though clearing the Duras decks in order to start his life over, he affirmed that he wrote *M.D.* not for reasons of personal interest or through *mimétisme* but simply out of solitude, and that it was Duras herself who encouraged publication.Yet almost three years later, in an interview for the magazine *L'Evénement*, Andréa offered a very different insight into the extremes of his relationship with Duras which he framed in terms of *Leidenschaft*, or a mixture of passion and suffering.[31] To the question of whether he desired her body in the same way she did his, he answered: 'It was prohibited to pretend. I had to go at it with my body. To make love … The non-relationship of man to woman, she lived it with a passion, also with a fatigue, because she knew it was a failure … She attempted something, however. To invent, to write. That was the infinite grace of MD, her humility.'[32] Andréa admits that he had tried to kill himself several times following her death and had experienced complete emptiness, his illusory fusion with Duras (her body and not just her name) having been destroyed. The main thrust of this second interview, however, remains the same as that of the first, with Andréa, in his role as Duras's literary executor, recommending a resurgence of general interest in her work in the face of hostile forces like Sollers. He remarks with disarming generosity: 'I, YA, was her favourite, *à jamais* and *pour jamais*, yet anyone can be her favourite.'[33]

The publication in 1999 of Andréa's *Cet amour-là* would seem to complicate unnecessarily this admirable intention.[34] The book presents a behind-the-scenes view of his strange and tortured life with Duras from the moment he moved in with her in 1980, as well as his difficult and painful attempt to come to terms with her death. By invoking his wish to recover his individual voice after having felt for so long silenced like a 'Nobody' by Duras, *Cet amour-là* appears to bear out the hypothesis I proposed at the end of *The Erotics of Passage*, namely, that by speaking out and writing for himself, Andréa might potentially 'reduce the compulsive terror and excitement of the later Duras corpus' (p. 158). For while *Cet amour-là* is still remarkably discreet, notably around Andréa's own gay identity and desire (briefly alluded to in passing references to a certain Frédéric), it reads as a kind of exposé revealing in extensive, even banal detail the personal tyranny of Duras and his own extreme, masochistic passivity. Moreover, despite the many obvious qualities of *Cet amour-là*, such as its fully assumed first-person narration and its sincere tone, at once naive and tragic, eloquent and raw, the text reads very much like *M.D.*, that is to say, as sub-Duras. Not only are many of its main themes clearly second-hand (for example, Andréa's insistence on both an impossible personal love and a generalized love for the world), but also the style and idiom remain quintessentially late Duras. I am thinking in particular of the obsessive invocation and reworking of a name ('Duras'), the recurring motifs and inversions, the sudden formalization of relationships with a third party (e.g. Duras/Andréa/Balthazar), the confusion of subject and object positions (especially the first-person address to a second person), and the resort to an imagined scenario (the fantasy of Duras as alive in death). These various features are pushed to a desperate, at times even embarrassing level of excess (e.g. the account of Andréa's own birth on pp. 42–43), and the book becomes increasingly rambling and prolix (Andréa talks in an afterword of having maintained everything, 'the hotch-potch, the commonplaces', a luxury, of course, which Duras never actually herself permitted).

In the last analysis, Andréa exposes himself as a second-rate writer. The more traces one finds of Duras's texts and dialogues, the more one is impelled to return to the original. Hence, whatever the work's evident personal value—a statement of survival, a record of mourning and recovery, an attempt to redefine his identity, an assessment of Duras as well as self-assessment, a form of public confession—*Cet amour-là* demonstrates effortlessly that Duras's unique voice will always make its difference felt. Writing about Duras—a 'subject painted in gold' (p. 111)—just as she had foretold and indeed encouraged, Andréa still remains after her death her perfect foil (it is a small but not altogether insignificant fact that Andréa continues to write in the name invented for him by Duras). Ironically, yet perhaps not unintentionally in view of Andréa's continued humility and devotion to the singular genius of Duras, *Cet amour-là* will serve to ensure that the mystery and achievement of Duras's work remain intact and even enhanced.

This last point is crucial, for rather than attempting as critics to write 'over' Duras's dead body in order to retrieve a single voice—the essential, 'true' voice of Duras—we need now, if anything, to 'resurrect' the corpus in all its forms. That is to say, we should avoid approaches that maintain it as a living corpse and repetition of the same, and attempt instead to raise and extend it theoretically.[35] This will entail an examination of individual works in their own right rather than as part of an endless process of personal reclamation or intertextual elaboration, or even, as in the case of the later productions, as part of an ongoing process of interpersonal collaboration. What would it mean, for example, to read texts such as *La maladie de la mort*, *La pute de la côte normande*, *Emily L.* and *Yann Andréa Steiner* outside their original context of Duras's relationship with Andréa, and hence divorced from the issues of futurity and posterity which inevitably come to the fore in any discussion of Duras's relations with 'Y.A. homosexual', and indeed of homosexuality in general in Duras's work?[36] Similarly, rather than simply fall in line to produce, *à la* Sollers and Todd, a premature judgment of Duras's place in literary history, we need to return in imaginative and productive ways to the work itself which, barring the possible publication of new material, constitutes a now discrete corpus. While *C'est tout* cannot in any way be said to provide closure to the oeuvre, it does at least endow it with a certain finality which we ought to respect.

I would like to illustrate briefly some of the points I have been making by taking a small but instructive case of the problems faced in trying to attach biographical limits—any limits—to a critical study of Duras's work. Although not known as a letter writer, Duras corresponded regularly with the Italian writer Elio Vittorini during the 1940s and 1950s when the two belonged to the Saint-Benoît group of communist intellectuals that included (among others) Dionys Mascolo, her former husband Robert Antelme, and Edgar Morin. Many of these letters on a range of personal, political and literary matters are available for consultation at the Vittorini archives housed at the University of Urbino. What many of the letters from late 1952 to late 1953 bring to light is the profound unease felt by Vittorini and Mascolo at the publication of Duras's 1953 novel, *Les petits chevaux de Tarquinia*, which she dedicated to Vittorini and his wife Ginetta. This is a novel about frustrated sexual relations experienced by a group of friends on holiday in the stifling heat of Italy, and which, by Duras's own admission, caused a rupture within both her life and literary practice (coincidentally, it is also what first drew Andréa to Duras's work and, in his words, changed his life definitively).[37] The hope would be that by reading this series of letters one might be in a better position to appreciate the novel and its key importance in the corpus. However, the result is unsatisfying and ultimately of minor value since the letters offer no real insight into the work. One can agree or disagree with Vittorini's instinctive distaste for the novel, conveyed in a letter to Duras dated 2 December 1952, on account of its unconvincing characterization and its 'masking of truth to the point of parody by the prejudices of the period' (populism, disenchantment, persiflage). One can also trace in Mascolo's six-page letter to Vittorini dated 12 November 1953 his 'horror' of the book which he took not only as an indirect statement by Duras on recent holidays spent together with the Vittorinis, but also as a work of spite and malice directed against him personally. Mascolo writes with bitter irony that this is literature with base feelings, out of keeping with the normal character of Duras who has allowed herself to be taken in 'authentically' by the 'literary game' and its illusion of power. For Mascolo, the novel all but constitutes an anonymous letter of denunciation by Duras (there are echoes here of the débâcle in 1950 when he and Duras were summarily expelled from the Communist Party). Duras's response to these attacks is encapsulated in a brief letter to Vittorini dated 16 October 1953, where she states that she had not painted a portrait of anyone. All she had done was pay attention to her own and everyone's behaviour ('le bruit que nous faisons') and incorporated into the work the great love she felt for the Vittorinis.

What one is really left with after witnessing this intricate case of personal relations, where many of the key words and terms remain a stubborn mystery (the reference, for example, in Duras's letter to a 'polemic' is unclear), is Duras's insistence that her novel possesses no direct biographical intent and has everything to do with what Mascolo dismisses as the literary process, i.e. the *jeu* (as opposed to *je*) *littéraire.* She is effectively warning here of the dangers of an over-personalized, biographical approach to the activity of reading which, in her view, can have no direct claim or purchase on the act of writing. This fact is worth bearing in mind even when—and especially when—examining Duras's later works which play so seductively with the status of the first person, such as *L'amant* and *La douleur*. After all, to state poetically, as Duras so often did in the 1980s, that her texts 'were herself' is far from saying that her work contains definitive biographical truth.

To restate the central argument of this Introduction: what is in danger of being lost in the increasing 'embodiment' of the Duras corpus is a dynamic sense of its extraordinary range and complexity, as well as of its important theoretical and political implications. It is therefore crucial at this stage of Duras studies to resist such a move, before the texts are consigned to canonization in the Pléiade or else encased in the insights of previous criticism. Whatever the now well-documented depressive and destructive tendencies of individual texts, plays and films (and cycles thereof), the Durassian oeuvre dazzles in its sheer energy and emotional power, its experimental daring and assumption of risk, its unflinching drive towards clarity even through negation, its consummate command and intensive precision, above all, its defiant refusal to be categorized under one term, even one as capacious as *écriture courante*, Duras's answer in the 1980s to *écriture féminine* and an apparent all-inclusive transcription of anything personal, social or political that 'passes' during the scene of writing. Duras reinvested and changed irrevocably all media that she touched—literature, film, theatre, journalism. She also raised fundamental themes to the level of the momentous, making them a matter of life and death: the apocalyptic impact of love and sexual passion; the inescapable hold of the past and the unconditional nature of writing and act of bearing witness; the trauma of loss, violence and madness; human injustice and the catastrophe of colonialism; the horror of war, Hiroshima, the Holocaust; the wonder and brute force of nature. To underestimate such thematic weight would be at the same time to overlook the visceral qualities of Duras's style, by turns spare and poetic, elliptical and lyrical, elemental and delicate, absolutist and speculative, dramatic and formal, incantatory and clinical, seductive and teasing, but always in transition.

Revisioning Duras aims to do critical justice to Duras's unique body of work by deliberately eschewing a biographical and chronological approach. The tripartite structure—Film, Race, Sex—is a loose juxtaposition of formal and thematic categories wherein no one element is hierarchized and all notion of exhaustive coverage is banished. The three sections constitute broad areas of enquiry. 'Film', for example, brings together discussion of certain of Duras's films, her film criticism and her engagement with photography. 'Sex' includes analysis both of gender and sexuality, intersexual relations and sexual practices, issues which also feature in 'Film' and 'Race' but which are placed here in their full context, for example, the threat that homosexuality poses within the universalizing tradition of French thought and culture. 'Race' addresses questions of racial difference, immigration and the representation of the native Other in Duras's work, with particular emphasis on female identity and desire. This supple interweaving of formal and thematic concerns produces important new links and points of focus across the entire oeuvre which is no longer compartmentalized into early, middle or late Duras. This creates, in turn, a new architectonic alertness to the rhythms and varying levels of tone and contrast in the corpus, with immediate ramifications in the case of Duras's film work which has often been woefully undervalued, not merely because much of it remained unavailable prior to recent retrospectives in London and Paris, but also because it has been viewed by many as secondary to her literary work or as a mere extension of it (the unhelpful notion of Duras as a model literary film-maker still persists). Similarly, while issues of race have certainly been examined in relation to Duras's work, notably in the pioneering studies of Christine Holmlund and Panivong Norindr,[38] they deserve further detailed analysis and development, in particular regarding (post)colonial and ethnic subtexts such as the history of Indochina, African and Arab immigration in Europe, and Judaism.

To the question why one should pursue categories of representation like race and sex in the case of a writer and film-maker who continually veers, often sublimely, towards the non-representational, the answer proposed by *Revisioning Duras* is that this serves strategically to ensure a crucial shift away from the biographical towards the chief problematics of Duras's artistic practice. To take the example of *L'amant*, the novel is discussed by various contributors in different contexts—race, ethnicity and female fetishism—rather than from an autobiographical viewpoint which has, after all, already been extensively mapped out.[39] In the same way, when Duras's politics and media work are considered, it is for a specific purpose (e.g. to define her attitude to immigration) rather than out of a wish to confirm or disprove facets of her own personality. Moreover, whether using music theory to explore formally the soundtrack of Duras's films, or colonial texts and postcolonial theory to evaluate Duras's presentation of the *coloniale* from *Un barrage contre le Pacifique* to *L'amant de la Chine du Nord*, or feminist and gay theory to determine the status of lesbian desire in Duras's film and literary work, or a combination of psychoanalysis and photography theory to reappraise mother/daughter relations in Duras, the contributors to this volume remain always sensitive to the multiple ambivalences throughout Duras's work, particularly with regard to the use of sexual and racial stereotypes such as the chanting Indian beggar girl, the Jew with blue eyes, black hair, and the male homosexual in unconscious denial of difference. For the collection is not aiming simply to make Duras a testing ground for theory, a feature of much Duras criticism, whether Lacanian (inspired by Jacques Lacan's famous 'Hommage à Marguerite Duras du *ravissement de Lol V. Stein*'),[40] Derridean (cf. the work of Marie-Claire Ropars-Wuilleumier),[41] or Kristevan and anti-Kristevan, following Julia Kristeva's key study of the workings of melancholia in Duras's fiction, 'La maladie de la douleur'.[42] Rather, the contributors draw on the fruits of recent and current Duras criticism, including notably the work of Leslie Hill, Suzanne Chester, Yvonne Y. Hsieh, Lia van de Biezenbos, and Michelle Royer,[43] to establish how far Duras's work questions and redefines the very parameters of literary and cinematic form, as well as the conceptual categories of race and ethnicity, homosexuality and heterosexuality, fantasy and violence. In so doing, they not merely 'revisit' but 'revision' Duras in the widest sense of the term.

Revisioning Duras offers, then, less a distanced, objective view of Duras—as if that could at all be possible: Duras never leaves us untouched or secure as readers and viewers—than a fully engaged and accessible investigation of her work. Its primary objective is to avoid positioning the corpus along partisan lines or judging it through a narrow prism in order to open up a new critical dialogue and so stimulate further readings. For this reason, the collection runs directly counter to Vircondelet's ultimately sanitizing project of explaining—and explaining away—Duras. The contributors all share the view that if Duras's achievement is to be truly celebrated rather than simply consecrated, or at worst, dismissed, then Duras studies must pursue new theoretical paths and connections. Only then will it be possible to appreciate the real significance of Duras as a twentieth-century artist and thinker, just as it is only now in France that the legacy of Jean-Paul Sartre—whose cultural role and intellectual influence Duras arguably replaced—can at last be properly re-evaluated.[44] The Duras corpus, consistent in its intensity and provocation despite its many evolutionary turns, presents an urgent challenge to its readers and viewers. In responding directly to this challenge this collection will—it is hoped—also offer a new perspective from which to reconsider and revision the very links between theory and artistic practice.

Notes

1 See Marguerite Duras, *Le camion, suivi de Entretien avec Michelle Porte*, Paris, Minuit, 1977; Michèle Manceaux, *L'amie*, Paris, Albin Michel, 1997 (which complements and extends Manceaux's earlier *Brèves: Journal*, Paris, Seuil, 1984); Christiane Blot-Labarrère, *Marguerite Duras*, Paris, Seuil, 'Les contemporains' 14, 1992, which uses a vast amount of citation to endorse Duras's own view of her work as a liberatory aesthetics of the possible; Madeleine Borgomano, *L'écriture filmique de Marguerite Duras*, Paris, Albatros, 1985, and *Duras: Une lecture des fantasmes*, Brussels, Cistre 'Essais', 1985.

2 See Alain Vircondelet, *Marguerite Duras ou le temps de détruire*, Paris, Seghers, 1972.

3 Alain Vircondelet, *Marguerite Duras: vérité et légendes*, Paris, Chêne 1996, including unpublished photographs by Jean Mascolo. Already in 1995, no doubt in preparation for her imminent death a year later, Vircondelet had published *Pour Duras*, Paris, Calmann-Lévy.

4 Jean-Pierre Ceton, *La fiction d'Emmedée*, Monaco, Rocher 'Manifeste', 1997.

5 Frédérique Lebelley, *Duras ou le poids d'une plume*, Paris, Grasset, 1994.

6 See Philippe Sollers, 'Duras, par Sollers', *L'Evénement du Jeudi*, 3–9 September 1998, pp. 92–95. Sollers's slighting of Duras continues a long tradition of mutually hostile remarks by both authors, including Duras's equally sharp dismissal of Sollers in 'Duras est SEXY!' (interview with Pierre Bergé), *Globe*, No. 30 (July–August 1988), pp. 79–83. Parodies of Duras include Patrick Rambaud's *Virginie Q. de Marguerite Duraille*, Paris, Balland, 1988, and Dominique Noguez's extended skit, 'Aurélia Steiner (Trouville) de Marguerite Duras', in *Semiologie du parapluie et autres textes*, Paris, Différence, 1990, pp. 114–20. See also Noguez's 'La cuisine Duraille', *Le Nouvel Observateur*, 1–7 April 1999, p. 53. More disturbingly, in 1992 a journalist sought to expose what he considered to be her inflated worth by sending a sample of Duras's 1962 novel, *L'après-midi de Monsieur Andesmas*, to her main publishers, Minuit, Gallimard and POL. It was rejected unanimously as

'not of the highest literary quality'. Guillaume Jacquet of the magazine *Réaction* retitled an extract from Duras's novel *L'après-midi de Monsieur Andesmas* as 'Margot et l'important' and dedicated it to Marguerite 'qui ne sait pas'. Duras did not take legal action. *Le Figaro* published a letter on 22 September 1992 written jointly by Antoine Gallimard, Jérome Lindon, and Paul Otchakovsky-Laurens, in which they defended their 'rigorous' standards of professionalism.

7 Margaret Sankey, 'The Duras Phenomenon', *Australian Journal of French Studies*, Vol. 34, No. 1 (January–April 1997), pp. 60–76; p. 73. See also Vicki Mistacco, '*Plus ça change* ...: The Critical Reception to *Emily L.*', *The French Review*, Vol. 66, No. 1 (October 1992), pp. 77–88, for further analysis of the critical and political reception of Duras's later work in France. Jane Winston has argued a little differently that it is because Duras's critics have been baffled by her refusal to explain the links between political activism, journalism, and literary production, that they disconnect her political commitments from her love life, resulting in a Duras recoverable by the Right even though she behaves in Leftist fashion. See 'Forever Feminine: Marguerite Duras and Her French Critics', *New Literary History*, Vol. 24, No. 2 (Spring 1993), pp. 467–82. It should be acknowledged that in America Duras's work has been attacked both from the right and the left of the academy. For an example of the former, see Antoine Compagnon's 'The Diminishing Canon of French literature in America', *Stanford French Review*, Vol. 15 (1991), pp. 103–15, which equates the shrinkage of PhD dissertation topics in the US with the expansion of the Marguerite Duras empire. In 'The Righting of French Studies: Homosociality and the Killing of "la pensée 68"', *Profession* (MLA Publications), No. 92 (1992), pp. 28–34, intended as a counter-response to Compagnon, Naomi Schor proposes in no less scathing terms that Duras's reputation 'is a symptom of an international fascination with female sexuality, madness, and short sentences' (p. 34).

8 Marguerite Duras, 'Sublime, forcément sublime Christine V.', *Libération*, 17 July 1985, pp. 5–7.

9 See Marcelle Marini, 'Transgressions', in *Duras, Dieu et l'écrit: Colloque international*, ed. Alain Vircondelet, Paris, Rocher, 1998, p. 83.

10 Marilyn Schuster, *Revisiting Duras*, New York, Twayne, 1993, p. 151. Schuster's 'revisiting' of Duras must be understood in the first instance as a return to Duras by the Twayne series which published Alfred Cismaru's early survey of Duras's work in 1971.

11 Schuster, *Revisiting Duras*, p. 151.

12 See Trista Selous, *The Other Woman: Feminism and Femininity in the Work of Marguerite Duras*, New Haven and London, Yale University Press, 1988.

13 See James S. Williams, *The Erotics of Passage: Pleasure, Politics, and Form in the Later Work of Marguerite Duras*, Liverpool University Press/St Martin's Press, 1997, which explores Duras's work post-*Le camion*.

14 *La Nouvelle Revue Française*, No. 542 (March 1998), Special Issue: Marguerite Duras. Included are articles by Blot-Labarrère, Manceaux and Vircondelet as well as Julia Kristeva, Nancy Huston, Patrick Grainville, Francis Marmande, Jacqueline Risset, Dominique Noguez, Pierre Mertens, Sylvie Doizelet, Brigitte Giraud, Aliette

Armel, Colette Fellous, Daniel Dobbels, Cécile Wajsbrot, Nedim Gürsel and Marie Anne Guerin.

15 See Susan D. Cohen, *Women and Discourse in the Fiction of Marguerite Duras: Love, Legends, Language*, Oxford, Macmillan, 1993.

16 The most substantive criticism has been made by Blot-Labarrère in the *Bulletin de la Société Marguerite Duras*, No. 4 (1999), pp. 44–47, where she castigates Adler for using Duras's fiction as so-called historical fact (e.g. *La douleur*), as well as for committing a host of errors and inaccuracies, resulting in confusion and a debased and vulgar image of Duras and her oeuvre. The editors of the *Bulletin* follow up this review with their own list of errors. Adler's book has inevitably provoked counter-claims and denunciations, including most notably a rejection by Duras's son, Jean Mascolo, both of the idea that Duras's mother was a prostitute in Indochina, and that Duras had an 'ambiguous' relationship with Delval. The writer Jorge Semprun stated in *Le Monde*, 26 June 1998, that he did not, as Adler claims, denounce Duras, Mascolo or Antelme to the Communist Party headquarters of the 6th arrondissement in Paris. For a compact account of Adler's biography, see the dossier entitled 'Duras, la vérité' in *Le Nouvel Observateur*, 20–26 August 1998, pp. 4–13, which includes extracts from the book, and her interview in *Lire* (June 1998), 'La vérité recomposée de M.D.' (pp. 46–48). In *Elle*, 20–26 August 1998, Frédérique Lantieri provided a helpful summary of the difference of views on the key issues held by Adler, Mascolo and Vircondelet: political engagement (notably on the question of colonialism), Vichy and the Resistance, the nature of her affair with a rich young Chinese man, the Delval affair, the torture scene in *La douleur*.

17 See Alain Vircondelet, *Duras: Biographie*, Paris, François Bourin, 1991 (*Duras: A biography*, trans. Thomas Buckley, Normal IL, Dalkey Archive Press, 1994).

18 Vircondelet, *Duras, Dieu et l'écrit*, p. 12. In his conclusion to the collection, Vircondelet adds the final highly contradictory statement that he and the other contributors have tried to approach Duras's oeuvre 'in its most appropriate area while maintaining our own independent judgment, as if in some way we were continuing its enterprise, making ourselves the decipherers of this invisible' (pp. 298–99) ('nous avons essayé de traverser cette oeuvre en son plus juste lieu, et cela en conservant notre propre indépendance de jugement, comme si nous continuions en quelque sorte son entreprise, faisant de nous-même des déchiffreurs de cet invisible').

19 See Alain Vircondelet, *Marguerite à Duras*, Paris, Editions No. 1, 1998, p. 11. The Château de Duras now boasts an annual Salon du Livre linked to Duras's work.

20 See Bettina Knapp (ed.), *Critical Essays on Marguerite Duras*, New York, G. K. Hall, 1998. It is perhaps a reflection of this ultimately regressive approach to Duras's work that only three of the chapters are new and written specially for the volume; most have been published in English before, and some even date from the 1960s. The contributors include: Schuster, Selous, Jacques Lacan, Maurice Blanchot, Viviane Forrester, Micheline Tison-Braun, John Kneller, Karen Kaivola, Sharon Willis, Leslie Hill, Michael Bishop, Liliane Papin, Sharon Spencer, Deborah Glassman, Jeanine Parisier Plottel.

21 Knapp, *Critical Essays*, p. 5.

22 Knapp, *Critical Essays*, p. 9.

23 'Je crois que c'est terminé. Que ma vie c'est fini./ Je ne suis plus rien./ Je suis devenue complètement effrayante./ Je ne tiens plus ensemble./ Viens vite./ Je n'ai plus de bouche, plus de visage' (Marguerite Duras, *C'est tout*, Paris, POL, 1995, pp. 54–55).

24 Vircondelet, *Marguerite à Duras*, p. 189: 'Il ne reste plus qu'à écrire dessus, sur ce "corps mort" de Duras, de son oeuvre, de sa vie, de ses lieux'. Duras's original sentence reads: 'I told myself that one always wrote on the dead body of the world, and likewise on the dead body of love' (*L'été 80*, Paris, Minuit, 1980, p. 67) ('Je me suis dit qu'on écrivait toujours sur le corps mort du monde, et, de même, sur le corps mort de l'amour').

25 Marguerite Duras, *No More*, expanded and bilingual edition, trans. Richard Howard, New York, Seven Stories, 1998, with foreword by Paul Otchakovsky-Laurens and afterword by Christiane Blot-Labarrère, pp. 93–123; p. 123. While Blot-Labarrère provides a convincing reading of the 'perforated text' (p. 117) of *C'est tout* as 'a book of love' (p. 93) with religious and apocalyptic features, she happily repeats some of the major truisms of Duras criticism, e.g. that the oeuvre is exceptionally homogenous (p. 108), that Duras's writing is redemptive (p. 93) despite being based on 'the notion of lack, of void, of the unspeakable' (p. 117). This approach is in direct contrast with that of Richard Howard, who, in his Translator's Note (pp. 9–11), presents the text perhaps more truthfully as a work of '*hargne*', as 'one of the fiercest little books in our culture, the converse of the Stoic manual of proper dying', a series of 'intermittences not of the heart, as in Proust, but of the spleen', and a reminder of 'the degradations or mortality: greedy, illicit, profound. *Odi et amo*' (pp. 10–11). (It is not insignificant to our discussion that Blot-Labarrère is presented in the text as 'among the very few whose writings were respected by Duras' (p. 123), as though again a personal endorsement by Duras accords greater value to critical work.) It should also be noted that the expanded version of *C'est tout* (longer by over 20 pages) ends on a very different note from the original in which the last two sentences placed at the top of the final page allowed the book to be swallowed up by the white void of silence which had encroached throughout in regular intervals of white spacing. By contrast, the expanded version, while for the most part no less despairing or aggressive in tone (for example: 'You are all a bunch of idiots./ You're completely fucked up./ It's all unbearable' (p. 75)), ends with these words by the narrator to Y.A.: 'I love you./ *Au revoir*' (p. 92) ('Je vous aime./ Au revoir' (p. 78)).

26 *La cuisine de Marguerite*, Paris, Benoît-Jacob, 1999. In fact, the status of this book, published with the authorisation of Duras's son and material executor Jean Mascolo, is currently in doubt. Mascolo has stated that his aim in publishing this selection of his mother's recipes was to show Duras 'in a daily routine which she described as being as creative as writing'. However, Andréa has since taken Mascolo to court in order to have the book banned on the grounds of 'violation of moral rights'. The case continues.

27 See Olivier Todd, 'Mon Charabia', *London Review of Books*, 4 March 1998, pp. 14–15. Laure celebrates Duras as a cook and comments on recipes in the April 1999 issue of *Elle*.

28 See Chapter 7 of Williams, *The Erotics of Passage*. In 'Mon Charabia' Todd cites as an example of Duras's personal unpleasantness the fact that in her will she elided Andréa (portrayed as naive and confused), leaving him only a small room facing the flat in the rue Saint-Benoît where they had lived together for 16 years.

29 Alan Riding, 'Scrutinizing a Legend's Studied Facade', *The New York Times*, 26 November 1998, pp. B1-B2.

30 Yann Andréa, 'Le survivant': interview with Philippe Lançon, *Libération*, 18 March 1996, p. 44.

31 Yann Andréa, 'Duras mon amour' (interview with Jean-Francois Kervéan), *L'Evénement*, No. 740, 7–13 January 1999, pp. 98–103; p. 102.

32 Andréa, 'Duras mon amour', p. 102: 'Il ne fallait pas faire semblant. Fallait y aller avec le corps. Faire l'amour … Le non-rapport homme-femme, elle le vivait avec une passion, une fatigue aussi, car elle savait que ça ratait … Elle tentait quelque chose pourtant. Inventer. Ecrire. La grâce infinie de MD. Son humilité.'

33 Andréa, 'Duras mon amour', p. 103: 'Moi, YA, j'étais le préféré *for ever et for never*, mais chacun peut être le préféré.'

34 Yann Andréa, *Cet amour-là*, Paris, Pauvert, 1999. Andréa gave several short interviews to promote the book, including: 'Je ne suis pas le veuf' (with Philippe Lançon), *Libération*, 2 September 1999 ('Supplément', p. v), and '"Elle était d'une jalousie atroce"' (with Jean-François Josselin), *Le Nouvel Observateur*, 26 August–1 September 1999, p. 12 (part of a special dossier entitled 'Duras mon amour', pp. 6–18). In the latter, Andréa explains that *Cet amour-là* is not a book of personal self-liberation but rather a letter to Duras, hence a continuation of the letters he had sent to her before they lived together. As I write, there are plans afoot to adapt *Cet amour-là* for the big screen with an international cast.

35 I have discussed at length elsewhere the theme of the Duras corpus as body and living corpse. See 'Marguerite Duras: "La mort du jeune aviateur anglais"', in *Short French Fiction: Essays on the Short Story in France in the Twentieth Century*, ed. John Flower, Exeter, Exeter University Press, 1998, pp. 102–21, which argues that the Duras critic would do better to 'desublimate' the 'sublimating turns' of Duras's work (pp. 120–21).

36 See, for example, Martin Crowley, '"C'est curieux un mort": Duras on Homosexuality', *Modern Language Review*, Vol. 93, No. 3 (July 1998), pp. 659–75, which presents Duras's long and troubled encounter with the theme of homosexuality in terms of her wish to address an absolute beyond of passion, i.e. the absolute, intransitive status of writing beyond the world of polemic and contingency.

37 See Andréa, 'Le survivant', p. 44, where Andréa talks of the novel as producing 'an almost physical belonging'.

38 See Christine Holmlund, 'Displacing Limits of Difference: Gender, Race, and Colonialism in Edward Said and Homi Bhabha's Theoretical Models and Marguerite Duras's Experimental Films', *Quarterly Review of Film and Video*, Vol. 13, Nos 1–3

(1991), pp. 1–22, and Panivong Norindr, '"Errances" and Memories in Duras's Colonial Cities', *differences*, Vol. 5, No. 3 (1993), pp. 52–78.

39 See, for example, Janice Morgan, 'Fiction and Autobiography/Language and Silence: *L'Amant* by Duras', *French Review*, Vol. 63, No. 2 (1989), pp. 271–79, and 'Rewriting Her Story, from Passive to Active: Substitutions in Marguerite Duras's *The Lover*', in Leah Hewitt, *Autobiographical Tightropes: Simone de Beauvoir, Nathalie Sarraute, Marguerite Duras, Monique Wittig, and Maryse Condé*, Lincoln NE and London, University of Nebraska Press, 1990, pp. 93–126.

40 See Jacques Lacan, 'Hommage fait à Marguerite Duras du *Ravissement de Lol V. Stein*', *Cahiers Renaud-Barrault*, No. 52 (December 1965), pp. 7–15 (reprinted in *Marguerite Duras* (1975), ed. François Barat and Joël Farges, Paris, Albatros, 1979, pp. 131–37).

41 See, for example, Marie-Claire Ropars-Wuilleumier, 'The Disembodied Voice: *India Song*', *Yale French Studies*, No. 60 (1980), pp. 241–68.

42 See 'La maladie de la douleur', in Julia Kristeva, *Soleil noir: dépression et mélancolie*, Paris, Gallimard, 1987, pp. 227–65 ('The Malady of Grief' in *Black Sun: Depression and Melancholia*, trans. Léon Roudiez, New York, Columbia University Press, 1980, pp. 219–61). According to Kristeva, who draws primaily on Klein's thoery of object-relations and Freud's 1915 essay 'Mourning and Melancholia', Duras's society of narcissistically depressed and doomed heroines unable to sustain erotic bonds exemplifies the bleaching of sense that takes place on the textual level in her work in the form of a sparse, paratactic style. Such an 'aesthetics of clumsiness', devoid of even the odd moment of narrative synthesis, constitutes for Kristeva the apotheosis of the postwar crisis of modernist literature.

43 Leslie Hill, *Marguerite Duras: Apocalyptic Desires*, New York, London, Routledge, 1993; Suzanne Chester, 'Writing the Subject: Exoticism/Eroticism in Marguerite Duras's *The Lover* and *The Sea Wall*', in *Decolonizing the Subject: The Politics of Gender in Women's Autobiography*, ed. Sidonie Smith and Julia Watson, Minneapolis, University of Minnesota Press, 1992, pp. 436–57; Yvonne Y. Hsieh, 'L'évolution du discours (anti-)colonialiste dans *Un barrage contre le Pacifique*, *L'Amant* et *L'Amant de la Chine du Nord* de Marguerite Duras', *Dalhousie French Studies*, No. 35 (1996), pp. 55–65; Lia van de Biezenbos, *Fantasmes maternels dans l'oeuvre de Marguerite Duras*, Amsterdam, Rodopi, 1995; and Michelle Royer, *L'écran de la passion: une étude du cinéma de Marguerite Duras*, Mount Nebo, Queensland, Boombana Publications, 1997.

44 The year 2000 saw a profusion of volumes dedicated to Sartre, including Bernard-Henri Lévy, *Le siècle de Sartre*, Paris, Grasset; Denis Bertholet, *Sartre*, Paris, Plon; Olivier Wickers, *Trois aventures extraordinaires de Jean-Paul Sartre*, Paris, Gallimard; and Michel-Antoine Burnier, *L'adieu à Sartre, suivi du Testament de Sartre*, Paris, Plon. Duras, of course, famously denied Sartre the sacred status of writer during her interview with Bernard Pivot on *Apostrophes*, 28 September 1984, describing him merely as a 'launcher of ideas'.

Part I
Film

CHAPTER 1

An Art of Fugue? The Polyphonic Cinema of Marguerite Duras

Wendy Everett

In this chapter, I shall consider the intimate relationship which exists between music and the multilayered and self-referential cinema of Marguerite Duras by investigating her films in relation to the concept of *fugue*, with its dual meanings of polyphonic musical structure and of flight, escape, or absence (as in *faire une fugue*, to run away). In so doing, I hope to identify ways in which her work relates to the wider modernist context, and to indicate a new perspective from which to view her films. Initially, it must be said, there seems little originality in applying the musical analogy to Duras's work, given that it already appears almost commonplace in the general critical canon, where it may serve to indicate either the lyrical qualities of her language, or the way in which the repetitive intertextuality that characterizes both her writings and her films constitutes a theme which confers coherence upon her entire corpus. Ishaghpour, for instance, considers that the musicality of Duras's language is fundamental to everything she does,[1] while Carol Murphy uses the musical analogy to discuss the tight intertextuality of her works, whereby 'fragments of the text reappear, are gently orchestrated, so as to confer upon the oeuvre a musical air which is the rhythmic reverberation of themes, characters, places and events'.[2] In similar vein, an article in the French journal *Le Point* comments that 'Duras constantly modulates her work, pulling out all the stops'.[3] Yvonne Guers-Villate even posits a link with fugue: 'It's a matter therefore of orchestrating certain themes in different ways ... as in a musical fugue',[4] although she neither justifies nor develops this almost throwaway comment. Discussion of Duras's films also inclines to musical simile, as when Alain Vircondelet likens their composition to that of a piece of music: 'her camera will create solemn and monotonous accents like a repetitive and haunting cello sonata'.[5] Madeleine Borgomano explores Duras's filmic metaphor in terms of the counterpoint between the soundtrack and the images,[6] and Sanford S. Ames directs the musical analogy towards the spectator for whom, he suggests, watching a film by Duras is like listening to music: 'We are suspended and remade like music in time.'[7]

However, whilst the musical analogy trips lightly and repeatedly off the critical tongue, there is remarkably little attempt to develop the analysis or to assess what its implications might be. Indeed, it is quite clear that musical comparisons and terminology serve primarily as a way of avoiding the problems inherent in using the standard critical vocabulary to describe or analyze Duras's repetitive, elliptical, and elusive work. Of course, musical terminology appears particularly apt, given its tacit acknowledgement of the inadequacy of language and its recognition of the powerful responses, physiological as well as emotional, which music is able to provoke in the listener.[8] It is frustrating, therefore, that while the above comments frequently appear to be hovering on the edge of an important aspect of Duras's work, their potential interest remains largely unfulfilled because of their failure to develop or assess the implications of the relationship they suggest. It seems to me that if the musical analogy can be applied to film (recognizing, of course, that the procedure is inherently problematic because of the traditional privileging of image over sound and the supreme importance accorded to the narrative in the majority of films),[9] it is only worth attempting if it leads to a fuller understanding of the works in question, by identifying, for example, the ways in which the mathematical rigour of musical structures may permit the expression of the inexpressible as well as the transgression of generic (and other) boundaries.

Within the general critical framework outlined above, there have, of course, been some attempts at a more systematic discussion of ways in which individual works by Duras might be approached via music. In literature this applies particularly to *Moderato cantabile* whose structure, developing through repetition, polyphony and modulation, is widely seen to reflect musical rather than narrative concerns, while close textual studies of *India Song*, for example, acknowledge most readily the centrality of music and its relationship with the narrative structure.[10] It is evident that one of the reasons for the widespread recognition of the importance of music in Duras's work is that she herself foregrounds it. Musical terminology colours many of her titles, and music is accorded an innovative and essential role in her films and novels. It is also repeatedly discussed in her various interviews and broadcasts, all this despite her insistence that it is impossible to talk about music, as during her conversation with Michelle Porte in *Les lieux de Marguerite Duras*.[11] In fact, it would be difficult *not* to be aware that in Duras's life as well as her work, her love of music, especially piano music and particularly Bach, is fundamental. With Porte, for example, Duras repeatedly speaks of her deep love for the piano, her delight in playing, and her regret that she is not a better pianist—comments which are frequently echoed by her characters, and haunt, in various ways, her writings and films.[12] In fact, she spends much of this particular conversation seated at the piano, playing fragments of the music from *Nathalie Granger* and *India Song* and even a few bars of a Bach fugue while declaring herself to be both fascinated and terrified by the power of music: 'Music terrifies me … moves me profoundly.'[13] While the power of music consists therefore in its ability to manipulate the listener's emotions, its fascination seems to reflect its locus beyond or outside chronological time and even beyond language itself, hence its mystery and unfathomability ('this language that we cannot decipher, the language of music').[14] Given that, as Duras recognizes, music, this 'symbolic language of the unconscious mind whose symbolism we shall never be able to fathom',[15] is centred on memory and desire and occupies the very spaces towards which her films and her writings reach out, it is through music, or by creating works which function as music, that she can best operate.

If Duras's love of music is reflected in the titles she gives her works, as well as in the complex and repeated references to music which they contain, in her films it also emerges in the central role accorded to music within the soundtrack, for here she can take full advantage of its emotive and motivic potency, and, in particular, of the way it functions in relation to other filmic elements such as image and voice. And although the range of music, and the frequency with which it is heard, may be relatively restricted (at certain points, the same few bars recur time and again, while at others the film remains stubbornly silent), its impact is huge, and it constantly transgresses the traditional rules governing film music listed in order by Gorbman, for example, as '[i]nvisibility; 'Inaudibility'; Signifier of emotion; Narrative cueing; Continuity; Unity', in recognition of the fact that music should support and clarify the narrative without ever drawing attention to itself.[16] For Duras, on the contrary, music forms an integral part of the film's structure and is foregrounded as one of its primary signifiers. Moreover, far from supporting the visual images and clarifying the narrative, music in her films serves to destabilize, decentre, and complicate.[17]

India Song, for instance, is structured by and around two strongly contrasting but equally powerful musical compositions: Beethoven's fourteenth *Diabelli Variation* and the banal but evocative blues melody 'India Song' specially composed for the film by Carlos d'Alessio. Together these compositions establish the film's three-part structure and create its internal rhythms, as well as multiply and extend its complex layers of meaning. For example, it is 'India Song' which, in relation to the variously 'scored' off-screen voices, both creates the (unseen) reception which constitutes the central section of the film, and evokes a vivid sense of period and place (colonial India, late 1930s), in addition to becoming a powerful leitmotif of desire through its association with the slow dance sequences and the languid gazes of the characters. In a clear acknowledgement of the power of music, the tune is cited by the Vice-consul as his reason for having come to India and having experienced love for the first time: 'I love "India Song". I came to India because of "India Song". This tune makes me want to love' ('J'aime "India Song". Je suis venu aux Indes à cause de "India Song". Cet air me donne envie d'aimer'). The *Diabelli Variation*, whose contrapuntal relationship with 'India Song' lies at the heart of the film's structure, itself develops complex layers of introversion, memory and desire due to its association with the death and absence of the main character (Anne-Marie Stretter), as well as with (the memory of) her life, since she was a pianist for whom music had become unbearably painful. Moreover, the shifting tensions between the two musical voices contribute to the film's powerful emotional undercurrents. Given that neither 'voice' can be clearly situated within the diegesis, and that each role, now emotive, now motivic, now descriptive, switches constantly, we can begin to appreciate that music actually replaces narrative construct in this film rather than merely supporting it.

Nor is *India Song* unique among Duras's films in its reliance upon music. The imperfectly played snatches of a Czerny study, along with Nathalie's seven notes (an arpeggio construction which Duras herself composed for the film), perform similarly multiple functions in *Nathalie Granger*, creating and deepening the film's layers of meaning (particularly in relation to violence, desire, and loss), as well as determining its rhythms, even establishing the pace at which the actors move. Music thus constitutes the film's physicality as well as its narrative form.[18] The powerful relationship at the heart of *Une aussi longue absence* is both set up and simultaneously evaluated by the Mozart and Rossini arias which structure the soundtrack, whilst music is used by Duras to provide the concluding voice in a number of films including, for example, her last, *Les enfants*.

The concept of music as a subjective, non-discursive, non-representational discourse whose power lies in its ability to appeal directly to the emotions, and through them to memory, has of course dominated the classical tradition of narrative film making, where the (Wagnerian) leitmotif, a repeated musical theme that enables us to construct memory patterns within the narrative, is central. To a certain extent, the tight musical repetitions in Duras's films function as leitmotifs, and certainly the relationship between music and memory, and music and desire, is fundamental. But again, Duras subverts the rules of the game. As we have seen, the range of music used in a given film is restricted, often to one or two fragments heard over and over again, and—even more daringly—these may well be repeated from film to film, and from book to film to book. For instance, Beethoven's *Diabelli Variations* are heard in *Des journées entières dans les arbres* as well as in *Le camion* and *India Song* (and we should not forget, of course, that the child in *Moderato cantabile* is learning the *Diabelli Sonatina* in the piano lessons which both structure the novel and are mirrored in its title). Similarly, *The Art of Fugue*, which, as we shall see, is represented visually in *Nathalie Granger* and repeatedly discussed by Duras in interviews and articles, forms an integral part of the closing section of *Détruire dit-elle*. This extreme musical intertextuality both infinitely extends and radically attacks the notion of leitmotif, first by the self-consciousness of the process (by which we are made aware of the music we are hearing), and second by its supreme indifference to generic boundaries. A consequence of this is that the memories which the music evokes and explores cannot be contained by a single text, but spill out across her entire oeuvre. In so doing, they involve the spectator directly and creatively within the process. Each time they are heard they acquire still deeper resonances of meaning.[19]

The music which Duras includes in her films is thus of central importance, and there is room for far more extensive treatment of this topic. However, my purpose here is to consider the degree to which her films can themselves be analyzed as music, or—more specifically—as fugue. While I am not suggesting that Duras deliberately set out to create films which function as music (in the way that, for example, Jean-Marie Straub, André Delvaux, Alain Robbe-Grillet and Georges Perec have done),[20] nevertheless it is clear that she herself recognizes and even points us in the direction I have suggested. In 'Les yeux verts', a special double number of *Cahiers du Cinéma* in 1980 devoted to her work, Duras describes a film she admires (George Lucas's *American Graffiti* (1973)) as 'a joy: cinema like one says: music',[21] clearly indicating that film, at its best, can indeed function as music by creating a powerful and lasting response. To appreciate fully the significance of this remark, one needs to recognize how dismissive of mainstream cinema Duras frequently is ('this rotten thing called cinema'),[22] and how limited she finds, for example, its unambiguous, closed images: 'Cinema limits the text, brings to a halt the imaginary process'.[23] Film as music, it follows, is a way of overcoming these limitations, of destabilizing the self-defining image and opening it up to the imagination.[24] I would like to link that very positive and telling statement by Duras—i.e. film = music = joy—with another in which she claims that the most successful of all her film shots occurs in *Nathalie Granger*, as the camera pans in close-up across various scores lying scattered across the floor:

> Of all I've ever done, of all the films I've made, the shot that moves me most is the shot of music, of sheet music, of scores, in *Nathalie Granger*. We placed a pile of scores on the floor, and the camera wanders across the scores, finishing, I think, on *The Art of Fugue*, on the cover of the score. It must just pass close to the *Chaconne* to end up on the hardest of all, *The Art of Fugue*, or possibly the *Goldberg Variations*, I'm no longer sure, while the child plays her scales ...
>
> (De tout ce que j'ai fait, de tous les films que j'ai faits, le plan qui me bouleverse le plus, c'est le plan sur la musique, sur l'écriture musicale, sur les partitions, dans *Nathalie Granger*. On a mis une masse de partitions par terre, et la caméra se balade sur les partitions, elle finit, je crois, sur *L'Art de la fugue*, sur la couverture de la partition; elle doit passer très près de la *Chaconne*, elle finit sur la plus dure, c'est-à-dire sur *L'Art de la fugue*, ou peut-être sur *les variations Goldberg*, je ne sais plus, tandis que l'enfant fait des gammes ...)[25]

Duras therefore believes that her own films work best when image *is* music. We are not talking here of simply a close correlation between music and images, but about music *being* the visual image. The written score, with its complex pattern of black notes on the stave, represents the mystery of music, the complicated and unfathomable relationship between its written form and the affect and nature of its sound. We are being *shown* music, since what is normally perceived as sound is instead being expressed as sight. In other words, *music has changed voice*. This provides us with a key to the language of Duras's films, to the way they can indeed be approached as musical structure and fugue. What is more, Duras again gently points us in the right direction when she explains that the work which the camera finally reaches, via a Bach *Chaconne*, is his supremely complex *Art of Fugue*, or 'possibly his *Goldberg Variations*'. This is a kind of meta-polyphonic description of film's acknowledgement that the polyphonic fugues of Bach are its inspiration, direction and expression.

Nor is Duras alone in her fascination with the complexities of fugue which, widely acknowledged to be 'the most intricate expression of the complex language of western music',[26] seems to exert a powerful influence over contemporary culture far exceeding the realm of music. It is indeed possible that some understanding of its form and nature may provide insight not only into Duras's films, but also into the modernist context in which they belong. Why is it that this apparently traditional and tightly regulated structure should exert such a fascination? What, indeed, is a fugue? As soon as we attempt to answer that apparently simple question, we become aware of a whole range of contradictions and complexities, for although it is possible to identify the main characteristics of fugue as polyphony and counterpoint, it rapidly becomes clear that fugue is not really a form at all, at least not in the sense, for instance, that a sonata is a form (in fact, fugal treatment can be found in many large-scale musical works, including the sonata). Rather, it is a *procedure* or *texture* that is always unfolding and expanding. *The New Grove Dictionary* emphasizes the dangers, even the impossibility, of attempting to define fugue, commenting that the classics, particularly Bach's fugues, are so diverse in structure as to defy classification, and insisting that despite all that has been written about fugal form and the complexity of the harmonic considerations which appear to govern its intervals and key structures, fugue actually precludes any such prescriptive treatment.

It is interesting that even its formal elusiveness is perhaps hinted at in its name, for 'fugue' means, quite literally, flight (Italian *fuga*; French *fugue*) and its musical application was initially to compositions in which each voice entering in turn appears to chase the preceding one. And this idea suggests some of the conventions which serve to identify, if not to define, the notion of fugue. In the exposition with which the work opens, the subject is announced by a number of different voices in turn, usually entering at different pitches (although neither the length and complexity of the exposition, nor the number of entering voices, is fixed). There may be more than one subject, and the subject(s) may well be incomplete. Furthermore, the initial exposition may be followed by a passage (or episode) from which the subject is entirely absent. In the course of the fugue there may be any number of episodes or expositions, and again there is no established or obligatory form. After the exposition, the themes or subjects are, as it were, played with, explored, reflected, inverted, transposed, mirrored, and so on, in different voices and in different keys, all of which in some way relate back to the original. For example, Bach's *Art of Fugue*, so admired by Duras, is an amazingly complex cycle of 14 fugues, each of which, though different, explores the potentialities of the initial subject of the first fugue. Bach's 'idealized world of uncompromised invention' thus sets the tone for the contemporary notion of fugue as not so much a form as 'an invitation to invent a form relevant to the idiosyncratic demands of the composition'.[27]

A musical form that is not a form; a musical texture that eludes definition whilst being characterized by its complex polyphonic and contrapuntal voices; a musical process that is 'never ending' but open-ended, and which is essentially self-reflexive—it is easy to identify both why fugue should fascinate Duras, and why it might be tempting to examine her works within its terms of reference. But before applying this idea directly to her filmic texts, I want to consider briefly the significance of Barthes's contention that it is through studying the relationship between music and other art forms that an understanding of contemporary culture in general may best be reached (Barthes states that 'analyzing music, even more than literature or painting, helps us to understand modernity').[28] In the light of this, the statement in the section on fugue in *The New Grove Dictionary*, to the effect that the current widespread interest in fugue reflects the 'essentially contrapuntal outlook' of the twentieth century, is particularly intriguing. For although this comment prefaces an account of the place of fugue in the works of twentieth-century composers such as Hindemith, Shostakovich and Bartok, it is clear not only that the modernist fascination with fugue which it identifies widely exceeds the domain of music, but also that within this fascination we might (if Barthes is right) obtain a clearer understanding of modern culture in general. Examples of overt recognition of the fascination exerted by fugue might include Perec's film *Les lieux d'une fugue*, whose autobiographical reference is to a childhood memory of playing truant, whose locations are mainly those where this escapade actually took place, whose soundtrack is based on Schumann's *Kreisleriana*, and whose editing is governed by precise musical permutations like a 'rhythmic repetition of elements in a sestina-like sequence'.[29] Moreover, Perec's remembered childhood self is not represented in the film, thus creating a strong sense of absence or escape. Film as fugue, we might say.[30] Aldous Huxley's 1928 novel *Point Counter Point* provides an interesting literary example of experimentation with musical form, for the construction of its complex, large-scale and elaborate plot is closely modelled upon Bach's *Suite No. 2, in B Minor.* Even in critical theory, the notion of fugue appears, for instance, in Julia Kristeva's desire to analyze the 'Other', the foreigner, in terms of 'the harmonious repetition of the differences it implies', as part of her proposal that Bach's fugues can provide a model for approaching contemporary issues.[31] In art, Paul Klee's conviction that the language of art could be understood and reworked in terms of fugue, and that eighteenth-century counterpoint could be translated directly into gradations of colour and repetitions and changes of shapes in order to accord to visual motifs the unfolding and modulating quality of aural ones, is highly significant. It is also beautifully illustrated by Klee himself in paintings such as *Fugue in Red* (1921). As a final example, we can see in Glenn Gould's experiments with Contrapuntal Radio an attempt to create a radically new form of radio documentary that would escape the linearity and predictability of traditional broadcasting by creating the verbal equivalent of musical counterpoint. What is particularly interesting about this project, undertaken by one of the century's finest performers of Bach, and whose composition *So You Want To Write A Fugue* (a fugue about fugue) provides a playful and helpful insight into the nature of fugue, is that the techniques which he uses, the way in which voices, music, and sounds all function as equivalent signifiers within a polyphonic pattern, is remarkably close to those which characterize Duras's films. In Gould's documentary about Schoenberg, for instance, the voices of a number of composers and conductors are heard simultaneously, while a Gregorian Chant and the music of Guillaume Dufay, Guillaume de Machaut, and Karlheinz Stockhausen are all mixed together in the background. Gould suggests that the real interest of this polyphonic approach arises from the fact that the listener must choose which of the many competing voices to follow. The 'composition' offers then total freedom of choice and interpretation, and requires an entirely creative and original response from each listener.[32]

With this in mind, we can understand Edward Said's suggestion that it is the simultaneity of the multiple contributing voices, their ability to provoke confusion and uncertainty, their inherent expressive freedom, and their demand for an essentially creative listener, that accounts for the contemporary fascination with fugue.[33] Indeed, it is this notion of simultaneity which is of central importance to Duras's film technique, for by making the visual image simply one amongst many competing polyphonic voices, and by constantly exploiting both their immediacy (which for Duras constitutes one of the few advantages of film over literature) and their simultaneity, she is able to attack and weaken the simplistic unambiguity of the filmic image, and to satisfy her desire to portray everything at once, 'all things confounded into a single one'.[34] The result is to ensure both that the film remains entirely mobile and that its 'meanings' will be a function of the creativity of each individual spectator. Seen in this way, fugue is a 'form' particularly suited to the conflicting and contradictory viewpoints of modernism.

While I do not have the time in this chapter to provide a sustained analysis of Duras's films as fugal textures, I should like to offer a brief example of the direction of my findings by referring to the opening and closing scenes of *India Song*. If we break these down into their basic (and simplified) components, certain key structural patterns can be observed. The opening scene (3′45″) presents us with an exterior view of a still landscape over whose hazy blue/green contours the sun is very slowly, almost imperceptibly, setting. The camera remains entirely static throughout, and beyond a very gradual darkening of the colours the eye detects almost no movement. (In fact, a bird does fly across the screen, but it is not foregrounded in any way and its visual impact is minimal.) The soundtrack, on the other hand, is busy. There is a lively contrapuntal play between the song, chants, cries, and chattering of the (unseen) beggar woman, in an unknown, impenetrable language, and the sustained dialogue in French between two unseen and unidentified female narrators. These voices, with their insecure status and shifting tenses, provide a context for the beggar woman, tracing her long journey of misery and loss to Calcutta and introducing the main subject material of the film: madness, loss, death, suffering and 'elles', the unknown women of whom more will be heard in the next scene. As their voices pause, we hear 'India Song' played on a piano, and the music carries us into the second scene of the film. We can already glimpse the radical disjunction between sound and images, for the information we expect of an establishing shot is conveyed not to the eye but to the ear, where, moreover, its status is uncertain and insecure. However, the dialogue is disturbing as well as puzzling since it sets up in the viewer a conviction that it is the off-screen space—the invisible element of film, the area beyond representation—which is the locus of the action and which contains the key to the film's subject matter.

What, then, of the concluding scene? This time it is the eyes, rather than the ears, that are kept busy. What we see is a map in extreme close-up (a representation of landscape rather than its visual depiction). The camera now moves constantly as it traces the contours of the map, examining its coastline and towns before following the long meandering course of the Mekong river. The dominant colours are pinks and orange. This time there are no voices apart from a very faint sound of the beggar woman's chant at the beginning which, like the flight of the bird in the first scene, links the visible and the invisible spaces of the shot. There is no narration although we do hear music, 'India Song' again, on the piano, and this music continues during the credits which follow. Just as it was hard to see the setting sun of the opening scene as a beginning, so, too, it is difficult to take this scene as a conclusion. There is no tying-up of loose ends, no narrative climax. But there does seem to be an important relationship between the two scenes. By depicting the various elements in diagrammatic form and then superimposing them, Duras produces some interesting contrasts, and this further substantiates my earlier claim that the key to understanding her technique, and the way in which we can apply the musical analogy to her work without encountering any of the traditional problems, lies in the fact that she does not consistently (either from film to film or within any film) privilege any single filmic element; all elements are considered equivalent carriers of meaning. Thus, in comparing the opening and closing shots of *India Song*, we can see that the narration has, quite simply, passed from voice to camera. It is the camera now which traces the beggar woman's painful journey, but in reverse, and it is our eyes, our reading of the names written on the map which transfer the tale of that dreadful journey to our imagination, for the names we read evoke the memories which we have formed during the course of the film. The names then, whose sounds have become familiar through their extensive repetitions in the film, act here as a visual leitmotif (although we have not actually read them before). In offering not a landscape but a map, Duras is again shifting the visual voice. The setting of the film, which we have previously created in our imagination almost entirely through the voices and music we hear, is now imagined afresh as we read the map. (We could establish a direct link here with the shot of the scores in *Nathalie Granger* discussed earlier.) But it is not only the place of narration which has changed. In the first scene, for example, we concentrated on the sun, as visual symbol of the heat which plays so central a role in the film (in its relationship with light/Calcutta/the monsoon/madness/heat/illness/death, and so on). In this scene (which is in fact immediately preceded by Duras in voice-over describing the heat), the sun is now represented by colour; the pink and orange shades of the map have replaced the blues and greens of the landscape at dusk. The period and setting which were introduced by the narrating voices in the first scene are here expressed through the music of 'India Song' which is now heavy with our own memories of death, sadness, loss, suffering (the very themes that were introduced by the two women's voices in the first scene).

Although we can thus analyze the two scenes in terms of modulation and change, and can even approach the last as a mirror fugue or inversion of the first, it would be impossible to approach them in terms of narrative development. There is no narrative reason why the opening shot, with its setting sun and growing darkness, and its narrating voices striving to recall past events, marks the beginning of the film, or why the map, with its promise of journey, should be the end. The two scenes are in fact dealing with the same subjects, but this does not imply stasis for movement or change has occurred both in our reading of those subjects, which gathers new intensity with each new repetition, and, of course, in the treatment they are accorded (voices, keys, intervals, constantly switch roles). Thus, it would be quite possible to look at the relationship between each of the scenes in *India Song* in this way, and to see how Duras, like Bach, constructs endless variation within the same restricted subjects, and how the motivic material of her films is itself structured through reflection, superimposition and modulation. This places them securely within the fugal tradition whilst radically excluding them from the filmic one. Similarly, if we consider the essential open-endedness of fugue which never reaches a point of resolution and conclusion but simply ends when the composer has had enough ('Fugue must perform its frequently stealthy work with continuously shifting melodic fragments that remain, in the "true" sense, perpetually unfinished'),[35] we can establish further parallels with almost the entirety of Duras's creative work which avoids narrative closure.

By rejecting a stable narrative structure, by undermining and ultimately destroying the self-defining certainty of the filmic image, and by situating the locus of the action in an off-screen space which lies ultimately within the imagination of each spectator, Duras is creating film which functions as music, film whose meaning is consequently situated beyond vision and language and so expresses the inexpressible. Blanchot, noticing this quality, sees Duras as a writer whose works strive to attain the 'pure' language of Mallarmé, 'language ... without power, without subterfuge'.[36] But Mallarmé's 'pure' language was, of course, a striving for the condition of music, for language untrammelled by definition and unsullied by utilitarian function, for language as endless and perfect potential. Given that Duras's films also strive to work as music, it is through the multiple voices of film as fugue, with their constantly shifting referents and their creation of perpetually deferred desires, that they can offer the spectator an unlimited creative potential, an absolute open-endedness.

Coda

Even this brief glance has, I hope, indicated some of the many ways in which the concept of fugue offers a helpful and exciting attractive framework in which to view Duras's works, both individually and as related elements within the corpus. However, by way of conclusion, and bearing in mind Barthes's comments about music as a key to understanding modernity, I should like to introduce yet another voice into this discussion by juxtaposing Duras's *L'homme atlantique* and Cage's *4′33″* (1952) because of the way in which each explores and renews the medium used by means of what appears to be the total destruction of that medium. The screen remains entirely blank for over half of *L'homme atlantique,* while Cage's composition in three movements for an (unspecified) solo instrument (a work which he describes as his 'own best piece',[37] inevitably inviting comparison with Duras's 'best shot' which we discussed earlier) is composed of 4′33″ of silence. In other words, music offers not patterns of sound in these examples but an absence of sound, and film offers not visual structures but an absence of visual structures.

Let us develop our comparison a little further. Cage maintains that his composition highlights the audience's assumptions in a concert that the moments between the notes, the 'non-notes', are silence. But he insists that listening is a matter of hearing the structured silences as much as the notes; there is, he claims, no silence. The ambient noises which we try to exclude or ignore in a performance are an integral part of that concert, much as the acoustic is a feature. Thus, in taking away the props which are the notes, he forces us to listen in a new way and to question our concepts of sound and silence and of the divisions between them. Ultimately, we must accept the fact that the music will be created by each of us within our own heads, and that our role as listeners is not passive but active, i.e. that we are the ultimate creators. Duras sets herself a similar, if arguably harder task. The audience's expectations of film are that it should provide a good narrative, that the sounds and music which accompany the images should be mutually supportive, and that nothing must get in the way of the story. By removing images altogether and putting us in front of a dark screen (variously 'la nuit noire', 'la chambre noire'), Duras, too, is removing the image prop and forcing us to look inwards by using our imagination. The limitations of the image as sign are thus overcome. Like Cage's audience, Duras's spectators must play an essentially active and creative role and question the concepts of listening and looking, as well as the relationship between the two.

So what of fugue then? Via Duras and Cage, we have slipped from the first to the second of our initial definitions, i.e. from musical texturing back to the word's original meaning of escape and absence. In *4'33"*, as in *L'homme atlantique*, the subject has disappeared ('a fait une fugue'). Or has it? Bringing together Cage and Duras surely pinpoints the articulation of silence/invisibility at the core of modernism. And given that the spaces or silences which all of Duras's films articulate—and which constitute the locus of their most complex meanings (of desire, memory and loss)—are exactly those areas which, although problematic in film, are traditionally the domain of music, we can perhaps begin to understand how Duras's films, while they may exclude themselves from cinematic tradition, fit quite comfortably into the fugal tradition. Cinema: une joie, comme on dit: musique. Film: an art of fugue.

Notes

(N.B.: All translations from the French texts are my own.)

1 Youssef Ishaghpour, *Cinéma contemporain de ce côté du miroir*, Paris, La Différence, 1986, p. 274.

2 Carol J. Murphy, 'Duras' *L'Amant*: Memories from an Absent Photo', in *Remains to be Seen: Essays on Marguerite Duras*, ed. Sanford S. Ames, New York, Peter Lang, 1988, p. 172.

3 Jacques-Pierre Amette, 'Duras, la reine Margot', *Le Point*, No. 1008, 11 January 1992, pp. 57–60; p. 58: 'Duras ramifie systématiquement son oeuvre et joue de tous les claviers'.

4 Yvonne Guers-Villate, *Continuité/discontinuité de l'oeuvre durassienne*, Brussels, Editions de l'Université de Bruxelles, 1985, p. 159: 'Il s'agit alors d'orchestrer différemment ... certains motifs, comme dans une fugue musicale'.

5 Alain Vircondelet, *Duras: Biographie*, Paris, François Bourin, 1991, p. 201: 'sa caméra rendra des accents graves et monotones, comme une sonate pour violoncelle, répétitive et obsédante'.

6 Madeleine Borgomano, *L'écriture filmique de Marguerite Duras*, Paris, Albatros, 1985, p. 121.

7 Ames, *Remains to be Seen*, p. 7.

8 Anthony Storr, *Music and the Mind*, London, Harper Collins, 1977, p. 149.

9 See David Bordwell, 'The Musical Analogy', *Yale French Studies*, No. 60 (1980), pp. 141–56.

10 For an example of close analysis, see John Phillips, 'The mathematics of meaning: Marguerite Duras's *Moderato cantabile*', *Nottingham French Studies*, Vol. 34, No. 2 (Autumn 1995), pp. 41–54, in which Phillips argues that the novel is 'meaningfully structured according to a mathematics of music', although his ultimate conclusions, based around a fairly rigid elaboration of binary oppositions, suggests a rather frustrating exercise in closure rather than an exploration of text as opening, as other. For an analysis of *India Song* which recognizes musical techniques, see Marie-Claire Ropars-Wuilleumier, 'The Disembodied voice: *India Song*', *Yale French Studies*, No. 60 (1960), pp. 241–68.

11 'Bien sûr, on ne peut pas parler de la musique' (Marguerite Duras and Michelle Porte, *Les lieux de Marguerite Duras*, Paris, Minuit, 1977, p. 29).

12 See, for example, *L'amant*, Paris, Minuit, 1984, pp. 137–38.

13 Duras and Porte, *Les lieux*, p. 39: 'La musique m'épouvante … me bouleverse'.

14 Duras and Porte, *Les lieux*, p. 30: '[c]e langage-là que nous ne pouvons pas décrypter, le langage de la musique'.

15 Anton Ehrenzweig, *The Psychoanalysis of Artistic Vision and Hearing*, London, Sheldon Press, 1975, pp. 164–65.

16 Claudia Gorbman, *Unheard Melodies: Narrative Film Music*, Bloomington IN, Indiana University Press, 1987, p. 73.

17 For a traditional account of music's supporting role in film, see, for example, Maurice Jaubert, 'Music on the Screen', in *Footnotes to the Film*, ed. Charles Davy, New York, Oxford University Press, 1937, pp. 111–15.

18 See Duras and Porte, *Les lieux*, p. 38.

19 One consequence of the way Duras uses all aspects of film language as equivalent signifiers is the creation of the visual leitmotif, i.e. images such as Anne-Marie Stretter's red bicycle which are accorded the same function as their musical counterparts.

20 In, for example: *Chronik der Anna Magdalena Bach* (Straub and Huillet, 1968); *Rendez-vous à Bray* (Delvaux, 1971); *L'Eden et après* (Robbe-Grillet, 1971); *Les lieux d'une fugue* (Perec, 1976).

21 '[U]ne joie: cinéma comme on dit: musique' (Marguerite Duras, 'Les yeux verts', *Cahiers du Cinéma*, Nos 312–13 (June–July 1980), p. 31).

22 Duras, 'Les yeux verts', p. 173: 'ce truc pourri qu'on appelle le cinéma'.

23 Marguerite Duras, *Le camion, suivi de Entretien avec Michelle Porte*, Paris, Minuit, 1977, p. 75: 'Le cinéma arrête le texte, frappe de mort sa descendence: l'imaginaire.'

24 See Wendy Everett, 'Slipping in and out of focus: words and images in the filmic discourse of Marguerite Duras', *Nottingham French Studies*, Vol. 34, No. 2 (Autumn 1995), pp. 55–66.

25 Marguerite Duras, *Nathalie Granger, suivi de La femme du Gange*, Paris, Gallimard, 1973, pp. 29–30.

26 See Alfred Mann, *The Study of Fugue*, Oxford, Faber & Faber, 1958 p. v.

27 Glenn Gould, 'Art of the Fugue', in John McGreevy, *Glenn Gould, Variations, By Himself and His Friends*, New York, Quill, 1983, pp. 201–14; p. 205.

28 See Roland Barthes, 'Analyse musicale et travail intellectuel', *Le Monde*, 2 March 1978 (republished in *Oeuvres complètes*, Vol. 3, Paris, Seuil, 1995, pp. 819–20; p. 819): 'l'analyse musicale, mieux encore que celle du texte ou de la peinture, nous conduit à comprendre la modernité'.

29 See David Bellos, *Georges Perec, A Life in Words*, London, Harvill, 1995, p. 598.

30 David Bellos, *Georges Perec*, pp. 597–98.

31 Julia Kristeva, *Strangers to Ourselves* (1988), trans. Léon. S. Roudiez, New York, Columbia University Press, 1991, p. 3.

32 Robert Hurwitz, 'Towards a Contrapuntal Radio', in McGreevy, *Glenn Gould*, pp. 253–63.

33 Edward W. Said, 'The Music Itself: Glenn Gould's Contrapuntal Vision', in McGreevy, *Glenn Gould*, pp. 45–54; p. 47.

34 Duras, *L'amant*, p. 15: 'toutes choses confondues en une seule'.

35 Gould, 'Art of the Fugue', p. 205.

36 Maurice Blanchot, *Le livre à venir*, Paris, Gallimard, 1959, p. 44: 'le langage ... sans pouvoir, langage du rapport nu'.

37 Richard Kostelanetz, *Conversing with Cage*, London, New York and Sydney, Omnibus Press, 1988, p. 65.

CHAPTER 2

Screening the Vampire: Notes on *India Song* and the Photographic Images of *La mer écrite*

Gill Houghton

> For the scenes in front of the mirror we'd shoot without knowing what the mirror was going to do, because it had a life of its own. We treated the mirror like a stranger—and the person in the mirror as someone we did not know. I knew what Delphine Seyrig would do in front of the mirror. But I'd no idea what that would lead to inside it. And that, too, was fantastic. Even for me, when I see the film sometimes, I'm caught up as a spectator in a kind of vertigo.[1]

In what follows I speak from the position of an artist rather than theorist, and I explore the ways in which this locates me in a different methodology and different relationship to theory and practice. My reading of Duras's work is thus initially through visual imagery. The concepts which make up the chapter's main headings—Reflections and Distortions, Borders/Mist, Glass, Darkness, Day/Light, the Photograph, Murder—refer to the way I might use concepts or materials in my own practice in order to think about the relationship of time and space. These can often be fragmentary and are concerned with the temporality of moments of everyday life. Arranged in sequence as one might see an image in a film or photograph, they are intended deliberately not to give a clear linear reading, and thus may present contradictions, repetitions, interruptions and blurrings in the reading of the text. My reason for doing this is to present a new way of looking at Duras's work, one that leads from a linear sense of time and space in *India Song*—a film consumed by its own narcissism and doomed, I will argue, like the vampire—to a never-ending place of repetition of that time. This will lead me in turn to consider *La mer écrite*, a book of photographs which presents clues, fragments and parts of events having no fixed linear time and containing a temporality and open space of looking in both image and text.

Reflections and Distortions

India Song is a film that presents a reflection and re-reflection of itself. It devours both its dead self and repeats and devours the interior space which Marguerite Duras presents. It is a film in which, I think, Duras fails ever to go beyond an internal, all-consuming work, for it fails to present any resolution or catharsis. However, from this failure Duras manages to begin to map a way forward for the image in her future visual work and, most interestingly, to provide a framework and dialogue for the relations between moving images and stills, film and photography. Obviously, in the period since *India Song* there are numerous works to consider, but it is my aim to focus on some key points of comparison and difference between this film and *La mer écrite*, where the images wander and meander, uncontained, and thus create a different kind of reflection. *La mer écrite* highlights, in fact, the relation in *India Song* between narcissism and vampirism, the way in which the film reflects itself narcissistically as a reflection on—and reflection of—a never-ending vampirism.

What is a vampire? The vampire exists in many guises and is able to travel through time and space, existing in different places at the same time. It can take the form both of bats and wolves and thus reflects the double, or rather distorted mirror image. In *The Old Man and The Wolves,* for instance, Julia Kristeva creates an allegorical image of the wolves as the struggle between East and West. Kristeva has said of the story: 'Here importantly the wolves are contagious; they inject people to the same extent that one can no longer make out their human faces.'[2] She writes at one moment in the book that 'the old man realized the wolf had injected him with its venom',[3] and: 'I saw fang marks'.[4] This is similar to the bite of the vampire which injects and claims its victims for vampirism. The characters in Kristeva's book do not embody stable identities, hence the presence of the doppelgänger.[5] The vampire is caught in a never-ending repetition in order to survive.

The idea of a living dead has great significance within the film *India Song*, for although in love with love and compliant with pleasure, Duras's characters are fond of the death they believe they bear within themselves. In her major study of Duras in *Soleil noir: dépression et mélancolie*, Kristeva has suggested that due to its repetition of depression and melancholia, Duras's written work is non-cathartic. She contrasts this with the compensatory nature of Duras's films due to the filmic image's 'uncontrollable proliferation of associations rich or poor in meaning and emotion depending on the viewer'.[6] Filmed depression, Kristeva claims, always seems a 'foreign artifice': in the case of Duras's cinema, where the seductive power of the characters is increased, depression is acted out and thus less contagious than in her written work.[7] I will show, however, that non-catharsis also extends to the film works and in particular to *India Song*, a repetitive, reflective, cyclical film that allows no reprieve for Duras's characters or her viewers. Indeed, we are saturated, doubled and reflected as we absorb the melancholia of the image, and the film could be regarded, therefore, as a form of necrophilic, narcissistic vampirism. As an undead, the vampire repeats, never ends and reflects. It sucks and devours, caught in a never-ending repetition without resolution. This forms the basis of a non-cathartic practice for Duras, since she does not allow the viewer a resolved position in the film.

Let us establish first some conceptual areas for reflection in *India Song*. Ideas of time are represented through a series of opposites: darkness/light and day/night. The Image is formed by the absence and presence of the dead/undead in the film and the photograph, moving and static time which in turn focuses the viewer on the space of the film through the mirror. The mirror provides reflection and non-reflection through light/dark and forms the double of bodies and space or, in the case of the vampire, the absence of reflection in the mirror. It also contains time, image and space together, just as time will at points contain image and space. I say at points because this is deliberately part of the discussion that surrounds Duras's work. Is the black/blank time, for instance, actually containing the image or space? Through the appearance/disappearance of the body during the day/night, I will consider the space between these times and how this will be created through a mist or fog, as seen in many horror films. It is here, through the mirror, that Duras sets up spatially a question of distance, or of what will be in the distance—distance in terms of time and a spatial, formal distance, between reflections, objects and their distortions. As is crucial to vampire films, the mirror detects the presence or absence of being. To take the containment of borders within space/time: how does one create a space within the confines of interiority, that is to say, states of occurrence and non-occurrence of the image that create a limit yet also location for the image both as negative and as positive, thus creating an *other space*? The representation of space in the film *India Song*, a space of dead *other*, is a space that appears to be indecipherable yet from which, as I will show, a through-space is created, a split in the boundary, a tremor between interior and exterior.

Borders/Mist

I would like to consider the first frame of the film *India Song* as mist.[8] Mist is referred to in the film as a surround for darkness, as a relation to dampness/rain, and a reference both to the wet and the dry, Venice and Calcutta. But mist also refers to something hidden, something unknown, a shroud of *ethereal* form like breath on a mirror. In a film by one of Duras's favourite directors, Carl T. Dreyer, the poetically austere *Vampyr* (1932) about the strange adventures of young Allan Gray who is inspired by studies of devil worship and vampire terror in earlier centuries, mist similarly pushes the image to the limits of decipherabilty.[9] Out on the lake, for example, calling and voices are heard within the mist almost detached from Gray and Gisèle. The mist dissolves all boundaries between themselves and the point of landing, creating a space which seems infinite but in which one is contained. As viewers, we, too, become contained within this space and share the characters' experience of blocked vision and of doubled and repeated echoes. In *India Song* one of the anonymous voices says of the vice-consul: 'Perhaps he didn't see that there were people in that garden … in that light … in that kind of *mist*'.[10] Mist creates a point between dark and light, day and night in both films. Given that vampires usually inhabit night and remain covered during the day, it is significant that this mist shrouds the point between appearance and disappearance, similar to the relation to shadows and the movement of extra-corporeal experience which Dreyer presents as shadows in *Vampyr*.

If mist marks the point between appearance and disappearance, as also in Werner Herzog's *Nosferatu: the Vampyre* (1979), the vampire emerges directly from it. Before the mist all actions occur during the night, and after the mist we see daylight restored. Duras uses relations of black to white, dark to light, and night to day in *India Song* which mirror the associations made in *Vampyr*. Indeed, she alludes to the association of a living dead at night-time not only in the film but also in the film script and play. There is a specific relation between sun rising and sun setting. In her notes on *India Song* Duras writes: 'The exterior shots also present a scarcely changing image, always immersed in night.'[11] We have a relation between day and night, with Anne-Marie Stretter being seen mostly at night:

> *Voice 2*: Speaking of her past—She arrived at the dance late … in the middle of the night …[12]

And again of the vice-consul:

> *Voice 2*: … he comes every night …[13]

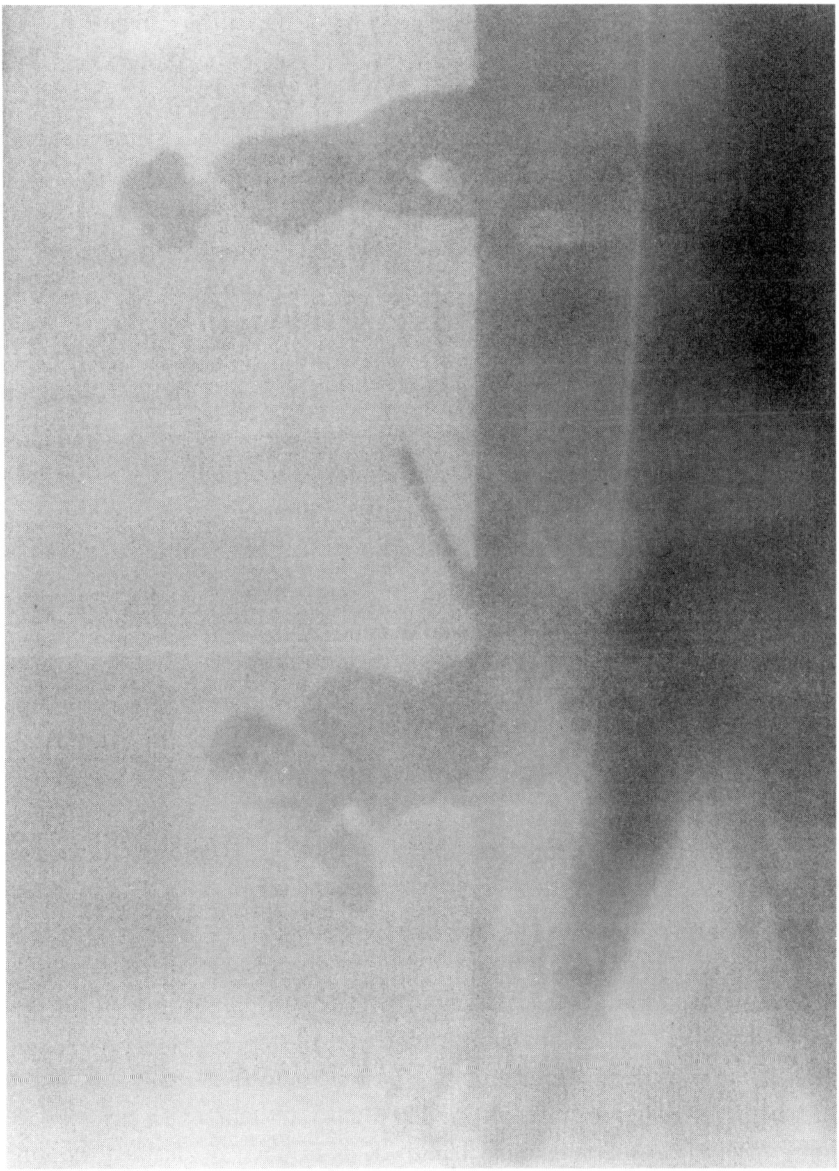

Vampyr (1932). Courtesy of BFI Stills, Posters and Designs.

Interestingly, the chattering voices in *India Song* are set up to narrate and, as surveillants, watch what happens in the Embassy. In a study of vampires in the Old and New World, and with specific reference to Anne Rice's *Vampire Chronicles*, Ken Gelder has noted that 'self-discovery is no longer personal (or familial), but organizational. [The vampire] Lestat has to negotiate with the Talamasca to access his archives; he realizes, in the meantime, that he has come into contact with an organization which knows more about him than he knows about it. That is, he realizes that he has been all the while under surveillance'.[14] Gelder goes on to say that 'this is also a feature of vampires themselves, which constantly monitor each other's movements and read each other's thoughts (or conversely try to 'cloak' their thoughts from each other). In [Rice's] *The Queen of the Damned* they are likened to radio receivers ... A tension is worked out in the novels between the vampires' need for anonymity or privacy, and their nagging sense that someone—another vampire, usually—is watching them, that they are part of a larger network of "airwaves"'.[15] Duras sets up this difference between events happening during the night and during the day, although this situation changes with the development of the postmodern vampire by Abel Ferrara in his film *The Addiction* (1997). This film merits our attention.

The Addiction is shot in black and white and has a haunting starkness. Kathy Corklin, a philosophy student at New York University, is researching for her PhD thesis and is dragged into an alley at night by a stranger who bites her on the neck and sucks her blood. Kathy recovers from the attack but develops an appetite and addiction for blood. At first she can only draw blood from others via a syringe, an analogy both to drug culture and to the spread of the AIDS virus in the late twentieth century. Kathy's life is shown with all the withdrawal symptoms of addiction. Interspersed with her own life and her philosophical readings are shots of the Holocaust, recalling those of Hiroshima victims in Alain Resnais's 1959 film, *Hiroshima mon amour*, scripted by Duras. Kathy speculates at one point on the reason for all these deaths. *The Addiction* explores the addiction of life, politics and power, and the complicated life of a vampire who has no escape from the very thing which she strove to acquire in the first place. Christopher Walken offers an important contrast to Kathy's addiction since as a vampire he is able to exist for periods both during the day and at night (the night allows for a build up of resistance to light). As a postmodern vampire he has learned to live, 'to blend in', as he says, by 'fasting', working and eating as humans do, rather than being addicted constantly to blood. He treads the uneasy boundary between the living and the living dead. Towards the end of the film Kathy invites all her colleagues and supervisors of her thesis to a party at night. She thanks them and with other vampires bites them. They

Hiroshima mon amour (1959). Courtesy of BFI Stills, Posters and Designs.

all become involved in the same addiction. Kathy then strives to find some sort of redemption.

In *India Song* Duras points to a similar presence of the living dead:

> *Voice 2*: ... Out. Every evening. She comes back when it's dark [i.e. before light].[16]
>
> *Voice 1*: No one can sleep?
> *Voice 2*: No.[17]

The story of Anne-Marie Stretter as a memory of the past evokes a timelessness yet it is contained within this never-ending, moving, repeated inability to sleep. Again, Duras gives as directions in the text the space between appearance and disappearance: 'It is getting darker. The bodies grow less and less distinguishable. Above them the fan goes on turning, the blades gleaming slowly. You can no longer tell any one body from another'.[18] Most of the film takes place during the time of darkness at night as if night were day and one could only exist during this time. The languor and torpor of movement suggest an equivalence to somnambulism and floating:

> *Voice B*: We saw him at night through our bedroom windows, walking ... at night as if in the middle of the day ...
>
> (Repeat) ... at night as if in the middle of the day ...
>
> He called down death on Lahore ... fire ... he shouted too ... disconnected words ... he was laughing.[19]

Three things are important here: the fact that it is night, the repetition by Duras of this fact, and the relation to fire (fire as light, heat and combustion). Vampires combust on contact with dawn or daylight. So, although the thinking here is often of lepers, there is clearly also the idea of self-combustion before light. Duras refers to lepers falling into dust—burning ashes, dust and leprosy:

> —Then beyond the garden, gleams in the sky. Either day or fire—rust-coloured fire. The voice is slow: a calm acceleration
>
> *Voice 1*: Those gleams over there?
> *Voice 2*: The burning ghats
> *Voice 1*: Burning people who've starved to death?
> *Voice 2*: Yes
>
> It will soon be daylight.[20]

In her notes to *India Song* Duras describes seeing the film as a double rectangle. I perceive this as a representation of the relationship between light/dark, day/night and black/white. The reference to the double rectangle also as an image is related to the double in the film, i.e. the mirror, its reflection and distortion, a relationship which can be represented thus:

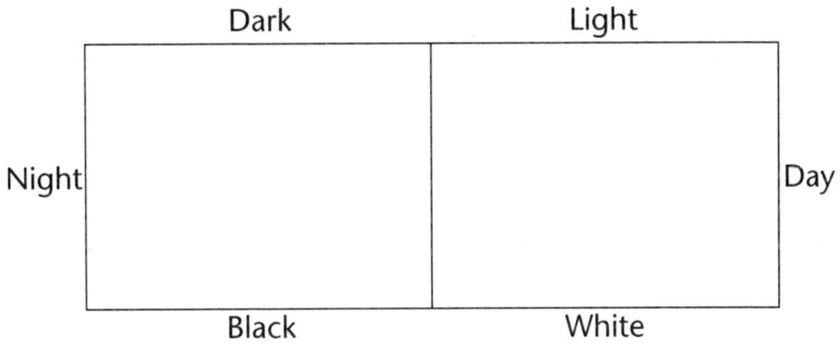

Duras creates a form of geometry through mirrors, glass and windows in order to organize the spatial temporal relationship of image and time in her films. *India Song*, in particular, produces specific co-ordinates in space which thus become both subject and object within the image. Beginning with dark from the drawing above it can be seen in the following terms, where the co-ordinates of the double rectangle present a sense of linear time-space:

Dark	Light	Day	White	Black	Night
Light	Day	White	Black	Night	Dark
Day	White	Black	Night	Dark	Light
White	Black	Night	Dark	Light	Day
Black	Night	Dark	Light	Day	White
Night	Dark	Light	Day	White	Black

Viewing this double rectangle from left to right, beginning with Dark, we can read each column below around to the right and back again, creating a never-ending form of linear time-space. Therefore, what first appears to be an open set of co-ordinates does, in fact, create a contained logic with no diversions or wanderings. Once the viewer returns to Dark the sequence begins again. As Kristeva has pointed out with regard to the coupling of doubling of characters in Duras's fiction, this is a 'blocked repetition', or 'reduplication':

> While what is repeated ripples out in time, reduplication lies outside time. It is a reverberation in space, a play of mirrors lacking perspective or duration. A double can hold fast for a while the instability of the same and give it a temporary identity, but mostly it throws the same into a great gulf that opens up an unsuspected, unfathomable substance. The double is the unconscious substance of the same, that which threatens it and can engulf it.[21]

That which is engulfed opens itself up to failure and to ruin. This is avoided in *India Song* (although not in *Son nom de Venise dans Calcutta désert*, made a year later with the same soundtrack) precisely because each interdependent section and relation of co-ordinates relates specifically to spaces and clues in the horror genre. The drawing of the relationship of each of these co-ordinates creates visually both a transparent screen, almost like a mirror or glass in its vertical/horizontal plane, and a plan of the edges and boundaries seen as a flat plan (of the embassy ballroom, for instance). This boundary between inside/outside is important in Duras's later films such as *L'homme atlantique*, and in the photographs of *La mer écrite*. Duras draws out the space so that the edges—for instance, the mirror against the wall, the window between inside and outside—form in relation to the volume of interior space or exterior space a spatial relationship: a relationship between intimacy and different relations of distance, and between solitude and different relations to proximity. Reflections in the mirror and shadows also create an ethereal, geometric volume. The first part of the drawing can be viewed as 'Glass'.

Glass

> That is the point of the glass, he wrote. Not a *surface* to be *covered*. Not an *object* to be *made*. Not a *picture of*, he wrote, and *not the thing itself. Shadow* and *projection*, he wrote. *Present* and *absent* at the same time. *Existent* and *non-existent*. A shadow has to be cast by something, he wrote. Every shadow implies an object and a source of light. On the glass the shadow, but shadow of what? What will the viewer see? He wrote. Something on the glass. The wall of the gallery, the other exhibits hanging on it. People moving, standing, leaning forward. And his reflection. Himself bending forward and looking. Looking at. Looking through. Looking back at himself looking. *Shadow of what?*[22]

Immediately following Duras's invitation, like Alice through the looking glass, to step into the frame in the form of the large mirror which encompasses the first image of *India Song*, Durassian cinema employs windows, glass and mirrors as a reflection of the gaze, of borders and of space, with each mirror or window operating as a screen. The mirror in *India Song* reflects all these possibilities; indeed, as a silver glass it focuses our gaze on the reflections of this interior. The mirror gives us an unreal reflection of ourselves; it reflects what we presume to be an image of body and space. It provides a space for love, love of the self, love of the body and love of space. This is where Duras's narcissistic love of the film in love with itself as film is also reflected. The film haunts itself. Anne-Marie Stretter exists both as non-reflected and then reflected in the mirror. Duras presents her almost as a kind of *film noir* vamp who devours and reflects devouring. As a *vamp*ire she entices (and devours) her male companions during the night. We see them towards the end of the film walk together as vampires through the film in the hotel. She reflects devouring whilst reclining in her sleep, presenting her naked breast as an erotic form of devouring and an invitation to devour or suck.[23] The Mirror thus exists to double and contradict, to show the ethe*real* and the *ethe*real as both same and other. The vice-consul is referred to as shooting himself in the mirror, although at this point all mirrors are unbroken. Vampires are immune to the effects of bullets and cannot be penetrated by them to any detrimental effect.

The lake in *India Song* acts as a double to the mirror, a shimmering, moving, reflective pool. We see the vice-consul walking around the edge of the lake seeing himself reflected as Narcissus once did. The reference here is surely to the shots in *Vampyr* of Gray walking around the edge of the lake in his search for the vampire. Could Duras have been thinking here of the narcissistic indulgence created in *India Song* by one vast mirror? Of the film itself as the embodiment of Narcissus? If so, then perhaps this love of the film will become important for our consideration of how it comes into being from the dead. As a detective might put it, how can we solve this death?

Darkness

With night-time comes darkness and this constitutes a connecting thread in Duras's films. It seems that darkness creates a space for death and desire. It enshrouds *India Song* and we are aware of its full impact due to Duras's use of light through chandeliers, candles, glass and mirror. It permeates the night so that the living dead of the film function within the artificial light of night. Anne-Marie Stretter's suicide takes place just as darkness is ending—a self-combustion when stepping out into the daylight? Duras has also discussed her relation to darkness and the viewer in a chapter of *Les yeux verts* entitled 'Le Noir'. She quotes Isi Beller on the experience of watching her films: '"In reading, we discover ourselves and in going to the movies, we lose ourselves"

India Song (1975). Courtesy of BFI Stills, Posters and Designs.

… when we go to see your films we do not lose ourselves. It is in the dark that we discover ourselves.'[24] In *India Song* the knowledge gained is specifically of death as desire. Anne-Marie Stretter desires death in an overwhelming sense as she goes to take her life. As a reflection of the undead she can never die. She is in limbo and unable to die, unless she is exposed to daylight. Jalal Toufic has pointed out the following:

> Darkness scares us, more because we feel a *presence* than because it is already a matte making possible a telepathy that undoes locality. The black of the iris is a matte that could not later be replaced by a visible element, hence the iris in Murnau's *Nosferatu* points to the presence of an invisible (that can not be reached even by telepathy or the uncanny ability of the dead/undead to materialize whatsoever in the Bardo state)—or better to a *presence*—and hence belongs to a phenomenon whose other manifestation is the absence of the vampire in the mirror.[25]

The iris allows the pupil to regulate the amount of light entering the eye and therefore form a large or small sphere of darkness. Darkness envelops the film in the form of the shadow which casts a dark patch across the space outside the embassy, in moonlight or in dawn light, between day and night. The shadow in *India Song* is cast by the beggar woman whom we do not see other than in shadow. (Similarly in *Vampyr*, Dreyer presents Gray and the Guard as shadows outside themselves.) As black space creates a space within Duras's film, so darkness and blackness become intertwined, thus allowing the viewer to experience darkness as moving time, i.e. time passing as darkness.

Duras extends the importance of blackness/darkness in *L'homme atlantique*. This film contains twenty minutes of black screen, dark spaces and several blanks of blue space. It begins with the sound of the sea and dark screen. We flit between dark/light and black screen, the light, sea, sand and beaches. Duras then directs Yann Andréa to look at the camera: 'until your gaze is blinding [*l'extinction de votre regard*], you must keep trying to look'. Yann is looking not only at the camera but out past the space while encountering his own double reflected in the blue light of the window, which functions as a mirror and screen between inside and outside. *L'homme atlantique* is about the desire to capture, to hold on to the desire for something, some image. Like the vampire active at night-time we are left sitting in this dark space. There is a constant shift in temporality of each shot. As one begins to focus, the image is removed. Duras frustrates the viewer and creates an uneasy vertigo; spectatorial pleasure is both contained and disrupted. Constant allusions to blinding, disappearance and darkness show us that nothing is permanent. Indeed, the changing of the image and blackness is so rapid that no vampire could survive this exposure. The film begins to look away from the interiority of night-life as presented in *India Song* where, as well as the relation to dark space, other areas of blackness are created which can be seen alone or in relation to darkness:

> A *black* pond C Look at the sky … sickness
> … this density … this filth
> … through the night.[26]

And in the text of *India Song* Anne-Marie Stretter is introduced in black.[27] In addition to numerous directions to black,[28] we also read, for example:

> *Voice 1*: (as before) What time is it?
> *Voice 2*: (pause) Four o'clock.
>
> Black Night.[29]

And:

> *Voice 4*: Yes. Didn't go out till after dark.[30]

Black is present both in the negative of the film and in the black and white photographs of Anne-Marie Stretter at the beginning of the film.

Day/Light

At the beginning of *India Song* we are reminded of the closing of the day by its absence. The film constantly reminds us of day by the presence of night, darkness and black. The viewer is claustrophobically contained within the space without day, and there is no relief from the weight of night. There are glimpses of a partial day/night through windows, before the evening begins in the embassy. This opposite of day and night is mirrored in the relation between black and white and light and white. During the film black and white are seen together, they reflect and mirror each other. White creates an image of starkness, flatness and blankness, and again references to colonial life infer containment and claustrophobia:

> It's strange—Most women in India have very white skins …
> —they lie out of the sun. Closed shutters … they're recluses.[31]

White also refers to death in the way that black can refer to death:

> *Voice 3*: That white patch … in a bend in the Ganges …? There …?
> *Voice 4* (hesitating): The English Cemetery—[32]

India Song (1975). Courtesy of BFI Stills, Posters and Designs.

There are countless images of reflection and light in white India.[33] References are made to Anne-Marie Stretter being dressed in white and to the whiteness of her dress,[34] and eventually four men will enter also dressed in white. White inhabits the space of night in a way which indicates and enhances its own reflection, since, for Duras, white must be viewed not only in its contrast to black.[35]

Richard Dyer has suggested that vampirism is expressed in colour as ghastly white and disgustingly cadaverous, without the blood of life which would give it colour.[36] Duras stresses the colonial other through the white of light and the negative and positive of film, and in particular through darkness/light as it relates to the vampire film. References to light are mostly artificial in *India Song*, particularly indoors. References to spaces outside the embassy all contain painful effects, such that natural light is dangerous. Here, vampires are destroyed by light:

> *Voice 1*: That Light?
> *Voice 2*: The monsoon.
> *Voice 1*: … no wind …
> *Voice 2* (continues): … it will break over Bengal …
> *Voice 1*: The dust?
> *Voice 2*: The middle of Calcutta.[37]

And again:

> *Voice 2*: … dead in the islands …
> *Voice 1*: … Eyes dead, blinded with light.[38]

This damage on contact with light and dust refers again to combustion and death on contact with daylight, to the disintegration of vision, the look and the gaze: 'the light perhaps, it's so harsh … and her eyes are so pale.'[39] If I emphasize again the details of this particular imagery, it is because it is crucial to understand the relevance of the relationship between black and white which Duras sets up in the film. This double rectangular relationship is effectively what allows Duras to claim that the epicentre of *India Song* is the photograph of the dead woman on the piano.

The Photograph

Why would a photograph be the focus of the film? It is presented as a black and white image, eternalized as a still image, caught in time, frozen behind glass, reflective yet static. The actress Delphine Seyrig does not incarnate or recreate Anne-Marie Stretter but rather, by standing next to her photograph, indefinitely embodies her. Toufic, who suggests that the maintenance of the image of the dead in *India Song* constitutes a forgery and may even be said to inspire a more extreme forgery, that of the whole image track of *India Song* by *Son nom de Venise dans Calcutta désert*,[40] points to an interesting idea of immobilization of images in vampire films. Anne-Marie Stretter, Michael Richardson, the vice-consul and her lovers can be said to possess this sense of immobility, but, as Toufic points out: 'Unlike Roland Barthes, we are not concerned with the still, but with the immobilization of characters or of film images *in* the motion picture'.[41] Why, then, should this film (in motion) contain the image of stasis, the photograph, for Duras? What is significant here about the photograph in relation to the moving image, and how does it connect to the idea of an undead?

The photograph contains for us a representation, a still of the living and the dead. The undead can never be captured in this way; there is an inability to capture in the lens something ethereal. The lens, like the iris, focuses through looking, gazing, opening and closing in an attempt, but fails ever to capture the image. The underlying question here, I think, is less one of forgery than of looking for evidence or clues, almost like the scene of a crime. The image of Anne-Marie Stretter acts as a host shrine to this evidence, a still tomb for the image, the portrait of a loved one. If we turn finally to *La mer écrite*, we see that only three of the 31 photographs included are of internal spaces. The outside images are of the sea,[42] of rivers,[43] of the borders and edges of surrounding land (walls, fences, gates, railings);[44] of images of the horizon,[45] sky, and changing times of the day.[46] There are close-ups and details of cut-down trees (*Honfleur—Le Poudreux*, p. 39), and literal images of death.[47] The image of the house (*Colleville—Montgomery-plage*, p. 63) is a poignant reminder of haunted houses, Dracula's castle and the shadows (*'Les Roches Noires'—Trouville*, p. 21), and of the appearance and disappearance of things. The three interior images (*Vauville—l'église*, p. 23; *le hall des 'Roches Noires'*, p. 65; *'Les Roches Noires'—Trouville*, p. 68), are all dark interior shots with a door-way or window as a way of looking out from inside, from the dark to the light. The photographs are matched by elliptical statements and reflections of varying length, and together these represent a series of directions and clues inviting the viewer to become a detective. As we traverse the textual space we are given pointers but each one seems to remain unsolved. Each still image gives us a point but we have no route in between. We are left almost with the traces and places of someone who has been followed.[48]

Murder

Dana Brand has discussed this idea of pursuit in relation to Edgar Allan Poe's stories, noting in the case of 'The Murders in the Rue Morgue' that the detective Dupin has many similarities to the *flâneur* and that his preference for gaslight over daylight recalls the *flâneur*'s fascination with the city evening in 'The Man of the Crowd'. Brand adds that Dupin and the narrator prefer darkness when engaged in any form of contemplative activity. Their days in the artificially darkened mansion are spent 'in dreams—reading, writing, or conversing'. Their evening activity seems interchangeable with those of the daytime. For them, as for the *flâneur*, urban observation is a kind of escapist reading in solitude, demanding darkness for concentration.'[49] As with the vampire, the detective has a double. In a discussion of Brand's essay Gelder suggests that when 'Dupin solves his crimes … "distance" is collapsed and, vampire-like again, he actually *inhabits* those inhabitants—that is, he occupies their consciousness (in order to get at the truth they are concealing)'.[50]

Although no large crowds are pictured in *La mer écrite*, each image conveys a similar, profound unease. The ebb and flow of tides causes erasure and produces flotsam and jetsam, leaving neither a trace nor an accumulation of traces. What *La mer écrite* does is to play with these products. The image, in conjunction with the text, both hides and reveals, pointing to murder in almost every instance—political, theological and personal. An image at low tide of an industrial space of emptiness becomes, for example, a reminder of the trauma of Chile and the atomic bomb on Hiroshima. These spaces, ordinary perhaps, seemingly useless, have another meaning than just another seascape/landscape, yet this depends directly on the viewer ('Ça dépend de vous, cher spectateur' (p. 26)). The image here is closer to Barthes's *punctum*, 'the feeling of an off-frame space, the point of sudden and strong emotion, of small trauma: it can be a tiny detail'.[51] It is the point of disturbance here which reminds us as spectators that we are not simply looking at the sea. Duras uses the sea to refer back to all the reflections and distortions of her work. On the one hand, it is doubled as still and glassy, blue, green and grey, and reflected in the images just as the mirror and glass in space reflect back. On the other, it is the space of the dark and the vast unknown, the deep, the void. The claustrophobia of internal dwelling in *India Song* has thus become an open house, a ruin without windows (*Colleville—Montgomery-plage*, p. 63), where anything contained is shattered and free-flowing.

La mer écrite plays additionally on the idea of *la mer/mère écrite*. Ivone Margulies has discussed this role of the mother's writing in Chantal Akerman's 1976 film *News from Home*, stating the following:

> For Akerman to give voice to her mother's letter raises ambivalent issues of inheritance and of indebtedness: in order to sign them, she must appropriate them, betray them. The original signature is erased, as if, through repetition, one could bypass repetition. Akerman's voice silences her mother's in a simulacrum of communication.[52]

The process of repetition in Duras's early film work has allowed her to bypass the never-ending process to repeat. Now, through the photographic image, Duras creates a visual form that stills the process of writing and forces us to focus on the trauma of each image. Our gaze as viewers and anxiety of a space of murder is focused, figuratively speaking, as a disturbance, more literally as a death. Duras silences the m/Other in these images and showcases the trauma and anxiety of a stilled event. The images do not repeat here but draw our attention to the details of all Duras's repeated concerns throughout her work. Even in the last stage of her practice there is no cathartic effect. One would perhaps have hoped for a resolution, a happy ending, a solved crime, but stasis assumes here a greater menace. The images are constant reminders of our anxiety, of our lives, of our dreams, of disquiet. The final image in *La mer écrite* is a reduced photograph of a window. *Through the glass* the shutters are half open and half closed; light filters through. For a vampire this would signal the end of a living death and truly close off a thousand repetitions of a lifetime.

Notes

1 Jan Dawson, '*India Song*: a Chant of Love and Death' (interview with Marguerite Duras), *Film Comment*, Vol. 11, No. 6 (1975), pp. 52–55.

2 'The Old Man and the Wolves', in *Julia Kristeva: Interviews*, ed. Ross Mitchell Guberman, New York, Columbia University Press, 1996, p. 164.

3 Julia Kristeva, *The Old Man and the Wolves* (1991), trans. Barbara Bray, New York, Columbia University Press, 1994, p. 8.

4 Kristeva, *Old Man and the Wolves*, p. 85.

5 In a discussion of *The Old Man and the Wolves* Kristeva talks about the doubling of some of her characters and the doubling of their identities as a form of metamorphosis. She speaks of this as part of the Gothic *roman noir* (*Kristeva: Interviews*, p. 165).

6 See Julia Kristeva, 'La maladie de la douleur: Duras', in *Soleil noir: dépression et mélancolie*, Paris, Gallimard, 1987, pp. 227–65; p. 234 (my translation): 'une profusion immaîtrisable d'associations, de richesses ou de pauvretés au gré du spectateur'.

7 Kristeva, 'La maladie de la douleur', p. 235.

8 Joël Farges and François Barat, for instance, have seen the film *India Song* as invisible. In 'PATHS: *India Song*', their introduction to *DURAS by DURAS*, San Francisco, City Light Books, 1987, they ask 'What image do we have of *India Song*? What do we see in it? The image of what body rushes by and flies into the mirror? Going where? Beyond the frame? Who returns in this mirror-hole with its virtual, false, true, and oblique images that shut off representation as one stops a haemorrhage? We make every effort to see *India Song*: but finally what was aimed at—" the threshold of the interval between deaths"—can only be glimpses. We hear them behind us, invoke and evoke them without meeting a living soul; so it is true then, that the gaze cannot be returned? That this film is invisible?' (p. 3).

9 Nina Auerbach has described *Vampyr* as '[t]he first canonical vampire film not based on *Dracula*; it claims to be, instead, a loose adaptation of "Carmilla" [from Sheridan Le Fanu's *Through A Glass Darkly* (1872)]. Despite its source, *Vampyr* scrupulously avoids not only erotic intimacy, but all contact between its characters, whether they are human or preterhuman; its key images involve a solitude so solemnly intense that it is scarcely a vampire film at all' (Nina Auerbach, *Our Vampires, Ourselves*, Chicago and London, University of Chicago Press, 1995, pp. 53–54).

10 '*India Song*' Shooting Script, Reel IV (10 shots) 17′26″ p. 51 (my emphasis).

11 '*India Song*' Shooting Script, p. 14.

12 Marguerite Duras, *India Song*, trans. Barbara Bray, New York, Grove Press, 1976, p. 13.

13 Duras, *India Song*, p. 23.

14 See 'Vampires in the (Old) New World: Anne Rice's Vampire Chronicles', in Ken Gelder, *Reading the Vampire*, New York and London, Routledge, 1994, p. 120.

15 Gelder, 'Vampires in the (Old) New World', p. 120.

16 Duras, *India Song*, p. 26.

17 Duras, *India Song*, p. 28.

18 Duras, *India Song*, p. 43.

19 In the Shooting Script, p. 51, and in Duras, *India Song* (text), p. 69: '(In one breath). The report said people used to see him at night through his bedroom window, walking up and down as if it was broad daylight … always to himself …
— … At night … as if it was broad daylight …
— Yes …

20 '*India Song*' Shooting Script, p. 44.

21 Kristeva, 'La maladie de la douleur', p. 253 (my translation): 'Alors que le répété s'égrène dans le temps, la réduplication est hors temps. C'est une réverbération dans l'espace, un jeu de miroirs sans perspective, sans durée. Un double peut fixer pour un temps l'instabilité du même, lui donner une identité provisoire, mais il creuse surtout le même en abîme, il ouvre en lui un fond insoupçonné et insondable. Le double est le fond inconscient du même, ce qui le menace et peut l'engloutir.'

22 Gabriel Josopovici, *The Big Glass*, Manchester, Carcanet, 1991, p. 22. Josopovici states at the beginning of his book that the work is not a fictionalized biography

of Marcel Duchamp, yet it could not have been written without the existence of Duchamp's *Large Glass.* The importance of the text here is also the nature of the making of a work.

23 Joan Copjec's psychoanalytic work on vampires and breast feeding is pertinent here. In 'Vampires, Breast-Feeding, and Anxiety', *October*, No. 58 (Fall 1991), pp. 25–43, she takes as an example the moment in Bram Stoker's *Dracula* when Van Helsing and the others burst into Harker's bedroom and witness Mina sucking blood from a wound in Dracula's bare breast. The Lacanian context of Copjec's article is well summarized by Gelder: 'although the mother may invoke vampirish images to describe the process ("being drained", etc.), the image of the sucking infant at the breast does not in itself usually produce anxiety. In fact, for Copjec, anxiety comes only *after* the breast has been drained, that is, when it no longer functions as a fantasy support for the infant, as its "object-cause of desire" ... one separates oneself from the breast in order to become a subject, but in doing so it must be recognized that what was a part of oneself is now other to oneself. Subjectivity and anxiety are thus intimately related; in order to become more "at home" in our bodies, anxiety is managed only by maintaining a *distance* from the breast-as-it-was, by figuring the breast as a "lost part of ourselves" about which we say nothing. But "whenever we too closely approach the extimate object in ourselves", an uncanny effect is realized: that extimate object now belongs to "a complete body, an almost exact double of our own, except for the fact that this double is endowed with the object which we sacrificed in order to become subjects"' ('Vampires and the Uncanny: Le Fanu's "Carmilla"', in Gelder, *Reading The Vampire*, pp. 50–51).

24 Marguerite Duras, 'The Dark', in *Green Eyes*, trans. Carol Barko, New York, Columbia University Press, 1990, p. 87 ('"Quand on lit, on se retrouve, et quand on va au cinéma, on se perd" ... quand on va voir tes films, on ne se perd pas. C'est dans le noir qu'on se retrouve' (Marguerite Duras, *Les yeux verts*, Paris, Cahiers du Cinéma, 1987, p. 114)).

25 See 'Asceticism and proliferation, or is the iris a halo or a matte?', in Jalal Toufic, *(Vampires) An Uneasy Essay on the Dead in Film*, Barry Town, New York, Station Hill Literary Editions, 1993, p. 107.

26 '*India Song*' Shooting Script, Reel V (7 shots), 14′13″, p. 51.

27 Duras, *India Song*, p. 13.

28 Duras, *India Song:* 'Sitting close to her is a man, also dressed in black. Away from the lovers there is another man in black. The woman in black and the man sitting near her begin to stir. Emerge from death' (pp. 14–15); *Voice 1*: Where's the one dressed in black?/ *Voice 2*: Out. Every evening. She comes back when it's dark' (p. 27).

29 Duras, *India Song*, p. 28.

30 Duras, *India Song*, p. 117.

31 Duras, *India Song*, p. 67.

32 Duras, *India Song*, p. 115.

33 Duras, *India Song*, p. 124.

34 Duras, *India Song*, p. 125.

35 Compare 'Le Blanc' and 'Le Blanc du Noir et Blanc' in Duras, *Les yeux verts.*

36 In *White*, London and New York, Routledge, 1997, p. 210, Dyer states: 'The vampire's bite, so evidently a metaphor for sexuality, is debilitating unto death, just as white people fear sexuality if it is allowed to get out of control (out from under the will)—yet, like the vampire, they need it. The vampire is the white man or woman in the grip of libidinal needs s/he cannot master. In the act of vampirism, white society (the vampire) feeds off itself (his/her victims) and threatens to destroy itself. All of this is so menacing that it is often ascribed to those who are not mainstream whites—Jews (see Gelder, *Reading the Vampire*, pp. 13–17), South East Europeans (Transylvania in *Dracula* and its derivatives) the denizens of New Orleans (Anne Rice's *Vampire Chronicles*). Horror films have their cake and eat it: they give us the horror of whiteness while at the same time ascribing it to those who are liminally white. The terror of whiteness, of being without life, of causing death, is both vividly conveyed and disowned.'

37 Duras, *India Song*, p. 16.

38 Duras, *India Song*, p. 27.

39 Duras, *India Song*, p. 65. Numerous other references to light include p. 35, p. 68, and p. 127.

40 Toufic, *(Vampires) An Uneasy Essay*, pp. 190–91.

41 Toufic, *(Vampires) An Uneasy Essay*, referring to Roland Barthes, 'The Third Meaning: Research Notes on Some Eisenstein Stills', in *Image, Music, Text*, essays selected by Stephen Heath, New York, Hill and Wang, 1977.

42 Marguerite Duras, *La mer écrite*, Paris, Marval, 1996, with photographs by Hélène Bamberger, p. 13, *Honfleur—Le Poudreux*; p. 27, *L'estuaire de la Seine*; p. 41, *les ducs-d'albe à Pennedepie*; p. 51, *Hennequeville*; p. 55, *Trouville—la plage.*

43 Duras, *La mer écrite*, p. 11, *la Seine à Berville*; p. 29, *la rivière Saint-Sauveur*; p. 33, *le bac rouge à Quillebeuf*; p. 35, *la Seine à Honfleur*; p. 67, *la Seine à Honfleur.*

44 Duras, *La mer écrite*, p. 9. *Colleville—Montgomery*; p. 17, *Putot-en-Auge*; p. 21. Les '*Roches Noires*'—*Trouville*; p. 25, *carte maritime*; p. 29, *la rivière Saint-Sauveur*; p. 47, *Vauville—l'église*; p. 55, *Trouville—la plage*; p. 59, *Trouville—les tennis*; p. 61, *la Seine à Honfleur.*

45 Duras, *La mer écrite*, p. 41, *le ducs-d'albe à Pennedepie*; p. 45, *vers Ouistreham*; p. 51, *Hennequeville*; p. 55, *Trouville—la plage*; p. 65, *le hall des 'Roches Noires'.*

46 Duras, *La mer écrite*, front cover, p. 11, *la Seine à Berville*; p. 13, *Honfleur—Le Poudreux*; p. 17, *Putot-en-Auge*; p. 27, *l'estuaire de la Seine*; p. 31, *la gare du Poudreux-Honfleur*; p. 33, *le bac rouge à Quillebeuf*; p. 41, *les ducs-d'albe à Pennedepie*; p. 51, *Hennequeville*; p. 63, *Colleville—Montgomery-plage.*

47 Duras, *La mer écrite*, p. 15, *Putot-en-Auge*; p. 43, *Vauville—le cimetière*; p. 63, *Colleville—Montgomery-plage.*

48 See Walter Benjamin, 'The *Flâneur*', in *Charles Baudelaire, A Lyric Poet In the Era of High Capitalism*, trans. Harry Zohn, New York and London, Verso, 1992, p. 37. Here Benjamin explains that 'the street becomes a dwelling for the *flâneur*: he is as much at home among the facades of houses as a citizen is in his four walls'. The act of looking and gazing at others comes into its own for the first time. The arcades gave space and place to the idle of the time. Here voyeurism and desire for the

'other' are carried with the walker so that there is always a gap between desire and what is desired. Lost amongst the crowds in a big city the *flâneur* was able to view and follow, becoming both detective and conspirator at the same time. Benjamin's essay on Baudelaire's text suggests that the individual maintains his/her anonymity in the crowded spaces of the city, and that even in terror crowds become an asylum to shield the criminal as well as giving freedom to the individual. As Benjamin asserts, it became the origin of the detective story.

49 Dana Brand, 'From the *Flâneur* to the Detective', in *Popular Fiction: Technology, Ideology, Production, Reading*, ed. Tony Bennett, London and New York, Routledge, 1990, p. 230.

50 Gelder, 'Vampires in the (Old) New World', in *Reading the Vampire*, p. 121.

51 Christian Metz, 'Photography and Fetish', *October*, No. 34 (Fall 1985), pp. 155–64, a discussion of the *punctum* in Barthes's *La chambre claire* and Freud on fetishism.

52 Ivone Margulies, *Nothing Happens: Chantal Akerman's Hyperrealist Everyday*, Durham NC and London, Duke University Press, 1996, p. 152.

CHAPTER 3

Hijacking the Hunter: Duras's 'La nuit du chasseur'

Catherine Rodgers

Duras's films have attracted much critical attention since Madeleine Borgomano's 1984 study of her cinematographic texts,[1] but her work specifically as a film critic has not. I intend here to analyze one somewhat eccentric but enlightening example of her film criticism, her article 'La nuit du chasseur',[2] often referred to but which, to my knowledge, has never been examined in detail. The article was published in 1980, 25 years after the release of Charles Laughton's film *The Night of the Hunter* which is its subject.[3] It opens with this extraordinary assertion: 'I always forget the beginning of the film' ('J'oublie toujours le début du film'). And although Duras insists she has seen the film four times, she proceeds to make numerous errors with respect to its content, even when telling us (perhaps unsurprisingly) what she claims to have forgotten. 'I forget that the real father has been murdered' ('J'oublie que le vrai père a été assassiné'), she asserts, although the father in the film was not murdered but tried by a court and executed for having killed two people in an armed bank robbery. She admits to confusing the father with his murderer. In reality, the Preacher (the central character, played by Robert Mitchum, whom Duras takes to be the father's murderer) at no point attempts to kill the father. Whether or not Duras saw the film dubbed into French, or with French subtitles, or in the original English version without subtitles (and thus even allowing for possible mistranslations or a linguistic misunderstanding on her part), such errors are not easy to explain, especially given the quite unambiguous, if rapid, movement of the story line during the opening scenes of the film. Nor can one readily believe Duras's claim that many others have admitted to her a similar confusion of the father with the (supposed) assassin. One may be tempted to conclude that such a claim is manipulative, an attempt in the introductory paragraph of the article to instil a certain doubt in the reader (by force of numbers) in order to forestall any censure of the uncommonly subjective approach to the film that follows.

These initial, fundamental misinterpretations are not Duras's only factual inaccuracies; many other examples are to be found throughout the article. She sees the mother 'killed by him [the father] as a result of child-bearing and drudgery, of misery' ('tuée par lui à force d'enfantements et de corvées, de misères'). No reference is made to these facts in the film, nor are they even implied. Willa, the mother, has only two children, Pearl and John, and hardly appears crushed by household chores.[4] Duras states that the children 'go down roads, then a river. Roads between the rice paddies, ridges, embankments' ('descendent des routes, puis un fleuve. Des routes entre les rizières, des remblais, des talus'). The children, in fact, flee only in a boat, not on foot, nor are they naked as she maintains (or, at least, only in a metaphorical sense). And while Duras imagines that the river might be the Nile or the Mekong, contending that the setting is a nameless country, the location of the film is almost unmistakably that of the United States even if one were to discount its specific references to Cincinnati and Parkersburgh. It is certainly not, in any event, Egypt or the Far East. She describes the Preacher as 'handsome and laughing, on his black horse' ('beau et rieur, sur son cheval noir'), whereas his stolen horse is white like that of death. Does Duras confuse the horse and its shadow? Or could it be that she somehow perceives only the stereotypical black horse of the Hollywood Western baddy? She describes Rachel Cooper's gun as picturesque, which is accurate enough, and the old woman does handle it in an amateur fashion, not only in her stance as she points it at the Preacher, but also in the awkward way in which she pokes his behind with it. But the idea that this gun cannot be put to use is patently erroneous, even disregarding the comic effect it produces. Rachel shoots the Preacher and wounds him, and she subsequently uses the gun to keep him at bay until the State Troopers arrive to arrest him, thus bringing about his demise and giving the lie to Duras's comment that 'the old lady has nothing tangible with which to fight the crime' ('la vieille dame n'a aucune force d'ordre matériel pour combattre le crime'). Near the end of her article, Duras declares that 'the children flee from the old lady and give themselves to the father' ('les enfants se sauvent de la vieille dame et se donnent au père'). John, the boy, does so (if Preacher is substituted for father), but at this point in the film Pearl does not (although earlier she had run to the Preacher's side). What is more, Duras seems utterly confused in her understanding that the mother has entrusted the money to the children, when the plot demands that it is the father who has done so. The father has hidden the money from the bank robbery in Pearl's doll, having made the children swear not to tell a soul about it, even their mother. How is one meant to take a piece of film criticism which contains so many factual errors?

Beyond such misunderstandings, Duras also seems wholly unconcerned with the art of the film. In this respect, the difference between her critique and that of Molyan Mills[5] is striking. Mills traces the various styles that influenced Laughton (expressionistic, realistic, fantastic, stylised) and the directors who may have inspired him (Wiene, Lang, Wells, Griffiths). Mills discusses the application of unusual camera angles and special effects such as those used to create the arresting sequence showing Willa dead at the bottom of the river, her hair flowing with the river weeds in the current. Duras makes no allusion whatsoever to the style or art of the film nor to its startling images, not even to the moments of prominent and self-conscious symbolism such as that of the inserted sequence in which an owl, hunter of the night, seizes a harmless, innocent rabbit. She contents herself with the declaration that, were it not for its last 10 minutes, the film would be a typical nondescript Hollywood production: 'when American cinematic product reaches this essential insipidness,' she asserts, 'it is perhaps at the height of its efficiency: a product for everyday consumption', adding: 'No author' ('c'est peut-être lorsqu'il arrive à cette insipidité essentielle que le produit cinématographique américain est au comble de son efficience: produit de consommation courante. Pas d'auteur'). True, the characters are stereotyped, but how can one deny Laughton's personal stamp on the film, each shot and effect plainly having been so carefully calculated? How is it that Duras, a maker of experimental films and a writer of texts dealing with the specificity of the cinema, chooses to relate to this film at the level of content alone? Could it be in provocative defiance of the kind of intellectual and artistic approach to film criticism found in *Cahiers du Cinéma*? As she writes in 'Woody Allen Chaplin': 'I saw *Annie Hall* last night so that I could keep up a little with you *Cahiers du Cinéma* people who are so educated in things of the cinema' ('J'ai vu *Annie Hall*, hier soir, pour être un peu à votre hauteur, vous, gens des *Cahiers du cinéma*, si instruits des choses de cinéma').[6] Is it her desire here to represent herself as an outsider to highbrow film criticism, to be seen as preserving a (supposedly) naïve, commonsensical approach to films?

If this is so, could it also be for a related reason that she makes no reference to the fact that the background to the film is the Great Depression of the 1930s? As Suzanne Liandrat-Guigues has demonstrated,[7] the Depression infuses the entire film, and to take no account of it is to leave out a crucial dimension: the story is set in the time of the Depression precisely because this economic crisis gave rise to extreme and perverted behaviours, as represented in the film by the fact that a supposed Man of God stands for Evil while the 'ordinary' Rachel Cooper stands for Good. And the undertones, more or less ignored by Duras, are self-evident. Laughton broadcast evangelical Bible readings on the radio,[8] and it is therefore to be expected that *The Night of the Hunter*—much more so than David Grubb's book on which it is based[9]—should be suffused with Biblical references, in particular to the Gospel According to Matthew, to the Old Testament and to the Book of Revelations. Duras does at times adopt a religious tone, writing, for instance, of the 'miracle' of the end of the film, and of the 'grace' which overcomes the Preacher, and she deals generally with questions of morality, yet she disengages all this from any biblical connotation. She has in many places commented on her continued interest in the Bible. It is therefore unlikely that she would have been unaware of the direct biblical quotations in the film, nor of the many indirect allusions.

Hence, it has to be said that Duras's analysis, with its factual mistakes and blind spots as well as apparent disdain both for its biblical inspiration and its context, results in a singular falsification of the film. And matters are made worse by what can only be described as some highly suspect conjectures. Duras announces that 'Charles Laughton did not dare directly to give the father criminal intentions towards his children. I am doing it for him instead' ('Charles Laughton n'a pas osé faire du père, directement, le criminel de ses enfants. Je le fais pour lui, à sa place'). This is not only to discount the fact that *The Night of the Hunter* is an accurate adaptation of Grubb's novel (Duras may not, of course, have known of its existence) but, more importantly, to impose a quite unjustified intention on Laughton. The Preacher does try to usurp the position of the father, for example by announcing to the young John his marriage to Willa in terms of being his future father, and, in front of strangers, convincingly plays a caring paternal role. Moreover, through the choice of camera angles and the framing of shots, the film itself suggests a parallel between father and Preacher. The sequence at the beginning of the film showing the father's arrest is repeated at the end when it is the Preacher's turn to be arrested: the same camera-shots are used, the State Troopers and the arrested man go through the same actions and make the same gestures, and John's lines in the script are virtually identical. The scene in the court room when the death penalty is pronounced on the father is mirrored almost precisely in the scene where the Preacher is condemned to prison for car theft: the same courtroom and exactly the same camera angle. The father and the Preacher even share the same hangman. That the two are to be identified with one another is therefore surely part of the intended meaning of the film, but it is difficult to see how the relationship can function in the way Duras perceives it. Part of the Preacher's evil is that he perverts the paternal function, and there is no intimation that the father means his children any harm. On the contrary, he has robbed a bank out of his desire to provide for them, to protect them in the severe times of the Depression, and knowing that he is to be executed nevertheless resists the Preacher's veiled threats, promises and interrogations as to the whereabouts of the money which represents his children's future.

Duras highlights the 10 minutes before the arrest of the Preacher as 'the real film' ('le véritable film'), implicitly defending her standpoint by seeing the crux of the film as the hymn which Rachel and the Preacher sing together as the latter waits outside her house. This scene is indeed a special moment, but there are other prominent scenes in the film that could be singled out as equally special, such as the one before the sacrifice of Willa in the bedroom, for which the set is constructed to suggest a church, or the shot, mentioned above, of Willa at the bottom of the river, or even the enchanted dream-like sequence of the children drifting downstream. To reduce the interest and importance of *The Night of the Hunter* to just its last 10 minutes seems remarkably idiosyncratic. In any case, Duras's reading of the hymn sequence leaves room for critical circumspection. In her interpretation, Rachel Cooper, in order to keep the Preacher at bay, 'comes up with the idea of singing' ('invente de chanter'), and Duras views the hymn first as a barrier between the hunter and his prey, then as a source of his liberation: thanks to the hymn, she maintains, he is freed from the evil which inhabits him such that the hymn no longer acts as a deterrent against the murderer but against Evil itself. Delivered, the Preacher can—at least until dawn—recover his innocence, and his childhood. However, in order to interpret the hymn sequence in this way, Duras yet again must ignore or deform several facts. It is the Preacher, not Rachel, who initiates the singing. And whereas Duras implies that this singing continues throughout the night, it actually lasts (within the diegesis) only the time it takes for Ruby, the eldest child, to get out of bed and come downstairs. Duras stresses that the children join in the singing: 'They sing together, loud and high as in a church. Together. Both of them know the song, the children too' ('Ils chantent ensemble, fort et haut comme dans une église. Ensemble. Tous les deux connaissent le chant, de même les enfants'). Yet, except for Ruby, the children are asleep in their beds during the singing. Duras states that at the end of this initiatory night, Evil has left the killer and moved on to inhabit others. But the spell cast by the singing of the hymn, which is certainly there, is in reality prematurely broken by Ruby's entrance. Accordingly, the Preacher has not been completely cleansed of Evil, the proof of which is that he then enters the house with the intention of grabbing John and Pearl. Only when Rachel shoots him does he take refuge in the barn, no longer representing any immediate danger. If there is a moment when Evil leaves the Preacher it is not at the end of the singing but when, wounded, he utters a cry reminiscent of the screams of evil spirits in horror films as they leave a body. One may legitimately ask if Duras gets anything right in her interpretation of this episode. Her apparent misunderstandings, together with her erroneous explanation of the timing of the events, serve to undermine her analysis of this sequence which she sees as being of such significance that it dwarfs the rest of the film.

It can hardly be doubted that this piece of criticism, with its misconceptions and unsupported hypotheses, results in a general misrepresentation of *The Night of the Hunter*. And yet, even if her instinctive insights are often marred by error, Duras does catch some of the film's essence. The moment at which Rachel Cooper starts singing in answer to the Preacher brings, as Duras rightly suggests, an intimation of grace into the terrible night when Good and Evil, Love and Hate briefly achieve transcendence through communion. This happens not only on the soundtrack, in the mingling of the two voices, but also visually: the film had hitherto presented Rachel in the light and the Preacher in the dark (throughout the film he is often portrayed as a menacing shadow). Light and dark are now inverted, leading to a single shot in which Rachel's face is cast in the dark foreground while the Preacher's face is lit in the background. Hence, Duras is right to claim that 'all the narrative elements of the film turn out to be false trails', and to ask: 'Where are we? Where is the good, the bad? Where is the crime? The film loses all morality' ('tous les éléments narratifs du film apparaissent comme des fausses pistes', and to ask: 'Où est-on? Où est le bon, le mauvais? Où est le crime? Le film devient sans moralité'). The clear separation between Good and Evil—symbolized in the Preacher's hands, one tattooed with the word *LOVE,* the other with *HATE*—had been undermined long before the singing of the hymn. As we have seen, the father becomes a criminal but for a worthy motive. The Preacher loves and hates women, being at once attracted and repulsed by their sexuality (he watches a titillating show but does not consummate his marriage). He thanks God—his phallic knife held erect between his praying hands—for putting him in prison with the father, thus giving him the opportunity to cheat another widow. He even murders in the name of God, calling out that the Lord cannot object to killing because His book is so full of it. He is a confidence trickster but in one sense not a fraud, since he salves his conscience by believing (or, at least, convincing himself) that what he does is not morally wrong. Willa becomes caught up in his perversion, ending up thanking God for her husband's rejection of her femaleness and even for her impending death at his hands. Under the Preacher's influence, Good becomes warped, while Rachel, although she immediately sees that the Preacher is not to be trusted, seems unable to grasp the full force of Evil in him, indeed in anything, by always transforming Evil into Good. Thus she exculpates Ruby who has told her lies to cover the fact that she goes out with men, explaining her behaviour as a worthy search for love. By the end of the film, the positions of

Good and Evil have been rearranged. If Duras is right (and it would seem that she is), Evil has left the Preacher and entered the lynch mob, while the 'good' Rachel has actually shot somebody. *The Night of the Hunter* does, as Duras sees, explore the complex relationship between Good and Evil, even if it does so principally in order to stress the difficulty of adhering to conventional morality in times of extreme hardship. This is clearly not as stereotyped a film as Duras would have us believe.

Duras's statement: 'At the end of this initiatory night, the children will have learned of the mystery of evil and at the same time of its infinite relativity' ('A la fin de cette nuit initiatique, les enfants seront instruits du mystère du mal et en même temps de son infinie relativité'), is equally discerning if, once again, one is prepared to allow some flexibility in her version of the facts, that is, if the 'night' is taken to be the full period covered by the film and not just the single night of the confrontation between Rachel and the Preacher (a plausible option), and if Duras's use of 'the children' is taken to mean John alone. Pearl is too young, too innocent, to be able to distinguish Good from Evil: she is ready from the first to offer her love to the Preacher, even calling him Daddy. John, who has lost his innocence, recognizes bad in the Preacher, but when the latter is arrested, relives the arrest of his father, realizing that the stolen money has been the root of all the harm. For this money, his father has been executed; by entrusting it to his children he has put them in mortal peril and has indirectly caused the death of his wife. When John rushes to the Preacher and rips open the doll to reveal the money, this is surely less a gesture of love—Duras maintains that the children run to him suddenly 'overwhelmed' ('foudroyés') by love—than a desperate need to purge the cause of so much Evil, and to divest himself of the heavy responsibility of knowing where the money is hidden. It is nevertheless credible that, as Duras suggests, John refinds his father in the Preacher, an idea supported by the strong resemblances between the arrest scenes, and that he recognizes the relativity of Evil. At the end of the film, John's gift to Rachel for Christmas is one of her own apples which he wraps in one of her doilies. In stealing for a good cause, he is repeating his father's gesture and obliquely illustrating the biblical saying quoted at the opening of the film: 'Ye shall know them by their fruit'. The apple is also a heavily laden symbol of the biblical fruit of knowledge. As a result of his dreadful experience, John has come face to face with Good and Evil, has somehow understood that they are complementary, and symbolically initiates Rachel Cooper into this knowledge. Further, Duras's sensitivity and that of the film coincide in giving childhood the highest value; as she says, 'the old lady's song has opened the floodgates of the infinite, childhood' ('le chant de la vieille dame a ouvert les vannes de l'infini, l'enfance'). Childhood, as represented by John and Pearl, is what, in the words of Rachel

Cooper, 'abides and endures'. When Rachel quotes from the Bible, surrounded by children's faces floating in a starlit sky, those faces are images of transcendence. And while Duras surely goes too far in claiming that the Negro spiritual they sing enables the Preacher to recover his childhood, there are moments in the film when he is deliberately presented as juvenile, such as when he snarls with childish rage at Pearl and John in the cellar. It is also worth noting that in Grubb's novel he is at one point directly likened to a child. Willa thinks to herself as she is about to be murdered: 'Why, he is so little. He is only a child. He looks like a little boy in his nightshirt' (p. 154).

In all, Duras offers some shrewd insights, even perhaps sensing (or, if indeed she had read Grubb's novel, consciously or unconsciously transforming?) what is in the book but not apparent in the film. But for the most part her text so disfigures the film that it could almost be said to have little to do with it. She unashamedly usurps Laughton's position from the outset, thus rendering her analysis more revealing of herself than of the subject of her article. Having flaunted her forgetfulness and her misconstruction, she signals: 'I have always viewed and constructed Charles Laughton's film in the light of this error' ('C'est sur cette erreur que j'ai toujours vu et construit le film de Charles Laughton'), and steps in to do what he supposedly had been too spineless to do, i.e. to make the father the killer of his children. Quite apart from the fact that at this point alone she appears correctly to separate father and usurper, is such arrogance justifiable in a piece of film criticism? Perhaps not, but Duras is no impartial film critic. She offers a quite different, highly subjective type of film criticism that she has defended in *Les yeux verts*. She writes in 'Renoir, Bresson, Cocteau, Tati':[10] 'Bresson is a very great director … Cocteau's films are very beautiful, but beautiful for others, not me … Godard is one of the greatest. The greatest catalyst in world cinema') ('Bresson est un très grand metteur en scène … Cocteau, c'est très beau, mais pour d'autres que moi … Godard? C'est un des plus grands. Le plus grand catalyseur du cinéma mondial'). Of this highly individual position she states simply: 'We ought to institute this kind of criticism: not to talk about a film in a timeless way, but about oneself in relation to it', adding: 'When I see *The Night of the Hunter* … for the fifth time, each time I feel renewed … and at the same time I am amazed at having been the same me throughout the years of my life' ('Il faudrait instaurer cette critique-là: ne pas parler du film de façon intemporelle mais de soi devant le film. Quand je revois pour la cinquième fois *La nuit du chasseur* … je me retrouve chaque fois comme renouvelée … et en même temps émerveillée d'être égale à moi-même à travers les années de ma vie'). She claims that more than the film at the moment of viewing, what matters for her is what *remains* of the film: 'the morning after, what has become for me of the film I saw yesterday, in the state it is in at the end of that night, this is the film I will have seen' (p. 46) ('Le lendemain matin, ce qu'est devenu pour moi le film vu la veille, son état après la nuit, c'est le film que j'aurai vu'). It is thus perhaps not at all unexpected that she should make no attempt to check the accuracy of her memory, nor that she should herself be the starting point for her analysis (significantly, the first word of the article 'La nuit du chasseur' is 'I'), nor, in the final account, that the analysis should turn out to be more revealing of its author than its subject. Conceivably, her models are the two characters in the essay 'Book and Film' which follows 'La nuit du chasseur' in *Les yeux verts*, who integrate into the film they are watching a news bulletin that has preceded it.[11] Duras does much the same with *The Night of the Hunter*, using it as a pretext for projecting her own universe and therefore writing not a conventional piece of film criticism but something approaching a piece of fiction. The way in which, throughout the article, she confuses, then substitutes, father for criminal—initially distinguishing between the 'criminal' and the 'father', then proceeding from 'criminal father', 'father child-killer', to 'father' and 'real father' when referring to the Preacher—belongs more to fiction than to what one normally expects of criticism. And she has no qualms about using fictional rhetorical devices and stylistic effects., For example, in dealing with the hymn, she repeats the words 'song' ('chant') and 'sing' ('chanter'), mimicking the function of the hymn in the film, and reaching a climax with: 'they sing at the top of their voices' ('ils chantent à tue-tête').

Even more so than at the level of style, one recognizes some of Duras's personal obsessions in her overall view of *The Night of the Hunter*. Some of her misconceptions, in particular the crucial one concerning the father's identity, appear to stem from her seeming inability to enter into another's work, as well as reveal her propensity continually to rework her own themes. She departicularizes the film the better to invest it with her own phantasms. America becomes a nameless land, enabling her to replace the film's space with that of her own childhood and some of her books, notably the Mekong and the paddy fields. Compare her description of the space of *The Night of the Hunter*:

> They go down roads, then a river. Roads between the rice paddies, ridges, embankments. They go down the Nile, the Mekong … All is flat, lagoonal, easily covered
>
> ('Ils descendent des routes, puis un fleuve. Des routes entre les rizières, des remblais, des talus. Ils descendent le Nil, le Mékong … Tout est plat, lagunaire, facile à couvrir')

with that of the opening of *Le vice-consul*:

> ... a kind of vast stretch of marshland criss-crossed every which way by a thousand embankments. She walks for days, follows the embankments, leaves them, crosses the water, walks straight ahead, turns towards other marshes
>
> (... sorte de vaste étendue de marécages que mille talus traversent en tous sens ... Elle marche pendant des jours, suit les talus, les quitte, traverse l'eau, marche droit, tourne vers d'autres marécages).[12]

The similarity between the two landscapes, and the inaccuracies in her perception of the space of the film, point up the creative misreading in which she is engaged. She depersonalizes the film so as to make it her own, stripping the characters of their names as is often the case in her creative works. She even dispenses with the film's director and writes of the film's 'essential insipidness' before bestowing on it the status of miracle. Several of Duras's misreadings stem patently from personal fixations of which there are distinct echoes in her creative work, such as the transformation of Willa into a harassed, worn-out wife and mother like the humdrum women of *La vie matérielle*. In 'La maison' she turns Woman into Martyr:

> But perhaps woman secretes her own despair with every maternity, with every marriage. Perhaps she loses something of her empire, over her entire life, in the daily despair. Perhaps the aspirations of her youth, her strength, her love drain from her through the very wounds caused and received within the purest legality. Perhaps it is so. Perhaps womanhood approaches martyrdom
>
> (Mais peut-être que la femme sécrète son propre désespoir tout au long de ses maternités, de ses conjugalités. Qu'elle perd son royaume dans le désespoir de chaque jour, cela au cours de toute sa vie. Que ses aspirations de jeunesse, sa force, son amour s'écoulent d'elle par justement les plaies faites et reçues dans la plus pure légalité. Peut-être que c'est ainsi. Que la femme relève du martyre).[13]

This is the view of motherhood projected on to Willa, whose treatment foreshadows the transformation Christine Villemin will undergo in Duras's notorious article published in *Libération* in 1985,[14] in which her judgment about Villemin outraged public opinion. She takes the same liberty with Willa. These 'creative readings' belong to the same brand of subjective journalism.

Duras vigorously upheld her right to such subjectivity. In her foreword to *Outside: Papiers d'un jour*, she insists: 'There is no such thing as objective journalism', and: 'I have rid myself of many prejudices and, in my view, this is the most important prejudice of all' ('Il n'y a pas de journalisme objectif. Je me suis débarassée de beaucoup de préjugés dont celui-là qui est à mon avis le principal').[15] It should therefore come as no surprise to find many other parallels between 'La nuit du chasseur' and Duras's creative works. The liberating, transcendent quality of music is a recurrent theme in Duras, from *Moderato cantabile*, *L'amour* and *Nathalie Granger* to *Détruire dit-elle*. In *Moderato cantabile*, the sonatina is 'worn like a feather by this barbarian' ('portée comme une plume par ce barbare'),[16] i.e. Anne's child, who remains untouched and unconscious of his own action in a way reminiscent of the Preacher who likewise seems unaware of the transformation the hymn brings about in him. Similarly, in *L'amour* the madman's body is taken over by music without his being conscious of it (his body 'is carried away, remembers, dances as the music dictates', 'he is subjected to … his own movement' ('s'emporte, se souvient, il danse sous dictée de la musique', 'il subit … son propre mouvement')).[17] In *Moderato cantabile* the sonatina acts as a link between the different characters: the child, the piano teacher, the mother and Chauvin who joins in at a distance by humming the tune. Like the hymn in *The Night of the Hunter*, it goes straight to the heart and possesses the same indomitable power. As Duras puts it, 'It [the music] spread out once more over the world, flooded one's heart with the unknown, overwhelmed it' ('elle s'étala dans le monde une fois de plus, submergea le coeur d'inconnu, l'exténua'), adding: 'As the music built up, the daylight faded, noticeably' (p. 55) ('A mesure qu'elle s'échaffaudait, sensiblement la lumière du jour diminua'). At the end of *Détruire dit-elle*,[18] music announces the advent of a new order. It starts at night: 'Only when the darkness is almost complete, does the music arrive in its clarity' (p. 135) ('Ce n'est que lorsque l'obscurité est presque tout à fait complète qu'elle arrive clairement'), and in a crescendo akin to the one Duras creates in her 'La nuit du chasseur', music 'with immeasurable power and sublime tenderness' (p. 135) ('avec une force incalculable, dans la sublime douceur') ends up 'in sovereign splendour … smashing trees, ripping walls apart' (p. 136) ('dans une amplitude souveraine … fracassant les arbres, foudroyant les murs').

Duras singles out dawn in *The Night of the Hunter* as being the moment when the spell created by the hymn is broken, and normal life must resume. Yet while darkness suits the hunter, and while his arrest takes place in the morning, there is no concentration on dawn as such in the film. This contrived stress on the dawn echoes that of *Le ravissement de Lol V. Stein* where it marks the end of the spell that united Lol, Michael Richardson and Anne-Marie Stretter. The relativity of evil is treated directly in *La douleur* where Duras contends that the only possible rejoinder to the Nazi crime is to make it into a universal crime,[19] and where the diary 'La douleur' and the story 'Monsieur X' show a virtuous Duras as victim of Nazism, counterbalanced by 'Albert des Capitales' and 'Ter le milicien' in which a much darker Duras is portrayed. As Gabriel

Jacobs has shown, this apparently neat division between two facets of Duras is itself questioned by *La douleur* which, taken as a whole, presents a more disturbing picture of her.[20] More explicitly, Duras has acknowledged her own violence in several interviews. For example, she confided to Jacqueline Aubenas in 1983 that she bore within her all the evil of the world and that the desire to kill represented a constant in her life.[21] In 1990 she declared that every day in her head she killed Le Pen with all her force, waking up only to start the process all over again.[22] As a result of her conviction of the ubiquity of evil, she had little time for morality, that 'most crushing boredom' ('l'ennui mortel').[23] The conception of evil as an entity is symbolized in 'La nuit du chasseur' by the phrase 'the malady of death' ('la maladie de la mort'), reused by Duras in 1982 as the title of one of her texts to describe the situation of the homosexual man of the story who is unable to love a woman.[24] Feelings, emotions, and psychological states are sometimes envisaged in Duras as being detached from individuals, such that the concept of Evil leading one person to possess others is far from alien to her thought. In *L'amour*, the woman's memory 'has spilled out' ('répandu') into the space.[25] One of the central themes of *The Night of the Hunter*, the depiction of childhood as a state both of innocence and knowledge, of frailty and power, would (as I have shown elsewhere)[26] have struck many chords in Duras, and clearly did. The most conspicuous reconstruction in 'La nuit du chasseur' is that of the father, and Duras's statement that she is unable to conceive of the father as living, while it refers specifically to Laughton's film, could just as well refer to Duras's own texts where fathers tend to be either non-existent, dead, dying or invisible. François Peraldi[27] has analyzed the absence of father figures in Duras, linking it to the disappearance then death of her own father in her early childhood. In *The Night of the Hunter*, the transmutation of father into killer finds counterparts in other Durassian texts, in particular *L'amant*. There, the elder brother Pierre, strong, handsome, attractive (like Robert Mitchum), comes to some extent to occupy the position of the father; as Duras puts it, 'it is he who represents the law' ('[la] loi [est] représentée par lui').[28] She even refers to the elder brother as 'the child-murderer of the night, of the night of the hunter' ('l'assasssin des enfants de la nuit, de la nuit du chasseur').[29] He has usurped the place of the husband in her mother's heart, and the young Duras cannot help but feel both attraction and repulsion for her handsome evil brother. Perhaps this is why she makes the criminal the father in Laughton's film.

It can be seen that Duras effectively creates her own film out of *The Night of the Hunter*. Her act of appropriation and creation is, of course, akin to what we all do to a lesser extent when watching a film, but here the result is a fascinating series of revealing distortions. Moreover, riddled with mistakes as it is, 'La nuit du chasseur' does make one want to see the film. Yet after seeing it, rereading her text induces a certain malaise. Is this due to Duras's almost total lack of respect for another film director's work? Is it due to a haughtiness which assumes—even if she were right—that readers will be interested in *her* version of the film, however removed from the film itself? Many were enraged at the liberties she took with Christine Villemin, transforming the latter into a Durassian heroine. In this piece of film criticism, she approaches Laughton's film in the same spirit. Does it perhaps cause such unease because it unashamedly reveals what we, as critics, covertly do in all our critical discourse, and particularly so with such a wilfully elusive writer as Duras?

Notes

1 Madeleine Borgomano, *L'écriture filmique de Marguerite Duras*, Paris, Albatros, 1984.

2 Marguerite Duras, 'La nuit du chasseur', *Cahiers du cinéma*, Nos 312–13 (June-July 1980) (reprinted in *Les yeux verts*, Paris: Éditions de l'Étoile/Cahiers du Cinéma, 1996, pp. 95–103). Further references in the text will be made to the later edition. All translations are my own.

3 *The Night of the Hunter* (b/w, 1955), directed by Charles Laughton, starring Robert Mitchum, Shelley Winters and Lillian Gish.

4 However, in the novel of which Laughton's film is a fairly faithful adaptation, there is strangely one reference to Willa's 'tired hands, grown old too soon' (see Davis Grubb, *The Night of the Hunter*, London, Hamish Hamilton, 1954, p. 122).

5 Moylan C. Mills, 'Charles Laughton's adaptation of *The Night of the Hunter*', *Literature/Film Quarterly*, Vol. 16, No. 1 (1988), pp. 49–57.

6 'Woody Allen Chaplin', in Duras, *Les yeux verts*, pp. 40–41.

7 Suzanne Liandrat-Guigues, 'La parabole de la nuit du chasseur', *La Licorne*, No. 36 (1996), pp. 155–62.

8 As noted by Liandrat-Guigues, p. 155.

9 See note 4 above.

10 'Renoir, Bresson, Cocteau, Tati', in Duras, *Les yeux verts*, pp. 53–55.

11 'Book and Film', in Duras, *Les yeux verts*, pp. 104–07.

12 Marguerite Duras, *Le vice-consul*, Paris, Gallimard, 1965, p. 9.

13 Marguerite Duras, *La vie matérielle*, Paris, POL, 1987, pp. 62–63.

14 Marguerite Duras, 'Sublime, forcément sublime Christine V.', *Libération*, 17 July 1985, pp. 4–6. For a detailed analysis of this article, see James S. Williams, *The Erotics of Passage: Pleasure, Politics, and Form in the Later Work of Marguerite Duras* Liverpool University Press/St Martin's Press, 1987, pp. 115–20, and Chapter 12, 'Consuming Passions: Marguerite Duras', in David H. Walker, *Insight and Outrage: Modern French Writers and the 'Fait Divers'*, Oxford and New York, Berg, 1995.

15 Marguerite Duras, *Outside: Papiers d'un jour* (1981), Paris, POL, 1984.

16 Marguerite Duras, *Moderato cantabile*, Paris, Minuit, 1958, p. 54.
17 Marguerite Duras, *L'amour*, Paris, Minuit, 1971, pp. 70–71.
18 Marguerite Duras, *Détruire dit-elle*, Paris Minuit, 1969.
19 Marguerite Duras, *La douleur*, Paris, POL, 1985, p. 61: 'la seule réponse à faire à ce crime—le crime nazi—est d'en faire un crime de tous'.
20 Gabriel Jacobs, 'Spectres of remorse: Duras's war-time autobiography', *Romance Studies*, No. 30 (Autumn 1997), pp. 47–57.
21 See Jacqueline Aubenas, 'Entretien avec Marguerite Duras', *Alternatives théâtrales*, No. 14 (March 1983), pp. 11–15; p. 14.
22 See 'La mort dans les yeux', in Marguerite Duras, *Le monde extérieur. Outside II* Paris, POL, 1993, pp. 32–33; p. 32.
23 Aubenas, 'Entretien avec Marguerite Duras', p. 14.
24 Marguerite Duras, *La maladie de la mort*, Paris, Minuit, 1982.
25 Duras, *L'amour*, p. 54.
26 Catherine Rodgers, 'Au commencement était l'enfant', *Actes du colloque Duras 3D*, Université de Lyon II, November 1997 (forthcoming).
27 François Peraldi, 'Waiting for the father: incidence of an interpretation on the work of Marguerite', in *Remains to be Seen: Essays on Marguerite Duras*, ed. Sanford S. Ames, New York, Peter Lang, 1988, pp. 31–50.
28 Marguerite Duras, *L'amant*, Paris, Minuit, 1984, p. 13.
29 Duras, *L'amant*, p. 12. The memory of the elder brother and of the terrifying hold he has over the young narrator inspires the following enigmatic—but in the context of this article pertinent—comment in *L'amant*: 'Surrounding the memory, the ghostly light of the night of the hunter' (p. 67) ('Autour du souvenir la clarté livide de la nuit du chasseur'). Duras also refers to her own family as 'the family of the Hunter' (p. 126).

CHAPTER 4

Excitable Silence: the Violence of Non-violence in *Nathalie Granger*

Owen Heathcote

> On dit souvent que, dans les œuvres de M. Duras, il ne se passe rien, ou que tout s'est passé avant l'avènement du texte … L'univers apparemment ouaté qui s'y construit est sillonné d'une extrême violence.
>
> (Najet Limam-Tnani)[1]

Violence, whether individual or collective, is one of the major problems of our time. And not only of our time if, as Wolfgang Sofsky has recently shown, 'the taste for blood goes through the ages. Men delight in the destruction of their fellow human beings. Cruelty is endless'.[2] It is also increasingly argued that there is a connection between actual violence and its representations. This connection can take two forms. First of all, there is what Daniel Sibony, echoing perhaps the Surrealists, sees as the violence of art itself, the 'violence of beauty': 'Skirting or crossing these instances of violence is that of beauty: it leaves us without recourse when it appears, abandoning us in our desire to attain it while snatching mute cries and reducing us to its silence'.[3] Secondly, there is the violence which seems to be exacerbated, if not induced, by its representations. Thus, according to Olivier Mongin, the production of images on the small and large screen is part of the recycling of violence in our societies,[4] and, in a telling video entitled 'The Killing Screens', George Gerbner addresses the psychological, political, social and developmental impacts of growing up and living within a cultural environment of persuasive, ritualized violent representation.[5]

It can be seen from these remarks that a recurrent preoccupation of research into violence and representation is the potential effect of repeated violent action, such as murder, torture and warfare, on the vulnerable in society, and on those who represent the future of that society: its children. In concentrating on the cumulative impact of violent action on the young, whether in cartoons or films like *Robocop*, George Gerbner reflects Lee Edelman's contention that 'the child has come to embody for us the telos of the social order and been enshrined as the figure for whom that order must be held in perpetual trust'.[6] It does, therefore, seem to be the ultimate in 'nature erring from itself' if children themselves become violent—even if, as has been alleged in relation to the James Bulger murder, the murderers were themselves influenced by violent representations.[7] As has been shown by the recent BBC1 television series, *Children of Crime*, the violent child is the ultimate deviant, beyond even the 'beasts' and 'monsters' by which the tabloids habitually designate those other 'unnatural' murderers, the serial killer and the violent woman.[8] For, as again Edelman writes: '[the] child seems to shimmer with the iridescent promise of Noah's rainbow, serving, like the rainbow, as the pledge of a covenant to shield us against the threat of apocalypse now—or apocalypse later'.[9]

The emphasis on these two forms of representational violence—the violence *endemic to* representation and the violence *promoted by* representation—has meant a questioning of traditional perceptions of art. However great the threat of the apocalypse, tradition had it that any such threat could be exorcized or at least contained by art. However complicitous with aggression and death, the symbolization of aggression and death could also involve a sublimation and a repair which could even apply to violence committed by a child. As Leo Bersani writes in *The Culture of Redemption*: 'Sublimation becomes, in this view, the infant's most sophisticated defense against its own aggressions.'[10] For, again according to Bersani, '[s]ublimations have now become symbolic reparations' and '[t]hese new sublimations are, as it were, at two removes from any real objects; they are fantasy reparations of fantasy destructions.'[11] Although Bersani is highly critical of any such 'culture of redemption', many art forms are predicated on the assumption that art can repair the very damage it describes. The replaying of Schubert's *Death and the Maiden* in Ariel Dorfman's play of the same name enables Paulina to relive—but also to begin to come to terms with—the torture with which the music is associated. If such art is painful, it is self-consciously dealing with the pain it evokes. By offering a *mise en abyme* of performance within a performance, art can thus both express and contain its own violence.

It can be seen from the above that there are two main aspects to the representation of violence which are relevant to Marguerite Duras's film and book, *Nathalie Granger*.[12] The first aspect is that it engages with the violence of children, whether the violence of boys as relayed over the radio or with the violence of a young girl, Nathalie Granger herself. Given that the violence of the boys and that of the girls seems different, with male violence resulting in murder and female violence being largely internalized, the work also seems to comment on the relations between violence and gender. The second aspect is that the nature of that representation itself is crucial to the way the violence is perceived, and, in the fullest sense of the term, in what way violence is *treated*. It is therefore important to ask what *Nathalie Granger* can contribute to the sensitive, even taboo, subject of the relations between children, violence and representation. Since education, and, in particular, a young girl's education, is a key theme in *Nathalie Granger*, it will be useful to ask whether, in a form of *mise en abyme*, *Nathalie Granger* is not only about education but also itself educative. As Susan D. Cohen has demonstrated, another of Duras's texts about violence and education, 'Le boa', 'is an eminently didactic text, in which all the characters, animal and human, function as teachers'.[13] In what way (or ways) can *Nathalie Granger* be seen as a similar didactic or at least illuminating text? What can *Nathalie Granger* teach us about violence and about dealing with violence?

When compared to other works of Duras such as *L'amant* and the Indochinese cycle of Lol V. Stein and Anne-Marie Stretter, *Nathalie Granger* has received relatively little attention. Even in relation to violence, other more erotically charged works, such as *L'homme assis dans le couloir* and *La maladie de la mort*, have provoked considerably more interest.[14] There are three possible reasons for this. The first is that the work offers very little insight into the violence attributed to the eponymous Nathalie Granger. For although Nathalie's mother is deeply disturbed by her headteacher's reports of violence –'this violence in a little girl …' (p. 34) ('Cette violence chez une petite fille …')—the evidence for this violence is strangely limited. As Catherine Portuges remarks, we see nothing to bear out such reports.[15] A second reason is that Duras's use of her own house at Neauphle-le-Château for the setting of the film, as for the ensuing book, has focused attention on the house as its principal character. Duras states to Michelle Porte: 'One always thinks that you have to start off with a story to make a film. It's not true. For *Nathalie Granger* I started off completely with the house. Really, completely.'[16] Thirdly, and partly because Duras herself repeatedly identified the house as 'la maison des femmes' (p. 18),[17] attention has concentrated on the intrusion into that space by the travelling salesman and his subsequent departure or eviction. Although the salesman's invasion is seen as violent, critics have understandably emphasized the success of the women's silent resistance to that invasion rather than the violence of the invasion itself.[18] In these various ways, *Nathalie Granger* has been seen less as a violent than non-violent, or indeed counter-violent, work. Silence about Nathalie combines with the silence of the women in an allegedly silent house to give an impression of control, containment and women's empowerment. In line with conventional approaches to violence, an absence of violent actions such as murder, mayhem and war, or of the verbal abuse that Judith Butler characterizes as 'excitable speech',[19] has led to a parallel reticence about the violence, alluded to but not shown, of *Nathalie Granger*.

In order to examine the question of violence in *Nathalie Granger*, it follows that the above three aspects need to be revisited. First of all, it will be useful to look at the violence of the travelling salesman and the (counter)-violence of the two women in order to reach some provisional conclusions about the relations between sexuality, gender and violence. Is there any indication, for example, that men are violent because they are 'outsiders', or 'outsiders' because they are violent? And if violence depends on a relation to outside/inside, does this mean that questions about the gendering of violence are questions of positioning rather than biology? Secondly, it will be helpful to look again at the violence not only of the 'insider' Nathalie but also those anonymous 'outsiders', 'les tueurs des Yvelines', asking why the main violence of *Nathalie Granger* should be associated with children, and how this, too, relates to the gendering of violence. Thirdly, it will then be possible to re-examine the violence associated with the house: does the 'maison des femmes' generate or resist violence, or possibly both? It will, therefore, be necessary to conclude by applying, but also questioning, the pervasiveness of these spatial metaphors and ask which is the 'inside' and which is 'outside' in the relationship between place, sexuality and violence. Is there an unchanging core within this triumvirate relationship, or does each element take its turn to occupy centre stage in a kaleidoscope of shifting hierarchies? And what is more important—the structural relationship between place, sexuality and violence, or the individual at the centre of such a structure?

The role of the travelling salesman in *Nathalie Granger* has been the subject of a number of interesting critical analyses. Three features of the salesman have been emphasized. After Isabelle Granger's husband makes what Duras claims is an unplanned early disappearance from the film,[20] the salesman is the only male in 'la maison des femmes' and certainly the only male to speak. His most important feature seems to be his maleness. For Catherine Rodgers he personifies the 'masculine order'.[21] Secondly, the way he personifies this order is through his language, a language which is insincere, repetitive and unconvincing. As Lynn Higgins has recently written: 'his prepared speech reveals its futility and awkwardly dwindles to silence in the face of the women's friendly but passive non-response'.[22] Finally, he personifies not only masculinity but male-dominated commerce with his sales pitch, what Rodgers describes as the gab of a salesman who wants to sell a washing machine.[23] His language is therefore not only that of the male but of patriarchy—that of 'the bankruptcy of institutional discourses'.[24]

While these aspects of the salesman are both interesting and important, they tend to downplay the similarities between the salesman and the two women. Although his entry has been taken as an invasion of female space which later ejects him, it is interesting that no attempt is made to inhibit that entry. Indeed, if the salesman is an outsider, he is an outsider whom the women immediately link with the outsiders whose reports have already occupied their space since morning—the killers on the run: 'In the look of the young man, in this smile, violence. Anything is possible: a man on the loose from the Dreux forest?' (p. 50) ('Dans le regard du jeune homme, dans ce sourire, la violence. Tout est possible: un échappé de la forêt de Dreux?'). If, moreover, the women are afraid of him, they do nothing about it: 'They look at him with unusual attention. Fear. *But fear against which they do nothing, which they don't stop, which they allow to work*' (p. 50) ('Elles le regardent avec une attention anormale. Peur. *Mais peur contre laquelle elles ne font rien, qu'elles n'arrêtent pas, qu'elles laissent agir*'), and he is equally vulnerable and fearful: he flees from the house at the end because 'the house of the women has frightened him' (p. 88) ('la maison des femmes a fait peur'). As Anne Kaplan writes: 'Suddenly afraid, he leaves the house abruptly, running to his car … and departing as if from something that terrifies'.[25] Even if this seems to show the power of the women over the salesman, it also shows what they have in common: fear and an inability or unwillingness to articulate and come to terms with that fear. Like Martha and George in Edward Albee's *Who's afraid of Virginia Woolf?*, both sexes are suffering from unspoken, even unmentionable fears. If the encounter between the women and the salesman reduces them all to silence, it is in part because in facing each other they are also face to face with themselves, with their fears of violence and the violence of their own fears. Fear and violence are shared equally by so-called insiders and so-called outsiders, and by men and women. Moreover, in addition to sharing the same emotions, men's and women's knowledge and values overlap more than some critics have suggested. For despite what some claim is the women's rejection of commercialism and commodification, the women do not really reject the salesman's goods—*they already had what he had to offer.* Nor does he reject their evaluation of him: *he already knew he was no salesman.* Hence, the outsider is not so much ejected as already absorbed and the insider's values are already shared by the outsider. Thus, even if Duras argues that a man would have listened differently to the salesman because 'a man's gaze *has not yet rediscovered* that submerging function which a woman's has, that of burying discourse in a space where it cancels itself out, *falls silent*, and suppresses itself',[26] she reveals that the sound of silence lies beneath and beyond sexual difference, simply waiting to be discovered and uncovered. By showing sexuality to be defined and represented in terms of permeable positionalities, Duras shows sexuality to be infinitely fluid and exchangeable.

However, at the same time as being fluid and exchangeable, male–female relations in *Nathalie Granger* are still dependent on positioning and this implies the creation and crossing of boundaries. Thus, while seeming infinitely 'deterritorialized', sexual identity also involves the establishment and invasion of frameworks, boundaries and territories. Since the processes of territorialization and deterritorialization are at once inseparable and in conflict, both are experienced as painful, fraught and violent. By associating sexuality and sexual communication with not only metaphorical but also literal spatial positions such as inside and outside, absorption and expulsion, Duras has created the potential for infinite sexual freeplay while at the same time welding a constantly reterritorialized sexuality to the pain and the violence of control. Moreover, the greater the freeplay, the greater the need for control; the greater the control, the greater the urge for release. Duras's characters are thus caught in a double bind of the violence of sexual (self-)containment and the violence of erotic release.

Having established this painfully paradoxical character of sexualities in *Nathalie Granger* it is possible to turn to the women characters themselves to see in what ways they, too, may be seen to illustrate this double bind of violent containment and release. The first point to note here is that the women are double, and both complement and yet contrast with each other in terms of the colours of their clothes, with 'l'Amie' appearing frequently in white and Isabelle Granger in a black cloak. Their personalities are also differentiated but complementary, with the friend more demonstrative and affectionate towards the children and the mother more withdrawn and affected by Nathalie. The two women are both unexpressive, robot-like and detached, and yet they act frequently in tandem, seem virtually inseparable from each other and their feminized space, and are both deeply locked into the intimacies of their everyday existence. The choreography of their silent moves and movements offers a symbiotic female ballet which is both intensely individual and yet depersonalized to the point of total anonymity. The symbiosis of the two women is both violently exclusive of all strangers—such as the salesman or the viewer—yet also violently inclusive since neither he nor the viewer can easily break free from it. In relation to each other and to their audience, the women embody an outside and an inside which are both interdependent yet in violent mutual attrition.

When discussing the women of *Nathalie Granger*, a number of critics have seen them as relating to Duras's fascination with Michelet's *La sorcière*.[27] Isabelle's black cloak, the stoking of the garden fire, and the use of the pole while rowing on the small lake, have, when combined with the presence of the black cat, given an impression of two women with potentially magical powers. What is perhaps particularly significant here is that this association brings the two women into an association with a third party, whether that third party is the male visitor or the viewer of the film, who can be brought under their spell and drawn into their world. It can also be argued that the women entrap each other, with the result that the women are not only self and other but exist in a tripartite mirroring of self-in-other and other-in-self: the mirrors of the house duplicate the self that, when added to the other who is also a duplicated self, makes any identity triplicate. The same tripartite scenario is reinforced by the fact that the main preoccupation of the two women is, in fact, a third woman, whether the Portuguese maid Maria or the young Nathalie. There is a sense, too, in which 'la maison des femmes' itself is a further third woman, a fact which again, as Catherine Rodgers has pointed out, picks up on Michelet: 'Michelet insists on the woman's dwelling, that hut which he reappoints as his palace, and out of which he makes his birthplace'.[28]

It can be seen that the pair of women in *Nathalie Granger* becomes a threesome in a variety of different but complementary ways, whether through an addition of their own duplicated or reflected selves, whether through other women such as Maria and Nathalie, whether through the salesman or through the house and its 'properties', or whether, indeed, through the third dimension that is magic itself. Indeed, via a kind of Benjaminian aura,[29] it could be said that all the characters are always already duplicated and only need the presence of another to become a threesome. The phantasmatic presence of 'the other' is, moreover, a leitmotif in Duras, from Anne and Chauvin's fascination with the corpse of the murdered woman in *Moderato cantabile* to the paradigmatic presence/absence of the unseen Lol watching Tatiana Karl and Jacques Hold naked at their window as they are about to make love. Similarly tripartite is what Kate Ince and others have seen as Duras's 'female genealogies', such as the mother–daughter relationship epitomized by the *mendiante* in the India cycle who, as both mother and daughter and herself, is in a sense an amalgam of three women.[30] Real, imagined or phantasized threesomes permeate Duras's work, whether these are configured by three women as in *Nathalie Granger*, by two men and a woman as in *Hiroshima mon amour*, or by two women and a man as with Anne-Marie Stretter, Lol V. Stein and Michael Richardson. Often, of course, different threesomes will overlap or alternate. In *L'amant*, famously, different groups of three are formed by the two brothers and the sister and, at other times, by the sister, lover and younger brother. In addition, both the younger and older Duras can form phantomatic presences around a given narrative point of view, with the result that past, present and future offer a tripartite structure as persistent in Duras as her ballets of sexual or sexually charged, triple partners.

What are the implications of this for the violence in and of Duras, in particular with regard to *Nathalie Granger*? The first implication is that the pervasiveness of the threesome creates a structure which is extremely difficult, not to say, impossible to dislodge. Although the components in the structure may change, with the threesome being formed either by the older women and daughter, the older women and salesman, or the older women and 'la maison des femmes', the changes take place within the structure but do not affect it. Indeed, the very variety of changes possible within the structure has the paradoxical effect of confirming the invariability of this pattern of structuration. The tripartite structure is both infinite and claustrophobic, both proteiform and infinitely oppressive. For example, the very expulsion of the salesman from the universe of the house confirms the power of the house he vacates. The intervention of that other outsider, the head teacher, is similarly rejected, in that Isabelle decides not to send Nathalie to a special school, yet that decision leaves Isabelle, the friend and Nathalie confirmed in their tripartite confrontation with violence. Moreover, the violent rebuttal of the third-party outsider has the effect of turning the violence itself into a kind of '*tiers exclu*', a kind of third party to the now increasingly violent relationship between the remaining couple. Violence itself is, like the above-mentioned mirror images and phantom presences, a kind of real haunting, like the shadow of the hunter that passes through during the lovemaking of the narrator and the lover in *L'amant*.[31] Violence is, then, a third party *within* the tripartite structure, at the same time as a dimension to the remaining two parties of that structure. There is a sense, therefore, in *Nathalie Granger* in which not only are the characters violent, but also that violence itself is a character.

A second implication from the above is that sexuality and gender are subsumed by a more important, overarching tripartite structure. Although different sexes have been shown to have different kinds of violence, these violences are essentially interchangeable within the particular structure. As we have seen, the violence of the salesman confirms, and is superseded by, the increased violence of 'la maison des femmes'. What has been seen as the male voice of authority in the headmistress leaves a similar vacuum which is filled by Isabelle's increased sense of responsibility for the violence of Nathalie. The ejection of a male element in the tripartite structure does not mean that the remaining women become less riven with violence or that the violences of the structure itself are in any way changed. Indeed, the ejection itself can be read as an act of violence which, paradoxically, intensifies the violence of the vacuum that remains. The active violence of rebuttal—the women's repeated monosyllabic 'non' to the salesman's insistence that he is a salesman—dissolves into the more persistent passive violence of the women's silent lives. Thus, at the same time that violence overrides male–female distinctions, it also overrides the distinctions between language and silence. One of the disconcerting features of *Nathalie Granger* is that it reveals that the violence of women's silence—of apparent non-violence—underlies and outlives the more obvious but more disposable violence of men's 'excitable speech'.

Although the gendering of violence in *Nathalie Granger* may be read as subordinate to its violent structure, or its 'violence structurelle', there are times when that structure does indeed seem to depend on sex rather than sex depending on the structure. A key example of this is the mother–daughter relationship in the work which a number of critics have seen as central to its violence. If, according to Najet Limam-Tnani, maternity in Duras is invariably problematic ('Penetrated by lack, the mother/child relation is tainted on both sides by guilt and rarely gives rise to feelings of happiness'),[32] it is not then inappropriate that, in Lia van de Biezenbos's view, Nathalie's violence derives from her mother: 'Here, as in *Moderato cantabile*, the child seems to double the mother in the sense that textually the refusal of the child announces that of the mother. The violence of the child is a projection of the mother who needs the child in order to be able to express her own violence'.[33] Furthermore, according to Biezebos, Isabelle's reluctance to allow Nathalie to go to a special school can be ascribed to Isabelle's own needs rather than her sense of the needs of Nathalie: 'This is why Isabelle does not want to separate from Nathalie—she cannot cut the bond of violence. Isabelle had first of all to be hungry for her daughter in order to assimilate the latter's violence'.[34]

The implications of such an approach are manifold. First of all—and this despite Duras's presentation of children's violence in *La classe de la violence* as endemic among children as a class—violence is again attributable to individuals in as much as they are locked into a structure.[35] Maternity is not seen as an individual relationship so much as a violence-inducing structure, and the reproduction of violence is, once again, seen in terms of projection and absorption. At the very moment when violence might be essentialized in terms of sexuality, it is overlaid with notions of inside, outside and the exchanges between the two. At the same time as the feeding and the giving associated with the mother is coopted as a metaphor for a fundamentally structural relationship of inside and outside, the sex of Nathalie can be downplayed: she becomes just a locus of violence as it moves between the various parties involved. As a child even more than as a daughter, she becomes, like the young boy in *The Go-Between*, essentially an emissary of violence. For as a child, she is, like the corpse in *Moderato cantabile*, between states, between birth and adulthood. She is the quintessential intermediary. She is a less an essence, whether human or female, than a nodal point in a structure for the reception and retransmission of violence. There are, as a result, more similarities than dissimilarities between Nathalie and the boys whose murderous actions are being regularly reported on the radio: here again the emphasis is on violence as *transmissible*: it is the insistent transmission of and about violence which both fascinates and aggresses the household, rather than the 'content' of the violence or the identity—which remains anonymous—of its perpetrators. Like the insistent playing of single notes from the piano which recurs throughout the film, violence is an oblique aural assault whose form and source are less important than the readiness with which it is purveyed and received.

It would seem, then, the effect of locating the primary violence of *Nathalie Granger* in the eponymous Nathalie is twofold. On the one hand, there is the shock value of associating violence not only with a young woman but with a young girl ('Cette violence chez une petite fille …' (p. 34)). As is clear from the recent resurgence of interest in the Mary Bell case, a young girl's violence is still perceived as more shocking and more 'unnatural' than violence committed by boys.[36] On the other hand, Duras also shows that the violence is by no means necessarily 'intrinsic' to Nathalie as an individual since it just one particularly salient example of a pattern of violent relationships which involve all the other characters, whether men or women, as well as the house of which they are an integral part. A similar combination of violence as essence and violence as structure is, moreover, to be found in the house, which, when compared to a prison, is both the embodiment of, and site for, violence. As Duras herself has written: 'Yes, I see Isabelle Granger as prisoner of this home, prisoner of herself, of her life … of this sort of infernal circuit'.[37] If, as Michelle Royer has recently reminded us, the house constitutes the primary subject matter of the film, if not its true subject,[38] it is because the twin character of violence, both essence and structure, can be captured by the notion of 'inhabitation': violence inhabits Nathalie and her mother in the same way that it, and they, inhabit the house. Violence is of the house and in the house, in them and of them; they are also of and in it. In *Nathalie Granger*, then, the relationship between character and violence is simultaneously one of equivalence or metaphor and contiguity or metonymy. At the same time, these metaphorical and metonymical relationships are no mere figures of speech. The modes of representation designated by metaphor and metonymy are, in *Nathalie Granger*, not simply representational or designatory, but lived relationships of identity (metaphor) and proximity (metonymy). If all the characters, finally, are reduced to silence, it is because they can no longer use metaphor and metonymy to describe their relationship to violence. They can no longer speak (of) the way they inhabit violence and the way it inhabits them. The descriptive and the distancing power of language is beyond them and all they can now do is live their identity with violence.

Given that the characters in *Nathalie Granger* are obliged to live violence because they cannot themselves *represent* violence through recourse to metaphor and metonymy, it is interesting that, as suggested above, the *content* of violence remains elusive in the work. As indicated above, violence lies in transmission rather than its acts. Indeed, as Najet Limam-Tnani points out, there is a general problem about separating content from container in Duras since there is 'a continuity between interior and exterior, a commutability between container and contained, and an equivalence between inhabiting and being inhabited'.[39] Since metonymy is an important device for expressing a relationship between 'content' and 'container', and, indeed, of expressing the distinction between content and container, it is worthwhile noting that there seems to be a fascination with containers and vessels in *Nathalie Granger*, from the house itself to the vessels in the house—such as the extended and much praised clearing of the table of its vessels in the opening scenes—and to the preoccupation with a different kind of domestic container, the infamous Vedette 008. As Lynn Higgins has shown, this preoccupation with cleaning or erasure marks a desire to 'make a clean sweep' and create a metaphorical as well as literal 'tabula rasa'. It also shows the failure, as she indicates, of the ability of the sales representative to represent, either commercially or linguistically.[40] More particularly, however, it marks a kind of attempt to inhibit metonymy, in that, as with the violence, the content of the vessel is less important than its status as vessel. Elsewhere, the vessel itself refuses to accept any content, as in the famous scene with Nathalie and the perambulator where she endeavours vainly to push the cat into the pram only to see it bound out and off. So angry is Nathalie with the cat or with the innocent pram that she hurls the pram away and stalks off. Although this has, quite rightly, been seen as a gesture of the rejection of maternity, it also expresses anger at the failure of the metonymical process of containment: here, as with the salesman, there is a failure to represent in the sense of express and contain, or inhibit and inhabit. Nathalie attacks the vessel for failing to fulfil its function: she cannot make the container contain. In the same way, Isabelle may be in the process of stifling her child because she senses she is failing as a mother, and the salesman too is thwarted because he fails in the marketing of his containers. Throughout *Nathalie Granger*, then, there is an association between violence and the failure of metonymical representation and containment.

It is possible to link this metonymical block to the frequently cited remarks by Julia Kristeva in *Soleil noir* that Duras fails to offer any cathartic resolution to the violence in her work: 'With neither cure nor God, without value or beauty other than the malady itself which is seized at the site of its essential fissure, never, perhaps, was art so lacking in catharsis.'[41] As Kristeva has written more recently, Duras 'couldn't care less whether her art was incapable of catharsis, since she wished precisely to contaminate the reader with her deathly passion, her passion for death'.[42] This metonymical block can also be linked to a lack of fetishization in Duras: neither objects, such as the pram, the dishes, the washing machine or even the house itself, can be said to be fetishized in *Nathalie Granger*, any more than can other celebrated containers in Duras such as the 'Léon-Bollée noire' in *L'amant* or the lorry in *Le camion*. For although vessels, vehicles and containers are so important in Duras, these containers neither represent (in either sense) a particular content, nor do they, like the fetish, operate as surrogate objects of conservation and compensation. Nor does it seem that photographs and films of these containing objects operate for Duras in a substitutive or reparatory fashion. Rather, like Hervé Guibert's *L'image fantôme* as discussed recently by Alex Hughes, Duras's photographs and filmic images seem to fail to offer 'an illusion of "presence"' and fail to 'constitute, like the fetish itself, reserves of (ambiguous) consolation'.[43] Thus, as James S. Williams has demonstrated in relation to *Le camion*: '[t]he endless reversals, split-selves and punctuations of image … have been replaced by Duras herself as the punctual source of meaning', making the film into 'a cycle of self-ironic remakes' if not 'a hoax'.[44] Does this mean that the equally unfilled and unfillable vessels in *Nathalie Granger* make *Nathalie Granger* itself an unfilled and unfillable, and thus essentially self-ironizing, film? With its loquacious but faintly ludicrous salesman and purportedly violent, yet possibly no more than temperamental, child, *Nathalie Granger* could indeed be a kind of self-conscious cinematic hoax, whose supposed violence simply masks and exposes its own artistic knowingness, its own surrealist game. As Williams again writes of *Le camion*: 'Ultimately, it is only the film's violence both to itself and the viewer that ensures that "it will have existed"; that the conditional perfect of indecipherable writing is transformed into the future perfect of readable cinematic fantasy'.[45]

What, then, can one conclude from the violence in and of *Nathalie Granger*? First, that there is a symmetry and a cross-fertilization between the violence 'within' the film and the violence 'outside' it. On the one hand, violence seems to come from outside: the salesman's intrusion; the delivery of the newspaper and the electricity bill which are torn up and destroyed; the reports of the child killers of the Yvelines. Violence can even be triply removed from 'actuality': in the case of Nathalie's wilful blotching of her writing lesson, her violence is reported but not seen; it takes place outside the film. Like the destruction of *Le Monde*, it destroys representation rather than 'the real'.[46] However seemingly removed from the film itself, such violence reverberates within the film's spaces, mesmerizing the women through the very language they are then impelled to eject or destroy. Although previous critics have, as has been indicated, welcomed the women's empowering, if reactive, silence, this silence is less effective than has been suggested: reports of the killings become more, rather than less, insistent, and Nathalie's 'outside' violence is addressed but not resolved. Moreover, there is, as has been shown, a complicity between the women and 'outside' violence: if the violences of salesman, killers and Nathalie find echoes within the house, it is because there is a kind of family resemblance between them all. In a move which transcends sexual or gender distinctions, all the characters, whether girls, boys, women or men, participate in the transmission, reception and retransmission of violence. One of the main messages of *Nathalie Granger*—and it is a disturbing one—is that violence is inseparable from representation, and that the violence of representation itself provokes further violence, most notably the attempt to eradicate the hydra of representation.

Although it has been argued that *Nathalie Granger* 'is most readily intelligible as an apocalyptic political allegory',[47] the second conclusion we must draw is that the film is certainly not apocalyptic, and thus not political in that sense. Had there been a sense of the apocalypse in *Nathalie Granger* it might almost have come as a relief, since change might then have been born out of the cataclysm. What characterizes the violence of *Nathalie Grange* is that it is both unnervingly repetitive—the violent acts of the killers are reiterated through the radio reports—and infinitely layered—the violences of the killers fold on to the violences of mother and daughter in cycles of mutual contamination and reinforcement. The violence of *Nathalie Granger* is therefore, like a Moebius loop—both inside and outside, both singular and unending. What characterizes the violence of *Nathalie Granger* is that it is both individual and serial, personal and structured. It is this which gives the work its particular political edge. For the representation of violence is political here through being associated with an exceptional individual—'cette violence chez une petite fille'—and, at the same time, through being structured into relationships, environments, and forms of communication, whether the language of patriarchal authority or the language of women's silence.

Two important observations follow from this. The first is that Nathalie and her violence are both marginal and central, both deviant and normal. The gendering—and more particularly the feminizing—of violence is, therefore, simultaneously foregrounded and subsumed into an overall structure of male and female relationships, environments and languages. The second is that the combination of individual and structural violence makes violence all-pervasive yet invisible: violence is all the more ineradicable for being impossible finally to locate or express. This elusiveness and incommunicability of violence does indeed thwart any move toward catharsis, either for the characters or for the viewer/reader. At the same time, and perhaps paradoxically, the very absence of direct violence and the resulting impossibility of catharsis create a vacuum for which the reader/viewer may wish to compensate by a reparatory *reading or viewing* of the work. The very gaps and silences of *Nathalie Granger* invite a compensatory move of replenishment and restored plenitude. The silent pain felt by Nathalie and the silent damage inflicted by Nathalie on her sorry perambulator, encourage one, as Eve Kosofsky Sedgwick remarks in her argument for new, anti-demystificatory, non-paranoid 'queer' readings, 'to use one's own resources to assemble or "repair" the murderous part-objects into something like a whole … Once assembled to one's own specifications, the more satisfying object is available both to be identified with and to offer one nourishment in turn.'[48] The power and the politics of *Nathalie Granger* is, then, neither to shock with its supposed exposure of a young girl's violence, nor to invite pity and terror leading to catharsis, but rather to offer a seemingly non-violent and yet unbearable violence which the reader/viewer will intuit like the silent characters, and thus, equally silently, seek and find repair and restoration. The lesson of violence in *Nathalie Granger* is not, therefore, that it should be demystified and explained, but, more crucially, that it should be soothed, cherished and healed.

Notes

1 Najet Limam-Tnani, *Roman et cinéma chez Marguerite Duras. Une poétique de la spécularité*, Tunis, Faculté des Sciences humaines et sociales/Alif-Les Editions de la Méditerranée, 1986, p. 9.

2 See Roger-Pol Droit's review of Wolfgang Sofsky's *Traité de la violence* (Paris, Gallimard, 1997), *Le Monde*, 13 March 1998, p. viii: '[l]e goût du sang traverse les âges. La destruction de leurs semblables réjouit les hommes. La cruauté est sans fin.'

3 Daniel Sibony, *Violence. Traversées*, Paris, Seuil, 1998, p. 353: 'En marge ou en travers de ces violences, il y a celle de la beauté; elle nous laisse sans recours devant son apparition, largués dans notre envie de l'atteindre, nous arrache des cris muets, nous réduisant à son silence'. For the relation between surrealism and

violence, see Jacqueline Chénieux-Gendron and Timothy Mathews (eds), *Violence, Théorie, Surréalisme*, Paris, Lachenal and Ritter, 1994.

4 See Olivier Mongin, *La Violence des images ou comment s'en débarasser?*, Paris, Seuil, 1997, p. 14. For other recent work on violence and representation, see *Image et Violence*, Paris, Bibliothèque publique d'information, 1997, and Stamatios Tzitzis, *Esthétique de la violence*, Paris, PUF, 1997.

5 *The Killing Screens* (an illustrated discussion with George Gerbner, Northampton Media Education Foundation, n.d.). Among the many discussions of the impact of media violence, see Martin Barker and Julian Petley (eds), *Ill Effects. The Media/Violence Debate*, London, Routledge, 1997, and for a summary of the different approaches to violence, gender and representation, see Owen Heathcote, 'Violence and Gender: Representation and Containment', *Journal of the Institute of Romance Studies*, No. 5 (1997), pp. 255–60.

6 Lee Edelman, 'The Future is Kid Stuff: Queer Theory, Disidentification and the Death Drive', *Narrative*, Vol. 6, No. 1 (1998), pp. 18–30; p. 21.

7 For analysis of the notion of 'nature erring from itself' see Jonathan Dollimore, *Sexual Dissidence*, Oxford, Clarendon Press, 1991, pp. 148–65.

8 *Children of Crime*, BBC1, 7 April 1998–5 May 1998. The first programme (7 April) dealt with the James Bulger murder and the second (14 April) with the murders by Mary Bell. On the treatment of latter as a violent girl, see Gitta Sereny, *Cries Unheard. The Story of Mary Bell*, London, Macmillan, 1998.

9 Edelman, 'Kid Stuff', p. 24.

10 Leo Bersani, *The Culture of Redemption*, Cambridge MA and London, Harvard University Press, 1990, p. 19.

11 Bersani, *Culture of Redemption*, pp. 19 and 20.

12 Marguerite Duras, *Nathalie Granger* (b/w, 1972); *Nathalie Granger, suivi de La Femme du Gange*, Paris, Gallimard, 1973. Page references to the latter will be given in parentheses in the text.

13 See Susan D. Cohen, 'The Beast in the jungle: longing, learning, loving and luck in Marguerite Duras's "Le Boa"', in *Marguerite Duras: Lectures plurielles*, ed. Catherine Rodgers and Raynalle Udris, Amsterdam, Rodopi, 1998, pp. 35–55. Duras stresses the brilliance of her mother as a teacher who could reach out to all children in *Le monde extérieur. Outside II*, Paris, POL, 1993, p. 202. See also Marguerite Duras, *L'amant de la Chine du Nord*, Paris, Gallimard, 1991, p. 117.

14 See, for example Kate Ince, '*L'Amour La Mort*: The Eroticism of Marguerite Duras', in *French Erotic Fiction. Women's Desiring Writing, 1880–1990*, ed. Alex Hughes and Kate Ince, Oxford, Berg, 1996, pp. 147–73.

15 Catherine Portuges, 'The Pleasures of *Nathalie Granger*', in *Remains to be Seen: Essays on Marguerite Duras*, ed. Sanford S. Ames, New York, Peter Lang, 1988, pp. 219–29.

16 Marguerite Duras and Michelle Porte, *Les lieux de Marguerite Duras*, Paris, Minuit, 1977, p. 36: 'On croit toujours qu'il faut partir d'une histoire pour faire du cinéma. Ce n'est pas vrai. Pour *Nathalie Granger*, je suis complètement partie de la maison. Vraiment'. For an interesting presentation of the house at Neauphle-le-Château,

see Aliette Armel, *Marguerite Duras. Les trois lieux de l'écrit*, Paris, Christian Pirot, 1998, pp. 53–96.

17 See also pp. 23, 32 and 75; for 'la demeure des femmes', pp. 86, 87 and 88.

18 See, for example, E. Ann Kaplan, 'Silence as female resistance in Marguerite Duras's *Nathalie Granger* (1972)' in her *Women and Film. Both Sides of the Camera*, London and New York, Routledge, 1983, pp. 91–103; Catherine Rodgers, 'Déconstruction de la masculinité dans l'oeuvre durassienne' in *Marguerite Duras. Rencontres de Cerisy*, ed. Alain Vircondelet, Paris, Ecriture, 1994, pp. 47–68; p. 53; Lynn A. Higgins, *New Novel, New Wave, New Politics: Fiction and the Representation of History in Postwar France*, Lincoln NE and London, University of Nebraska Press, 1996, pp. 137–38.

19 See Judith Butler, *Excitable Speech: A Politics of the Performative*, New York and London, Routledge, 1997.

20 See Duras, *Nathalie Granger*, pp. 89–90.

21 See Rodgers, 'Déconstruction de la masculinité', p. 54.

22 Higgins, *New Novel, New Wave, New Politics*, p. 138.

23 Rodgers, 'Déconstruction de la masculinité', p. 53.

24 Higgins, *New Novel, New Wave, New Politics*, p. 139.

25 Kaplan, 'Silence as female resistance', p. 102.

26 Duras's note in *Nathalie Granger*, p. 90: 'le regard d'un homme n'a *pas encore retrouvé* cette fonction, submergeante, d'enfouissement du discours en un lieu où il s'annule, *se tait*, se supprime—qu'a le regard d'une femme'.

27 See for example, Catherine Rodgers, 'Lectures de la sorcière, ensorcellement de l'écriture', in *Duras. Lectures plurielles*, ed. Rodgers and Udris, pp. 17–34.

28 Rodgers, 'Lectures de la sorcière', p. 19: 'Michelet insiste sur la demeure de la femme, cette cabane qu'il renomme son palais, et dont il fait le berceau de sa naissance'. On the theme of black and white it is worth noting that *Nathalie Granger* is indeed in black and white, perhaps because, in Duras's eyes, there is no white in colour films (see Marguerite Duras, *Les yeux verts* (1987), Paris, Editions de l'Etoile/Cahiers du Cinéma, 1996, p. 15).

29 For a useful presentation of the Benjaminian aura, see Yvonne Sherratt, 'Aura: the aesthetic of *redemption*?', *Philosophy and Social Criticism*, Vol. 24, No. 1 (1998), pp. 25–41.

30 On female genealogies in Duras, see Kate Ince, 'Woman, lover, daughter, mother: female genealogies in *Le navire Night* and *Savanah Bay*', in *Duras. Lectures plurielles*, ed. Rodgers and Udris, pp. 132–49.

31 See Marguerite Duras, *L'amant*, Paris, Minuit, 1984, p. 122. On the theme of triangular desire in Duras, see Diana Holmes, *French Women's Writing 1848–1994*, London, Athlone, 1996, pp. 240–41.

32 Najet Limam-Tnani, p. 22: 'Pénétrée par le manque, la relation mère/enfant est de part et d'autre entachée de culpabilité et donne rarement lieu à des sentiments de bonheur'.

33 Lia van de Biezenbos, *Fantasmes maternels dans l'oeuvre de Marguerite Duras*, Amsterdam, Rodopi, 1995, p. 131: 'Ici, comme dans *Moderato cantabile*, l'enfant semble doubler la mère dans la mesure où textuellement le refus de l'enfant

annonce celui de la mère. La violence de l'enfant est une projection de la mère qui a besoin de l'enfant pour arriver à exprimer sa propre violence'.

34 Biezenbos, *Fantasmes maternels*, p. 131: 'C'est pourquoi Isabelle ne veut pas se séparer de Nathalie, elle ne peut pas couper le lien de la violence. Il fallait d'abord qu'Isabelle soit affamée de sa fille pour assimiler la violence de cette dernière'.

35 *La classe de la violence* (1984), directed by Jérôme Beaujour and Jean Mascolo, part of *Les oeuvres cinématographiques de Marguerite Duras. Edition Vidéographique Critique*, Paris, Ministère des Relations extérieures, 1984.

36 See note 8 above.

37 Duras and Porte, *Les lieux de Marguerite Duras*, p. 20: 'Oui, je vois Isabelle Granger comme prisonnière de cette demeure-ci, prisonnière d'elle-même, de sa vie ... de cette espèce de circuit infernal.'

38 Michelle Royer, *L'Ecran de la passion: une étude du cinéma de Marguerite Duras*, Mount Nebo, Queensland, Bombana Publications, 1997, p. 84.

39 Najet Limam-Tnani, p. 204: 'une continuité entre l'extérieur et l'intérieur, une commutablité entre le contenant et le contenu et une équivalence entre habiter et être habité'.

40 See Higgins, *New Novel, New Wave, New Politics*, pp. 138–39.

41 Julia Kristeva, *Soleil noir: dépression et mélancolie*, Paris, Gallimard, 1987, p. 235: 'Sans guérison ni Dieu, sans valeur ni beauté autre que celle de la maladie elle-même prise au lieu de sa brisure essentielle, jamais, peut-être, art ne fut aussi peu cathartique.'

42 Julia Kristeva, 'Une étrangère', *La Nouvelle Revue Française*, No. 542 (March 1998), pp. 3–9; p. 3: '[Duras] s'en fichait que son art soit incapable de catharsis, puisqu'elle voulait justement contaminer le lecteur avec sa passion à mort, sa passion pour la mort.'

43 Alex Hughes, 'Reading Guibert's *L'Image fantôme/Reading Desire*', *Modern and Contemporary France*, Vol. 6, No. 2 (1998), pp. 203–14; p. 213. For a different view of metonymy in Duras, see Renate Günther, *Duras*, Le Ravissement de Lol. V. Stein *and* L'amant, London, Grant & Cutler 'Critical guides to French texts', 1993, pp. 74–76.

44 James S. Williams, *The Erotics of Passage: Pleasure, Politics, and Form in the Later Work of Marguerite Duras*, Liverpool University Press/St Martin's Press, 1997, p. 36.

45 Williams, *Erotics of Passage*, p. 37.

46 See Higgins, *New Novel, New Wave, New Politics*, pp. 135–36.

47 Leslie Hill, *Marguerite Duras: Apocalyptic Desires*, London and New York, Routledge, 1993, p. 89.

48 Eve Kosofsky Sedgwick, 'Introduction: Queerer than Fiction', *Studies in the Novel*, Vol. 28, No. 3 (1996), pp. 277–80; p. 278.

Part II
Race

CHAPTER 5

Durasie: Women, Natives, and Other

Marie-Paule Ha

In the last 10 years or so, increasing critical attention has been directed to examining the colonial narrative space that structures the Asian novels of Marguerite Duras. Such studies offer a critique of Duras's relation to her native land and colonialism.[1] In this chapter, I propose to explore further the colonial problematic in the Durassian Asian texts by revisioning her women characters within the framework of colonial gender politics. I start with an overview of the roles of white women and their native counterparts as articulated in the colonial discourse of the Third Republic. In the second part of the chapter, I will examine the extent to which Duras draws on colonial narrative stereotypes in her portrayal of both white and native women as two diametrically opposed groups. The last part of the essay shows how the colonial gender politics that underlies Duras's representation of women characters also finds itself disarticulated by the liminal positionality of certain of her female protagonists who, through their crisscrossing of social and racial divides, both challenge and reaffirm the colonial hegemonic structure.

Even the most cursory survey of colonial writings, both fiction and non-fiction, reveals a wide range of conflicting views surrounding the roles of colonial women, or *coloniales* as they were called in France.[2] At the level of official discourse, European women were held up as civilizing agents entrusted with the task of affirming and maintaining the cultivation of the European self in the outposts of the empire. One of the most outspoken promoters of the civilizing mission of French women in the colonies was Clothilde Chivas-Baron, who described her fellow *coloniales* as the 'torch-bearer of civilization' carrying out 'works of charity and humanity' among the natives. In her book *La femme française aux colonies* (1929), we find some of the most eloquent descriptions of the role of the *coloniale* as the '[o]ne who creates France everywhere around Her with habits and visions of France … with the grace and morality of France, kindness and courage of France'.[3] The theme of women as civilizing agents was also the focus of the speeches presented during the two-day meeting of the Etats Généraux du Féminisme at the 1931 Exposition Coloniale in Vincennes. The addresses given by longtime *coloniales* such as Mme Chivas-Baron, Mlle Karpelès, Mme Georges Hardy and Mme Maspero detailed French women's participation in the *oeuvre civilisatrice* in their capacities as doctors, nurses, social workers, teachers and missionaries. Their privileged fields of action were social hygiene and education, with the ultimate goal being to achieve 'the elevation of the native towards our civilization'.[4]

To this narrative of 'the white women's burden' was superimposed what came to be known as 'the myth of the destructive female'.[5] In many colonial writings, the *coloniales* were blamed for spoiling the amiable *rapport* between colonizers and colonized that existed before the arrival of white women in the colonies. The latter's negative relationship with the natives was often ascribed to their racism, arrogance and ignorance of local culture. In *Prospero and Caliban*, O. Mannoni contends that in Madagascar, the racism of white women was much more rabid than that of their male counterparts.[6] In 'La femme et la politique indigène', Georges Hardy, former director of l'Ecole Coloniale, establishes a long list of complaints traditionally levelled against the ill-prepared colonial wives and the damage the latter brought to their husbands' careers.[7] Colonial fiction also abounds in unfriendly European female characters, and Raymonde, the antipathetic colonial wife in George Groslier's novel, *Le retour à l'argile* (1928), is a telling example.[8] In evoking the difficult personality of the heroine, who refused to make the slightest effort to adapt to her new life in Cambodia, the narrator makes it clear that it was her intransigence that drove her husband, Claude, out of their home into the arms of a native mistress. One of the main causes of Raymonde's unhappiness was the '*ennui colonial*' a condition endemic to colonial society, affecting women more seriously than men. The cause of this *ennui* was attributed to their idleness as most colonial housewives had at their disposal a retinue of native servants who took care of the household chores for them. As a remedy to their boredom, colonial wives engaged in either malicious gossip, petty disputes,[9] or adultery, the latter being a dominant theme in colonial fiction. In Alain Robbe-Grillet's *La jalousie* (1957), for instance, the narrator, a white plantation owner in an unnamed tropical colony, is obsessed with the idea that his wife is having an affair with their neighbor Frank. Likewise, Jean d'Esme's *Ame de la brousse* (1923) recounts the story of the heroine Colette who destroys her husband by engaging in an adulterous relation with another young officer. As I argue elsewhere, these conflicting narratives surrounding the roles of the *coloniales* were instigated by the different political agendas of feminist groups,[10] the colonial lobby,[11] and the settlers,[12] among others.

The animosity of white women towards the native population was often attributed to a perceived rivalry vis-à-vis the indigenous women, known in the Indochinese colonial parlance as *congaï*, a term used in the colonial society to designate marginalized women who served as concubines to European men. The theme of European wives sharing their spouses with the *congaïs* is ubiquitous in colonial fiction. We have seen that in Groslier's novel, *Le retour à l'argile*, Raymonde had to share Claude with his Cambodian mistress Kâmlang. The same situation occurs in Jeanne Leuba's *L'aile de feu* (1920), whose narrator protagonist Françoise finds out that her husband has also fallen under the seductive power of a native servant within their very own home.[13] In many of the colonial novels, the native women are seen predominantly through the gaze of their white masters. They are usually presented as mute, submissive and passive characters. In fact, according to Eugène Pujarniscle, one of the major qualities of the *congaïs* which attracted European males is the former's animal-like submissiveness to men: 'when you go home, you will find a little cuddly animal that will keep you warm in the winter, fan you in the summer, bring you tea and liquors, rolls your cigarettes, prepare your pipes ….'[14] Such is also Claude's perception of Kâmlang whose life, he believes, can only revolve around him: 'Hardly does he step in the house than he is convinced that she was waiting for him, watching out for his arrival … she will take his topee, undo the laces of his shoes, anticipate every single one of his gestures and ensure his well-being by thousand and one ways … She does not exist for herself: she is Claude's double, driven by the sole egoism of Claude.'[15] Claude premises this view of his mistress on what he takes to be the universal lot of all Asian women: which is to serve men. Hence, Kâmlang's devotion to him is but an instance of an immemorial law governing the relationship of the two sexes in Asia: 'And whatever the moment at which he catches hold of this devotion, he is sure that it is not a tactic. The spontaneity, the conscientiousness, and the dexterity with which Kâmlang carries out her tasks show that her mother and all her foremothers and all those of all the Asian women who are breathing at this very hour—served thus for centuries their spouses and lovers, be they princes or peasants.'[16]

The importance of colonial Indochina in Duras's work and life has been recognized by an increasing number of critics in recent years. In his *Marguerite Duras*, Alain Vircondelet observes that 'her entire oeuvre feeds on sources in white Indochina'.[17] More recently, in her superb biography on Duras, Laure Adler likewise notes that 'Marguerite's life is filled with accidents, breaks …

But the motherland, the place of origin, the ultimate source of her being remains to be colonial Indochina until the end of her life.'[18] My task here is to examine the colonial world in the land of Durasie,[19] with a particular focus on Duras's representation of both white and native women. This is done through an analysis of some of the topoi of colonial narratives that Duras draws on in her depiction of the colonial society. One such topos is the theme of boredom which serves as a leitmotif in several of her Asian novels. In *Un barrage contre le Pacifique*, the main characters are described at the very beginning of the novel as being 'soaked in boredom and bitterness'.[20] Throughout the narrative, the young protagonist Suzanne is consumed by idleness and boredom as she spends endless hours dreaming of leaving the plain through some sort of sexual escapade. The same fate also befalls the adolescent narrator in Duras's 1947 short story 'Le Boa', who whiles away many a dull Sunday afternoon on the terrace of her pension in a colonial city surveying the passing French soldiers with the secret hope that one of them would notice her. Not only, though, is boredom the predicament of the young unmarried female characters, it also affects many Europeans in the colony. Tedium is, for example, the main complaint of the white society in *Le vice-consul*, a plight none can escape since '[b]oredom here means a feeling of cosmic desolation, induced by the vastness of India itself. This country generates a mood of its own'.[21] The boredom of the colonizers is a consequence of their idleness, a condition especially prevalent among women, most of whom, we read in *Le vice-consul*, 'spend their lives in shuttered rooms, sheltering from the deadly rays of the sun. In India they do virtually nothing. They are rested …' (p. 77) ('vivent volets clos à l'abri du soleil-qui-tue, elles ne font presque rien aux Indes, elles sont reposées …' (p. 100)). Their inaction is attributed, the narrator of *L'amant* explains, to '[the] marvellous domestic service provided by houseboys'.[22] The favourite activity to defuse their boredom is gossip, as seen in the unending speculations of the women at the Cercle Français about the life of the ambassador's wife Anne-Marie Stretter: 'At the Club, the other women talk about her. What does she do with herself? No one knows … What really happened that time towards the end of her first year in Calcutta? …' (*The Vice-consul*, p. 85) ('Au Cercle, les autres femmes parlent d'elle. Que se passe-t-il dans cette existence? Où la trouver? On ne sait pas … Que s'est-il passé à la fin de la première année de son séjour? …' (*Le vice-consul*, pp. 109–10)).

Another distraction from the monotony of colonial life available to Durassian female characters is sexual escapade. We have noted in *Un barrage* that Suzanne is constantly fantasizing that one fine day a great hunter will come to carry her away from the plain. Lina, her brother Joseph's wealthy mistress, is yet another colonial wife who, we read, 'was bored to death in this Colony, she said, very bored' (p. 206) ('s'ennuyait dans cette colonie, beaucoup, beaucoup' (*Un barrage*, p. 261)). It is this unbearable *ennui* that drives her into the arms of Joseph in a movie theatre. In *Le vice-consul* and *India Song*, much of the gossip about Anne-Marie Stretter also revolves around her affairs with a retinue of young lovers. Indeed, the story of her life is one of endless sexual pursuits. Rumour has it that 17 years ago she deserted her first husband to elope with Mr Stretter whom she later cheated on with younger men. Many of the white women Duras creates in her Asian writings are strongly reminiscent of the stereotypical *coloniales*, a class of unproductive and idle wives consumed with boredom and melancholy within their artificially constructed society.

In contrast to these women, most of whom enjoy a life of leisure, the native women in Duras are drawn almost exclusively from the most disenfranchized groups among peasants and domestics (the two exceptions being the mother and the fiancée of the rich Chinese lover in *L'amant*). The absence of Indochinese middle-class women in her depiction of the native world is all the more intriguing given that Duras must have been aware of their existence since her mother was a teacher in a French school frequented by middle-class indigenous young girls.[23] Moreover, though less commonly present than the *congaï*, middle-class native women do appear as protagonists in a number of colonial novels. For example, in her short story 'Mémoires de Thi-Vinh' (1922), Chivas-Baron recounts the eventful life of Thi-Vinh, daughter of an Annamite mandarin. Likewise, the eponymous heroine of *Le roman de Mademoiselle Lys* (1920) by Nguyên-Phan-Long is the western-educated daughter of a Vietnamese rich landowner. In their co-authored novel *En s'écartant des ancêtres* (1939) and its sequel *La réponse de l'Occident* (1941), Trinh-Thuc-Oanh and Margurite Triaire trace the trials and tribulations of a group of western educated middle-class Indochinese friends from their youth to womanhood.[24] Why, then, is this group of indigenous women so prominently absent in Duras's Indochina, which is instead peopled by their less fortunate sisters?

In her article 'From *The Sea Wall* to *The Lover*: Prostitution and Exotic Parody', Pascale Bécel draws our attention to the contrast between the sexual victimization and passivity of the native women, on the one hand, and the empowerment and self-formation of Suzanne and the narrator-protagonist of *L'amant*, on the other, within the terms of prostitution. Bécel rightly points out that the Indochinese women in *Un barrage* are visible only in their reproductive function and that their bodies are 'represented mimicking natural phenomena: their bellies growing 'with the rhythm of plant-life', 'by periodical tides, or, if you like, by crops or burgeoning'.[25] Reduced to serving as mere gestatory receptacles (to continue the vegetal metaphor) and incapable of any resistance, native women are seen as ensnared in the never-ending circle of prostitution and procreation. Such is, we read in *Un barrage*, the fate of the wife of the Corporal, Ma's native servant, which she shares with all her unfortunate sisters: 'During this time, as did all the wives of the recruits, the Corporal's wife gave birth to children one after another, thanks to the virility of the militiamen' (p. 195) ('Pendant ce temps comme toutes les femmes d'enrôlés, la femme du caporal enfantait sans arrêt et toujours des oeuvres des seuls miliciens' (p. 246)). Besides being part of the western masculine stereotyping of Asiatic women as docile and submissive, this representation of native women as defenceless victims of the brutal patriarchal native society has also been, according to Antoinette Burton, a favorite topos in the discourse of middle-class European feminists in which was invoked 'a degraded female Other to persuade audiences that the western, and specifically the British, women's movement was part of the march of western civilization'.[26] By juxtaposing the representation of an enslaved 'Oriental' womanhood, Burton further argues, Victorian feminists were able to construct the emancipated image of the western women.

In Duras's Indochinese world, the reduction of native women to the category of 'Oriental' and 'primitive' womanhood likewise serves the purpose of enhancing the self-determination and control that her western heroines have of their bodies. In both *Un barrage* and *L'amant*, the two female protagonists manage, in spite of their young age, to turn the *rapport de force* around in their relationship with men. As Bécel convincingly argues, the heroine in *Un barrage* exploits her position of prostitution to the point of transforming her role as object of the exchange into that of subject. From being the object of Mr Jo's voyeurism, Suzanne quickly becomes the gazer whose look annihilates him as a person, turning him into a mere obstacle to the fabulous wealth she and her family covet: 'Instead of going to dress, Suzanne sat down in front of him [Mr Jo] and looked at him with a certain curiosity. But she began to think of other things almost at once, while continuing to look at him without seeing him, as if he had been transparent, and she was obliged to look though his face to perceive the dizzy promises of wealth' (p. 80) ('Au lieu d'aller s'habiller, Suzanne s'assit devant lui [M. Jo] et le regarda avec une certaine curiosité. Mais elle se mit à se distraire de lui presque aussitôt, tout en continuant à le regarder sans le voir, comme s'il eût été transparent, et qu'il lui fallait passer par ce visage pour entrevoir les promesses vertigineuses de l'argent' (pp. 101–02)). Such a subversion is certainly not the prerogative of the Corporal's wife who has to endure years of prostitution in order to keep her husband in the chain gang for their survival. A similar gender role reversal also occurs in *L'amant* in which the young narrator-protagonist plays the dominant and controlling part in her relationship with the Chinese lover. If prostitution, understood as a form of transgression through which, as Martha Noel Evans describes, the whore 'becomes the looker, the chooser, the centre of power',[27] is almost a *sine qua non condition féminine* in the Durassian universe,[28] it takes very different forms for white women and for their native counterparts. In *Un barrage*, Suzanne prostitutes herself for superfluous consumer goods such as perfume, cosmetics, phonograph, diamond rings and cars, whereas the prostitution of the Corporal's wife is the price she has to pay so as to keep herself and her family from starvation. In *L'amant*, it is with defiance, if not arrogance, that the first-person narrator refers to herself as 'the little white whore from Sadec' (p. 35) ('la petite prostitutée blanche de Sadec' (p. 45)) and as she gets to know the Chinese better, she also arranges to have him treat her family to sumptuous meals in Chinese restaurants and nightclubs. Later, she manages to exact substantial sums from the lover to pay the opium debts of her older brother. A similar contrast between the white and native women's prostitutions is present in *Le vice-consul* and *India Song*: the 'prostitution' of Anne-Marie Stretter is presented as an expression of feminine empowerment as shown by the irresistible spell she exerts on men around her, whereas her native Other, the beggar woman, is subjected to the most abject form of degradation as she is forced to sell her body during her pregnancy for a bowl of rice. Under these widely contrasting circumstances, it is not surprising that only European protagonists attain female *jouissance*, something denied their indigenous sisters.

If, in her representation of the white and native women protagonists, Duras does indeed reproduce a great many of the colonial racial and gender stereotypes, she also creates a number of female characters whose liminal positions serve to disarticulate the colonial construction of gender roles. In this last section of the essay, I will now focus on this group of characters which includes the first-person narrator in *L'amant* and *L'amant de la Chine du nord*, Ma in *Un barrage*, as well as the mother in Duras's two autobiographical novels.

A number of critics have studied the liminal spatiality occupied by the young heroine of the autobiographies. In *Fantasmatic Indochina: French Colonial Ideology in Architecture, Cinema, and Literature*, Panivong Norindr discusses the significance of the '*errance*' of the first-person narrator in *L'amant* across the colonial city which he reads as a transgressive move that undermines the colonial boundaries drawn to fix the geographical, social and racial self/other divisions.[29] Indeed, on one level, the autobiographical narrator does seem to subvert the colonial social and gender order through her sexual and racial transgressions. As I pointed out earlier, the young heroine is highly conscious of the power of her body and knows how to exploit it to her advantage. The minute description of her provocative attire (running to nine pages in the French text) and the repeated evocation of the effect her look has on men bespeak the narrator's obsession with her own sexuality, a concern that was certainly considered quite inappropriate, not to say scandalous, for young girls of her age in the 1920s, who were expected to display a certain demureness and virginal innocence. More shocking still to the colonial society is that not only does the precocious heroine agree to play Lolita to a native man, she also publicly flaunts this illicit relationship when she rides in his black Morris Léon-Bollée to restaurants and nightclubs.

Yet, as certain historians argue,[30] interracial romantic relationships rarely, if ever, constitute a real challenge to the colonial power structure. Indeed, the theme of the white colonizer seeking erotic excitement through the 'penetration' of the exotic Other has a well established tradition in colonial narratives from the South Sea romances to the exotic tales *à la* Loti. Colonial literature abounds in stories of yellow, black, and brown Madame Butterflys since keeping a 'petite épouse' is part and parcel of living in the colony and 'knowing' the natives. And in the colonial context, 'knowing' the natives does not in general result in better treatment of the latter, only in their more effective control. At the narratological level, the love plot in *L'amant* shares a number of the functions inherent in the standard exotic romance which invariably starts with the meeting of a pair of interracial lovers, the white male acting as the material provider for his native mistress and ends with the former abandoning the latter to return to the Metropole.[31] As we noted earlier, in *L'amant* the traditional gender roles between the young narrator and her Chinese partner have been inverted and their romantic adventure concludes with the Chinese lover being transformed into a kind of 'Monsieur Butterfly' who, like his female namesake, is devastated when his white mistress leaves for the mother country. At the intertextual level, the love story in *L'amant* has numerous parallels with Pierre Loti's exotic novels such as *Aziyadé*. In both narratives, the white protagonists cross over into the native city to meet their native lovers. And in both stories, the native cities, the Muslim district of Eyoub in Loti's book and the Chinese city of Cholon in *L'amant*, constitute the site of the Other qua the locus of desire. In the French imaginary, Cholon has the reputation of being a latter-day Gomorrah which, with its gambling dens, brothels, and opium dives, seemed, in the words of Gontran de Poncins, 'a true caravanserai where all human activities are carried on as freely as the heart desires'.[32] Given its image in Indochinese colonial society, Cholon was indeed the most logical, if not ideal, site for the initiation of *L'amant*'s young heroine into the 'oldest profession' of the world. While the narrator's 'unbecoming' sexual escapade creates uproar among her French classmates and their parents, the scandal she causes is nothing more than a scandal that provides some good gossip in white society.

More than the interracial romance of the Durassian autobiographical narrator, it is the saga of the mother in *L'amant* and *L'amant de la Chine du Nord*, along with that of Ma in *Un barrage*, that most effectively exposes the contradictions of colonial gender politics since the role of these women as civilizing agents is constantly undermined by their failure to live by the bourgeois values. These contradictions, I argue, reflect the conflicting premises underlying the colonial order and ultimately bring about its self-fissuring and disarticulation. Like their real-life model Marie Donnadieu, *née* Legrand,[33] the mother and Ma were part of the small pioneering group of the Third Republic *institutrices* that responded to the call of the *mission civilisatrice* as well as to the lure of exotic adventure. In the three autobiographical novels, Duras's representation of the character of the mother partakes in more ways than one of the rhetoric of the 'white women's burden' that I discussed earlier. It is indeed interesting to note the magnitude of the transformation in the mother's role as a teacher in the three texts. In *Un barrage*, Ma is described as a simple teacher in a state school who, soon after the birth of her two children, leaves her job to become a homemaker, intermittenly giving private French lessons to supplement her income. In *L'amant*, the mother is likewise presented as the headmistress of the girls' school in Sadec who later starts La Nouvelle Ecole française, the financial success of which enables her to send money to her children in France. Yet curiously enough, the mother suddenly assumes an almost mythic aura in her role as educator in *L'amant de la Chine du Nord*, where we read that the mother was 'a great teacher … They worship her in Indochina because she's so dedicated to her profession. She has educated thousands of children …'.[34] The reason for the natives' adoration of the mother is the latter's selfless dedication to educating disenfranchized native children so that they might defend themselves against exploitation later in life: 'They say she has never given up on a child, not until he could read and write. She would hold classes late into the evening for children she knew would someday be workers, "manual labor", or as she put it: the exploited. She wouldn't let them go until she was sure they could read a work contract' (p. 108) ('On dit qu'elle n'a jamais abandonné un enfant avant qu'il sache lire et écrire. Jamais. Qu'elle faisait des cours tard le soir pour les enfants dont elle savait qu'ils seraient des ouvriers plus tard, des "manuels", elle disait: des exploités. Elle ne les lâchait que lorsqu'elle était sûre qu'ils étaient capables de lire un contrat de travail' (p. 122)).

Duras's transformation of the mother into a kind of secular missionary fighting on the side of the native working class is both perplexing and illuminating. According to Adler, Marie Donnadieu, the real-life model of the mother made a great deal of money in Indochina running a chic boarding school.[35] The profit from her educational establishment and her traffic in currency enabled her to buy several houses. Furthermore, Duras's presentation of the French school as the nurturing ground of the native underclass during the first quarter of the twentieth century is far from historical reality since French education remained for a long time the prerogative of the bourgeois elite.[36] In re-imagining the mother as a selfless educator devoted to the wellbeing of the natives, Duras reproduces the official discourse of colonial gender politics that promoted white women as civilizing agents dedicated to philanthropic work among the colonized.

In fact, besides the mother in *L'amant de la Chine du Nord*, several other Durassian women characters are also cast in the role of philanthropists. A case in point is Ma, who is presented as the protector of the peasants of the plain because she helps them to escape their misery by letting them participate in the building of the sea wall.[37] Ma is also known in the plain for her kindness to little children and even adopts a native baby girl abandoned by her own mother. The same story of adoption is later retold in *Le vice-consul* in which we read of the beggar woman giving up her baby daughter to a white woman. The philanthropy of the Durassian white women is meant to suggest a more benevolent form of colonial rule, i.e. a gentler and kinder feminine alternative to the traditional brutal phallocracy, exemplified by the corrupt and exploitative colonial government that ruins both Ma and the peasants in *Un barrage*. This form of colonial maternalism has a well-established tradition in colonial history as well as in the history of western feminism.[38] Some of the highly romanticized colonial maternalistic figures that bear a certain resemblance to the mother and Ma are Isak Dinesen/Karen Blixen in *Out of Africa* (1937) and Eliane in Régis Wargnier's film *Indochine* (1991). All these women, presented as advocates of native welfare, are said to inspire great affection and respect among the colonized who look up to them as their surrogate mothers.

While acting their part as civilizing agents, the mother and Ma also experience great economic and emotional difficulties that make it practically impossible for them to sustain such an image. In fact, the story of their lives belies the civilizing mission entrusted to them as they find themselves sinking deeper and deeper in the quagmire of 'going native'. In her study of the politics of gender and race in colonial Asia, Stoler has established the links between the construction of Europeanness and bourgeois civilities. The site that most centrally embodies bourgeois values, Stoler argues, is the domestic domain 'where essential dispositions of manliness, bourgeois morality, and racial attribute could be dangerously undone or securely made'.[39] Hence the importance of maintaining a well-cared-for European home that serves not only as an expression of superior western values, but also a manifestation of white prestige in the eyes of the natives. A perusal of the numerous pamphlets written by and for the *coloniales*,[40] as well as the latter's private letters,[41] shows their obsessive concerns with maintaining European ways in their attire, diet as well as home furnishings. Adoption of native adornments was strongly discouraged as it was seen as the first step on the way to the perdition of the European self. In an essay by Lottie Moon, an American missionary to China, the author warns her readers of such a danger: 'a man begins by wearing Chinese clothes, eating Chinese food, and adopting other Chinese customs; is there no danger that he may lose, by the constant habit of conformity, the power of prompt, manly protest against evil?'[42]

If these admonitions are correct, the mother and Ma certainly fail to heed them. In *Un barrage*, Ma goes about in her native accouterment that must surely have been disgraceful for a white woman: 'She was barefoot and wore a big straw hat pulled down over her eyes … Her loose, sleeveless, dark red dress was made from a *pagne*, a square of native cotton cloth' (p. 12) ('Elle était pieds nus et portait un grand chapeau de paille qui lui arrivait à la hauteur des sourcils … Sa robe grenat, taillée dans un pagne indigène, était large, sans manches …" (p. 16)). Indeed, one of the reasons for which the narrator in *L'amant* is so deeply embarrassed by her mother is precisely the latter's distinctly non-European look: 'her shoes are down-at-heel, she walks awkwardly … her hair's drawn back tight into a bun like a Chinese woman's, we're ashamed of her' (p. 23) ('ses souliers sont éculés, elle marche de travers … ses cheveux sont tirés et serrés dans un chignon de Chinoise, elle nous fait honte' (p. 32)). Besides the native attire, the mother also adopts the local custom of having herself photographed in old age and, in the portrait executed in native fashion, the narrator notices a striking resemblance between the mother and the Indochinese : 'all the men wore the same sort of turban, all the women had their hair scraped back into the same kind of bun … And they all wore an expression I'd still recognize anywhere. My mother's expression in the photograph with the red dress was the same' (p. 97) ('tous les hommes avaient le même turban, les femmes le même chignon, les mêmes coiffures tirées … Ils avaient tous le même air que je reconnaîtrais encore entre tous. Et cet air qu'avait ma mère dans la photographie de la robe rouge était le leur' (p. 119)).

Yet, more than their inability to maintain a French home and a French life style, it is the failure of the mother and Ma to raise their children 'properly' that constitutes the central irony of their situation. These women were supposedly entrusted with the mission to civilize the natives in their role as *institutrices*, yet what we find in the three texts are three seriously dysfunctional families. In each case, the mother uses extreme violence towards her children, by incessantly yelling and beating them. In spite of her reputation as a great teacher in the colony, the mother in *L'amant de la Chine du nord* is incapable of educating her own sons who both drop out of school. Worse still, the eldest of her children grows up to be a vicious scoundrel, beating his siblings, stealing from his mother to satisfy his opium addiction, raping Dô the native servant, and later leading the life of a pimp in Paris. Not only did the mother fail in her parenting role, like Ma in *Un barrage*, but also she did not hesitate to prostitute her daughter in order to obtain more money to pay for the oldest son's gambling and opium debts.

Undoubtedly, the tragedy of the mother and Ma is partly the result of their insolvent economic situation brought about by the corrupt colonial administration that cheated them of their life savings. The plight of these women cogently illustrates the contradictions of the colonial policy Stoler raises in her work: 'If the legitimation of European privilege and profit rested on a social taxonomy that equated Europeanness and bourgeois civilities … [w]as being poor and white politically untenable, a veritable colonial oxymoron?'.[43] But beyond their economic difficulties, the social origin of the mother and Ma, daughters of peasants, also disqualifies them from being the ideal torch-bearers of the mythically superior French civilization. The best testimony to this social discrepancy is given by the narrator of *L'amant* in her poignant outburst against the mother who opens herself to ridicule through her inability to transcend her peasant origin: 'My mother, my love, her incredible ungainliness, with her cotton stockings darned by Dô, in the tropics she still thinks you have to wear stockings to be a lady, a headmistress, her dreadful shapeless dresses, mended by Dô, she's still straight out of her Picardy farm full of female cousins, thinks you ought to wear eveything till it's worn out, that you have to be deserving, her shoes' (p. 23) ('Ma mère mon amour son incroyable dégaine avec ses bas de coton reprisés par Dô, sous les Tropiques elle croit encore qu'il faut mettre des bas pour être la dame directrice de l'école, ses robes lamentables, difformes, reprisées par Dô, elle vient encore tout droit de sa ferme picarde peuplée de cousines, elle use tout jusqu'au bout, croit qu'il faut, qu'il faut mériter, ses souliers' (pp. 31–32)). Obviously, the contradiction lies not just in being poor and white, but also having peasants embody a Frenchness that was constructed around bourgeois civilities. The cultural chasm separating the two classes that persisted until the First World War has been finely documented by Eugen Weber in his masterly work, *Peasants into Frenchmen: The Modernization of Rural France 1870–1914*.[44]

My revisioning of Duras's female characters within the framework of colonial gender politics elucidates the contradictions that underly Duras's own *rapport* with the colonial system as well as those of the system itself. As my reading shows, in her representation of white and native women Duras both reproduces and subverts the gender code that regulates the colonial society. These conflicting positions reveal Duras's relationship to her Indochinese motherland to be highly duplicitous, since her involvement with imperial ideology manifests elements of both resistance and complicity. Her portrayal of natives as passive and helpless victims reflects the colonialist ideas she expounded in *L'empire français*,[45] a propaganda treatise co-written with Philippe Roques, her senior colleague in the Ministry of Colonies where she worked from 1938 to 1940. Yet, due to the low socio-economic status of her family, she also experienced first-hand the exploitative side of the colonial system which she strongly criticizes in her Asian novels. The highly complex relationship Duras entertained with the colonial social order led her in her family narratives to expose the many racial, gender and class contradictions inherent in the colonial policy of the Third Republic.

Notes

1 See the two articles by Pascale Bécel, '*Le Vice-Consul*: Colonial Mimicry and Partial Writing', *Cincinnati Romance Review*, No. 13 (1994), pp. 218–27, and 'From *The Sea Wall* to *The Lover*: Prostitution and Exotic Parody', *Studies in 20th Century Literature*, Vol. 21, No. 2 (1997), pp. 417–32; and Chapter 4 of my *Figuring the East: Segalen, Malraux, Duras, and Barthes*, Albany, State University of New York Press, 2000.

2 For a detailed discussion of the socio-political circumstances surrounding the promotion of female settlement in the colonies at the turn of the century, see my article, 'Engendering French Colonial History: The Case of Indochina', *Historical Reflections/Réflexions Historiques*, Vol. 25, No. 1 (1999), pp. 95–125.

3 Clothilde Chivas Baron, *La femme française aux colonies*, Paris, Larose, 1929, p. 187: 'Celle qui, partout, crée la France autour d'Elle, avec des habitudes de France, avec des visions de France … avec de la grâce et de la morale de France, de la bonté et du courage de France.'

4 '[L]'élévation de l'indigène vers notre civilisation'. For a summary and commentary of these speeches, see '*Femmes et colonisation*', Aix-en-Provence, Institut d'Histoire Des Pays d'Outre-mer, 1987, pp. 15–40. Ann L. Stoler has written extensively on the relations between gender, race, and sexuality in Dutch Indonesia and French Indochina. Her work shows that European women were given the role of keepers of racial purity and cultural authenticity in the colonies. See her *Race and the Education of Desire: Foucault's History of Sexuality and The Colonial Order of Things*, Durham NC, Duke University Press, 1995.

5 A number of women historians address the myth of the destructive female. Besides Stoler, one may also consult Margaret Strobel, *European Women and the Second British Empire*, Bloomington IN, Indiana University Press, 1991, and Claudia

Knapman, *White Women in Fiji 1835–1930. The Ruin of Empire? …*, Sydney, Allen and Unwin, 1986.

6 See O. Mannoni, *Prospero and Caliban*, New York, Frederick Praeger, 1964. For another interesting and more subtle study on the subject, see Inglis Amirah, *The White Women's Protection Ordinance. Sexual Anxiety and Politics in Papua*, New York, St Martin's Press, 1975.

7 See Georges Hardy, 'La femme et la politique indigène', in Clothilde Chivas-Baron, *La vie aux colonies: préparation de la femme à la vie coloniale*, Paris, Larose, 1938, pp. 241–70.

8 See Georges Groslier, *Le retour à l'argile*, Paris, Kailash, 1994.

9 Examples of this highly critical view of colonial wives are found in Eugène Pujarniscle, *Philoxène ou de la littérature coloniale*, Paris, Firmin-Didot, 1931, and Charles Meyer, *La vie quotidienne des Français en Indochine 1860–1910*, Paris, Hachette, 1985.

10 In the early part of the twentieth century French feminists saw no objection to lending their support to the empire building project, which was a way for them to show that, by carrying out the imperial duties of *citoyennes*, they too deserved full citizenship and the right to vote. A case in point is that of *La Fronde*, one of the most prominent feminist publications of the *Belle Epoque*, which not infrequently carried articles promoting the works of colonial women in the outposts of the empire. While a history of the relation between French feminism and imperial ideology has yet to be written, since the mid 1980s a number of feminist historians have done excellent studies on the relations of resistance and complicity between western feminism and imperialism in the British and American contexts. For a good summary of the issues and the work carried out to date, see the introduction by Clare Midgley in *Gender and Imperialism*, Manchester, Manchester University Press, 1998.

11 At the turn of the century, the colonial lobby actively promoted female emigration to certain colonies. In January 1897, La Société d'émigration des Femmes was founded under the patronage of Joseph Chailley-Bert, journalist and General Secretary of the Union Coloniale, one of the most influential organizations of the colonial lobby. For a more detailed discussion of the work of the Société, see my 'Engendering French Colonial History'.

12 For a long time, the settlers had a rather ambivalent position vis-à-vis the presence of white women in the colonies. See Pujarniscle, *Philoxène*, and Meyer, *La vie quotidienne.*

13 See Jeanne Leuba, *L'aile de feu*, Paris, Plon, 1920.

14 Pujarniscle, *Philoxène*, p. 135: 'lorsque vous rentrez chez vous, vous trouvez un petit animal câlin, qui vous tient chaud l'hiver, vous évente l'été, qui vous apporte le thé et les liqueurs, vous roule les cigarettes, vous prépare des pipes …'.

15 Groslier, *Le retour à l'argile*, pp. 87–88: 'A peine entre-t-il qu'il est convaincu qu'elle l'attendait, surveillait son approche … elle lui prend son casque, délace ses chaussures, prévient ses moindres gestes et par cent actes assure son bien-être … Elle n'existe pas par elle-même: elle est le double de Claude, animée du seul égoïsme de Claude.'

16 Groslier, *Le retour à l'argile*, p. 88: 'Et quel que soit le moment où il saisit cette dévotion, il comprend qu'elle n'est pas une tactique. La spontanéité, la conscience, la dextérité enfin avec lesquelles Kâmlang s'y livre, prouvent que sa mère et toutes ses aïeules et toutes celles de toutes les femmes asiatiques qui respirent en cette même heure—servirent ainsi de siècle en siècle leurs époux et leurs amants, princes ou manants.'

17 See Alain Vircondelet, *Duras: A biography* (1991), trans. Thomas Buckley, Normal IL, Dalkey Archive Press, 1994, p. 13.

18 Laure Adler, *Marguerite Duras*, Paris, Gallimard, 1998, p. 17: 'La vie de Marguerite est pleine d'accidents, de ruptures ... Mais la terre maternelle, le territoire d'origine, le véritable lieu d'enracinement de son être restera jusqu'à la fin de sa vie l'Indochine coloniale.'

19 I borrow the term from Claude Roy in his interview with Duras, 'Duras tout entière à la langue attachée', *Le Nouvel Observateur*, 31 August 1984, pp. 66–67.

20 Marguerite Duras, *Un barrage contre le Pacifique*, Paris, Gallimard 1950, p. 13: 'saturés d'ennui et d'amertune' (*The Sea Wall*, trans. Herma Briffault, New York, Farrar, Strauss and Giroux, 1967, p. 9). All references in the text to Duras's work will be first to the listed English translation, then to the original French version.

21 Marguerite Duras, *Le vice-consul*, Paris, Gallimard, 1965, p. 116 : 'L'ennui, ici, c'est un sentiment d'abandon colossal, à la mesure de l'Inde elle-même, ce pays donne le ton' (*The Vice-Consul*, trans. Eileen Ellenbogen, London, Hamish Hamilton, 1968, p. 90).

22 Marguerite Duras, *L'amant*, Paris, Minuit, 1984, p. 27: '[le] service de ces gens, de ces boys, si parfait' (*The Lover*, trans. Barbara Bray, New York, Pantheon Books, 1985, p. 19).

23 For an excellent account of Duras's Indochinese childhood and her mother's career as *institutrice*, see Adler, *Marguerite Duras*.

24 See Clothilde Chivas-Baron 'Mémoires de Thi-Vinh', in *Trois Femmes annamites*, Paris, Charpentier, 1922; Nguyên-Phan-Long, *Le roman de Mademoiselle Lys*, Hanoi, Imprimerie Tonkinoise, 1920; Trinh-Thuc-Oanh and Marguerite Triaire, *En s'écartant des ancêtres*, Hanoi, Imprimerie d'Extrême-Orient, 1941; and Trinh-Thuc-Oanh and Marguerite Triaire, *La réponse de l'Occident*, Hanoi, Imprimerie d'Extrême-Orient, 1941.

25 Bécel, 'From *The Sea Wall* to *The Lover*', p. 423.

26 See Antoinette Burton, *Burdens of History: British Feminists, Indian Women, and Imperial Culture, 1865–1915*, Chapel Hill NC, North Carolina Press, 1994, p. 64.

27 See Martha Noel Evans, 'Marguerite Duras: the Whore', in *Masks of Tradition*, Ithaca, Cornell University Press, 1987, pp. 123–56; p. 124.

28 In 'Marguerite Duras: the Whore', Evans shows how in *Le ravissement de Lol V. Stein* the economy of Durassian desire, which is both anonymous and indiscriminate, pertains to the system of prostitution. Besides Lol and many of her doubles, the principle of indiscriminate replacement of partners underlies the relationships of desire of several of Durassian characters such as Anne-Marie Stretter who, in *L'amant de la Chine du nord*, is said to sleep with native princes as well as chauffeurs.

29 See Chapter 5 of Panivong Norindr, *Fantasmatic Indochina: French Colonial Ideology in Architecture, Cinema, and Literature*, Durham NC, Duke University Press, 1996.

30 See both Stoler, *Race and the Education of Desire*, and Strobel, *European Women*.

31 I use the term 'functions' as defined by Vladimir Propp. Functions constitute the fundamental components of the structure of a narrative.

32 Gontran de Poncins, *From A Chinese City*, trans. Bernard Frechtman, New York, Doubleday, 1957, p. 22.

33 Marie Donnadieu (then Mme Marie Obscur by her first marriage to a certain Augustin Obscur) went to Indochina in 1905 to teach in a girls' school and remained as *institutrice* for a few decades. For details, see Adler, *Marguerite Duras*.

34 Marguerite Duras, *L'amant de la Chine du Nord*, Paris, Gallimard, 1991, p. 122: 'une grande institutrice … Elle est adorée en Indochine parce qu'elle a une passion pour son métier … Elle a élevé des milliers d'enfants …' (*The North China Lover*, trans. Leigh Hafrey, New York, The New Press, 1992, p. 108).

35 See Adler, *Marguerite Duras*, p. 283.

36 In her study *Franco-Vietnamese Schools, 1918–1938: Regional Developments and Implications for National Integration*, University of Wisconsin-Madison, Media Center for Southeast Asian Studies, 1982, Gail P. Kelly points out that, before 1917, the French school system in Cochinchina was destined for 'children of European residents, Eurasians and, when space permitted, Vietnamese who served the administration and/or were notables (namely large landowners of the Mekong Delta)' (p. 8). In 1917–18, Albert Sarraut, the Governor General of Indochina, introduced a unitary educational system for all Vietnamese by the creation of Franco-Vietnamese schools with a curriculum adapted to so-called Vietnamese 'mentalities' and the colonial milieu. The 1917/18 reforms were put in place as a response to the economic and politic threat posed by the increasing number of French-educated Vietnamese. The creation of Franco-Vietnamese schools was a way to restrict the diffusion of French education among the Vietnamese. Even in missionary schools such as the Couvent des Oiseaux, the majority of the students were children of the native bourgeoisie as they alone could afford the steep tuition. For a description of the French schools in Indochina, see Kim Lefèvre's autobiography *Métisse blanche*, Paris, Barrault, 1989.

37 For a discussion of Ma's relationship with the peasants in *Un barrage*, see my *Figuring the East*.

38 Besides Burton and Midgley, see also Nurpur Chaudhuri and Margaret Strobel (eds), *Western Women and Imperialism: Complicity and Resistance*, Bloomington IN, Indiana University Press, 1992, and Jane Hunter, *The Gospel of Gentility. American Women Missionaries in Turn-of-the-Century China*, New Haven, Yale University Press, 1984.

39 Stoler, *Race and the Education of Desire*, p. 108.

40 See in particular Chivas-Baron's *La femme française aux colonies* and *La vie aux colonies: préparation de la femme à la vie coloniale*.

41 One good source is the doctoral dissertation of Geneviève Emmery-Rous de Fenerols, 'Itinéraire d'une famille française outre-mer Indochine-Algérie-Maroc au miroir d'une correspondance personnelle 1946–1969', University of Nice, 1987.

42 Cited in Hunter, *The Gospel of Gentility*, pp. 137–38.

43 Stoler, *Race and the Education of Desire*, p. 107.

44 See Eugen Weber, *Peasants into Frenchmen: The Modernization of Rural France 1870–1914*, Stanford, Stanford University Press, 1976.

45 For a discussion of *L'empire français* (Paris, Gallimard, 1940), see both Adler, *Marguerite Duras*, and my *Figuring the East*.

CHAPTER 6

Imaginary White Female: Myth, Race, and Colour in Duras's *L'amant de la Chine du Nord*

Kate Ince

Marguerite Duras's autobiographical writing is well known and now much written about. This, at least, is unquestionably true of *L'amant*, which was published in 1984 and very quickly became an international bestseller. The other texts usually held to make up the 'corpus' of Duras's autobiographical writings are—somewhat dubiously I feel, given that it is written almost entirely in the third person and presents a radically different version of what is similar material—*Un barrage contre le Pacifique*, *L'amant de la Chine du Nord*, and possibly also the 'Apostrophes' television interview Duras gave to Bernard Pivot in September 1984, which has now taken on the status of a text in its own right. (By the 'status of a text' I mean in this instance that the interview, in which Duras's spoken delivery resembled her often gnomic and lacuna-ridden written style, offers none of the guarantees of referential truth about a life which such an interview—following the publication of a revelatory and uncertainly 'autobiographical' novel as it did—might normally be relied upon to provide.) *L'amant de la Chine du Nord* followed *L'amant* to the top of the bestseller lists, at least briefly, putting Duras into the unusual, if not unique, position for a writer of having written her autobiography twice and achieved a double success. The composition of *L'amant de la Chine du Nord*, as is also widely known, was bound up with Jean-Jacques Annaud's adaptation of *L'amant* for the cinema, which had begun in the late 1980s and was to be released in France in January 1992.

Duras was at first involved in Annaud's production in an advisory capacity, but the two subsequently fell out and Duras was banned from the set, an exclusion which certainly fuelled, if it did not entirely account for, Duras's desire to write a second volume about her early life in French Indochina that might result in her own film of these events (a film she never made in the remaining years of her life). Although Duras intensely disliked Annaud's *L'amant* she was, at least according to Anne de Gasperi shortly after her death, pleased that the film was realistically convincing enough to enjoy a brief commercial success in France. According to de Gasperi, whom she sent to the cinema to see it for her, Duras's response to Annaud's financial gain was to think of how it would in turn increase her own: 'Good … my book will sell, then' ('Bon … mon livre se vendra').[1]

In addition to relating to Duras's 'autobiographical' corpus, this chapter is concerned particularly, although not exclusively, with relationships between women. This is an area of Duras's work which has received critical attention, in particular in Julia Kristeva's essay 'La maladie de la mort' in her study of melancholia, *Soleil noir: dépression et mélancolie.*[2] Kristeva's account of erotic relationships between women in Duras's work has recently been challengingly questioned by Emma Wilson's reading of *Le ravissement de Lol V. Stein* in her book *Sexuality and the Reading Encounter.*[3] Other critics to have paid particular attention to women's eroticism in Duras are Renate Günther, in her book on *L'amant* and *Le ravissement de Lol V. Stein*[4] and in subsequent work, and myself, in an article on *Le navire Night* and *Savannah Bay* included in the 1998 volume *Duras: lectures plurielles.*[5] However, the main focus of my chapter is race and colour, issues which Duras critics have only quite recently begun to consider. In most instances the axis of their investigations has been the colonialism of the Indochina of Duras's youth, given a particularly full portrayal in *Un barrage contre le Pacifique*, and the insights into it afforded by postcolonial theory. Panivong Norinder's 1993 article on Duras's colonial cities is an important reference here,[6] as is the work of James S. Williams[7] and Christine Holmlund[8] on the relationship to the (post)colonial Other in Duras's experimental cinema. Although the discussion which follows is informed inevitably by postcolonial criticism, I want to adopt an alternative approach and look not just at colonialism and postcolonialism as very different systems of structuring race relations, but directly at the representation of race and colour in *L'amant de la Chine du Nord*. My particular focus will be 'whiteness', the topic which has been explored for some time now by a number of cultural, literary and film critics, notably Richard Dyer in a number of papers and articles that came together in his 1997 book *White.*[9]

Before considering the relevance of Richard Dyer's writing on whiteness to Duras, however, I shall pay some attention to the one term in my title I haven't yet mentioned, 'myth'. Although this is a term which has been widely used in writing on Duras—for example, by Leslie Hill in *Apocalyptic Desires*[10]—to describe the peculiar status ascribed to the marginal figures of the Jew, woman, and the mad in certain of Duras's texts, and the mythical revelatory and destructive force possessed by these agents of apocalypse, I think it is appropriate to *L'amant de la Chine du Nord* in a way intimately connected to the text's autobiographical inclination. What is mythified in the text is, first and self-reflexively, the self and the story of the affair with the Chinese lover, and second, sexuality, both generally and in relation to the 'child', as the female protagonist of the novel is predominantly called. The most striking instance of the first kind of mythification occurs at the start of the fourth section of the text, which is the rewriting of the river crossing on which so much of the critical attention paid to *L'amant* has been lavished. This section opens with the short declaiming sentence 'It's the river' ('C'est le fleuve'), and continues: 'It's the ferry over the Mekong. The ferry *of the books*. Of the river. On the ferry are the natives' bus, the long black Léon Bollées, and the North China lovers, looking' ('C'est le bac sur le Mékong. Le bac *des livres*./ Du fleuve./ Dans le bac il y a le car pour indigènes, *les* longu*es* Léon Bollée noir*es*, *les* amant*s* de la Chine du Nord qui regardent' (my emphasis)).[11] 'The book', the fetishized Léon Bollée car, and the lover himself are all in turn pluralized here. This pluralization of both text and object(s)—privileged objects of the story told in *L'amant* and the story itself—can only be read as a mythification, an exaggerated fiction, of those objects and that story. There is one previous book Duras can be referring to, *L'amant*, but 'of the books' ('des livres') makes no sense unless read self-reflexively as a reference to both *L'amant* and *L'amant de la Chine du Nord*, and such a reading still fails to account for the pluralized car and lover. It is easier to find parallels to the kind of mythification Duras is engaging in here in the visual arts than in literature. Does Duras's multiplication of images contain, for instance, the same commentary on iconicity, stardom and consumerism as found in Warhol's pictures of Marilyn Monroe? Whether it does or not, the following paragraph contains several phrases of self-quotation (from *L'amant*) which indicate Duras's difficulty in matching the degree and perfection of self-image creation reached in her description of the river crossing in *L'amant*. The 'child' here is dressed in 'the soft-felt-rosewood-coloured-with-a-broad-black-ribbon "childhood and innocence" man's hat, in those black-lamé-if-you-please dancing shoes' (*L'amant de la Chine du Nord*, p. 35) ('du chapeau d'homme d'"enfance et d'innocence" … en feutre-souple-couleur-bois-de-rose-avec-large-ruban-noir, de ces souliers de bal … en-lamé-noir-s'il-vous-plaît'). Quotation marks and hyphenation indicate Duras's open self-quotation—of images rather than of precise words and phrases—in a kind of admission that the (non-)image of the 'absolute photograph' ('photographie absolue'), the photograph that was never taken, cannot be bettered or surpassed in this rewriting of her first meeting with the Chinese lover. And the only way in which the mythic status of the love of the lovers in this novel can be expressed is by matching it to the love portrayed in *L'amant*, which Duras does by writing, after the first scene of lovemaking, 'Now they're the lovers of the book' (*L'amant de la Chine du Nord*, p. 96) ('Devenus les amants du livre').

The second form of mythification in *L'amant de la Chine du Nord*, the mythification of sexuality, relates to two themes present in *L'amant* but given much more prominence in the second text: prostitution and incest. The 'child' of *L'amant de la Chine du Nord* tells both her lover and Hélène Lagonelle about the incestuousness of the love between herself and the younger of her two brothers, although this does not make the love of lover and 'enfant' itself any less incestuous. She is, in a generationally doubled version of this type of relation, '[h]is blood sister. His child' (*L'amant de la Chine du Nord*, p. 81) ('Sa soeur de sang. Son enfant'). The bodies of Paulo and the North China lover are explicitly compared—Paulo's will be like the lover's later in life (p. 91). Most strikingly, in *L'amant de la Chine du Nord* incest is given the status of a real event, or act, within the fiction. We are told that the 'child', after seeing Paulo's image in the bathroom mirror one day, and following much mutual embracing and kissing, undresses, lies down before him and shows him how to 'take' her. 'It was then that they took each other, for the only time in their lives' (p. 200) ('Ç'avait été là qu'il s'étaient pris pour la seule fois de leur vie'). It is this act that leads to the child's recognition 'that the love she had felt for the Sadec Chinaman and for the little brother was, and always would be, the same love' (p. 201) ('qu'elle avait vécu un seul amour entre le Chinois de Sadec et le petit frère d'éternité'). All boundaries between incestuous and non-incestuous love are here definitively blurred, if not erased.

Prostitution is another activity that becomes generalized in *L'amant de la Chine du Nord*, particularly through the new character of Alice, a dormitory supervisor at the boarding school who prostitutes herself with non-white men in the 'quartier' in a way that arouses both intense curiosity and envy in the boarders, including Hélène Lagonelle. A close parallel is made between Alice's sexuality and the child's, as what Alice also particularly likes is 'men who talk to her as they would to other women, who call her by other names' (p. 58) ('ceux qui lui parlent comme à d'autres femmes, qui l'appellent avec d'autres noms'). Prostitution between the lover and the child is emphasized by the extension of the plot in *L'amant de la Chine du Nord* to include the buying off of the mother and the whole family by the lover's father. In one instance, the child acknowledges that she is the element exchanged in this bargaining process by undressing after she and the lover have discussed his visit to her mother to pay for the repatriation to France of the elder brother (p. 147), a visit which was the lover's initiative, and to which the child at first reacts angrily. A little later, after the evening's dancing at La Cascade, an image of the child alone in the studio with envelopes of money is tellingly juxtaposed with Alice being watched prostituting herself at the boarding school. The doubling of the sexuality of the child in Alice and the enlarged role of economic exchange in her relationship with the lover, as compared with *L'amant*, already makes prostitution a far more important theme than in the first novel—although perhaps not much more significant than in *Un barrage contre le Pacifique*, where it is implicitly pivotal. A further instance of promiscuity, rather than prostitution, which occurs in *L'amant de la Chine du Nord* and adds to the mythification of sexuality, concerns AMS, the ghost of Anne-Marie Stretter who drifts through some early scenes of the novel, and is said here to have as lovers not just the men of the Embassy entourage, but chauffeurs and the princes of Laos and Cambodia who visit Cochinchine. This last point reinforces another strand of meaning about sexuality present in *L'amant* and also given more prominence in *L'amant de la Chine du Nord*, which is its 'royalty' or sovereignty, as it applied to AMS, the child, and Paulo.

One of the most difficult elements of *L'amant de la Chine du Nord*, as of *L'amant*, is the inclusion of characters from Duras's purely fictional work in texts which have at least some avowedly autobiographical content. The beggar woman of *Le vice-consul* and *India Song* appears briefly in *L'amant*, as does Anne-Marie Stretter, who has here lost her name completely (she regains the cipher AMS in *L'amant de la Chine du Nord*), and is referred to just as 'The lady' ('La dame'). The memory of 'The lady' in *L'amant*, and of the young man in Savannakhet who shot himself because she had to leave him, goes back six years before the main events of the story took place, to when the 'girl' was aged 10. What links the 'girl' to 'The lady', and motivates the narration of the latter's story at the point at which it occurs in *L'amant*, is, first, their shared isolation in scandal, and second, the deathliness of their desire:

> The same distance separates the lady and the girl in the low-crowned hat from other people in the town. Just as they both look at the long avenues beside the river, so they are alike in themselves. Both isolated. Alone, queen-like. Their disgrace is a matter of course. Both are doomed to discredit because of the kind of body they have, caressed by lovers, kissed by their lips, consigned to the infamy of a pleasure unto death, as they both call it, unto the mysterious death of lovers without love. That's what it's all about: this hankering for death.

> (La même différence sépare la dame et la jeune fille au chapeau plat des autres gens du poste. De même que toutes les deux regardent les longues avenues des fleuves, de même elles sont. Isolées toutes les deux. Seules, des reines. Leur disgrâce va de soi. Toutes deux au discrédit vouées du fait de la nature de ce corps qu'elles ont, caressé par des amants, baisé par leurs bouches, livrées à l'infamie d'une jouissance à en mourir, disent-elles, à en mourir de cette mort mystérieuse des amants sans amour. C'est de cela qu'il est question, de cette humeur à mourir.)[12]

A memory is recounted in *L'amant* of seeing 'The lady' on her terrace when returning from catechism with the little brother: in *L'amant de la Chine du Nord* this turns into AMS arriving with her daughters at a Latin lesson the child is taking with the Vinh-Long priest, asking who the child is, and commenting to the priest that she has 'a strange look' (*L'amant de la Chine du Nord*, pp. 108–09) ('un drôle de regard'). Although the presence of Anne-Marie Stretter (she is given her full name at this juncture) in Cochinchine rather than Calcutta is quite plausible within the fiction, if unexplained in terms of narrative (in *L'amant* we are led to assume that it was on a stopover in Calcutta that the girl glimpsed both the beggar woman and the colonial lady who was to become the fictional character Anne-Marie Stretter), her increased role in *L'amant de la Chine du Nord*, particularly at the moment of the meeting on the ferry and subsequent drive to Saigon, parallels and repeats, through the explicit comparison and identification of AMS with the child, the mythification of the sexual self Duras constructs in her rewriting of the story of her Indochinese adolescence. In the early part of *L'amant de la Chine du Nord* AMS is a particularly ghostly presence, wandering through scenes in a red dress where her appearance is realistically improbable, or playing (although not in view of the narrative eye) a 'Desperate Waltz' ('Valse Désespérée') at the piano. Her ghostliness is an effect Jean-Jacques Annaud tried (probably mistakenly) to capture in his adaptation of *L'amant*; the only successful visual effect which results from this attempt is AMS adopting the same posture as the child on the ferry, leaning on the balustrade with her foot on the lower bar of the railing, adrift on 'les routes du désir' ('the highways of desire').

Anne-Marie Stretter is, as has been widely noted, perhaps the dominant figure of fantasy in Duras's fictional writing, a highly sexualized woman who is also a mother of daughters, the perfect colonial 'lady' yet the lover of multiple members of the entourage at the Embassy where her husband is Ambassador, the ultimate object of desire and of the gaze. She is mysterious, scandalous and generous. A motif of 'charity' surrounds her which is both economic—in *India Song* she distributes leftovers to the destitute and leprous of Calcutta—and sexual, referring to her languourous 'prostitution' of her sexuality. In the film

India Song she is, as Deborah Glassman has amply illustrated,[13] both the focus and the blind spot of representation. One image in which many of these attributes come together is the dance with multiple partners, the activity that occupies the longest scene in *India Song*.

I have already quoted the part of *L'amant* in which the identities of Anne-Marie Stretter and the girl are explicitly compared in their solitude, scandalousness and deathliness, a comparison which breaks down fixed borders to their respective identities and allows these to overlap and merge. I wish to contend here that this merging is taken a stage further, and perhaps fully worked through, in *L'amant de la Chine du Nord*. The scene in which this takes place is, I think, the evening spent at La Cascade after the family meal, which is itself a scene that has undergone a radical change from the parallel occasion in *L'amant*, most notably in the very good relationship struck up between the lover and the child's mother, and the amicable (although perhaps enforcedly so) attitude of the elder brother towards the lover. At La Cascade the child progresses through a series of dances with multiple partners in exactly the same way as Anne-Marie Stretter in *India Song*, first with the lover, then with Thanh (the Siamese 'twin' of the little brother and an important additional character to *L'amant de la Chine du Nord*), then with the little brother himself. This dance is the centre of the sequence, and a reminder of the sovereignty of sexuality even (or perhaps especially) in incestuousness. The mother remarks on their dance, which is said to be like no other in their lives: 'Those two are like princes when they dance' (p. 166) ('Des princes quand ils dansent ces deux-là'), and the Chinese lover weeps and mutters the single word 'adoration'. The child then dances with the lover again, and finally watches him intently as he dances with 'the most beautiful of the hostesses' ('la plus belle des entraîneuses'), which he is doing at her command. Through this sequence of dances the child *becomes* what Anne-Marie Stretter is fantasized and projected as being in *India Song* and, by association, in all the other texts where she appears. Self-projection and fantasy merge, identities become indistinguishable, perhaps all the more so because AMS is nowhere mentioned in the scene at La Cascade. The representation seems to take place entirely under the sway of unconscious desire.

A footnote to the dancing at La Cascade specifies that if this scene were filmed, the camera should 'cancel' reciprocity by filming 'each person's solitude' ('la solitude de chacun'). There would be no two-shots or group shots: 'It's not worth doing group shots here, because here there is no group' (*L'amant de la Chine du Nord*, p. 166) ('Les plans d'ensemble, ici, ce n'est pas la peine parce que l'ensemble, ici, n'existe pas'). But shortly afterwards, when the narrative turns to detailing the child's departure from the colony, she is confirmed in her status as the centre of a community of desire which dancing at La Cascade grants her fantasmatically, if not in the conditional visuality of the filmed scene that Duras envisages as she writes. This occurs when Thanh tells the Chinese lover where he will go after the family has departed, having not hitherto had any conversation with the lover. When the child asks him why he has only now engaged in this conversation, Thanh responds: 'So that I'll see him again when you've gone … To talk about you, about Paulo, about our mother … to weep together for love of you' (p. 207) ('Pour le revoir quand tu seras partie … Pour parler de toi, de Paulo, de notre mère … pour pleurer ensemble de l'amour pour toi'). A projected community of mourning substitutes for an actual community of desire in an *après coup* temporality which confers upon the child the status of the central object in the narrative of *L'amant de la Chine du Nord*.

Race and/or colour are important aspects of Duras's self-portrayal in both *L'amant* and *L'amant de la Chine du Nord*. In *L'amant* self-designation is often made from the mother's point of view in the phrase 'the little white girl' ('la petite blanche') (in more affectively balanced passages, 'the white girl' ('la jeune fille blanche')), and in *L'amant de la Chine du Nord* a frequent expression is 'the white child' (l'enfant blanche'). As Yvonne Hsieh notes in an article on colonialist and anti-colonialist discourse in *Un barrage contre le Pacifique*, *L'amant*, and *L'amant de la Chine du Nord*, the explicit feminization of the lover's body in *L'amant* has disappeared in *L'amant de la Chine du Nord*, where, as well as being less timid and fearful than in *L'amant*, he is more robust, more healthy-looking and more beautiful, 'more "cinematic" than the one in the book' (p. 36) ('plus "pour le cinéma" que celui du livre').[14] But more significantly for my purposes here, he has, in the second novel, the white skin of the North Chinese, as does his fiancée. They both originate from the province of Manchuria, whose people are said to be characteristically fair-skinned compared to the majority of Chinese in Indochina. The lover has not lost the softness of skin which was such a crucial element to the eroticism of *L'amant*. He, the child, and Paulo are all said to possess 'rain skin' (p. 144) ('la peau de la pluie'), just as Hélène Lagonelle had 'Chinese skin' ('la peau de la Chine') in *L'amant*. But colour is a new and arguably very important element in the physical appearance of the lover: a less marked contrast in skin colour between the two lovers reduces the racial difference between them and contributes to a lessening of the supremacy of female subject over feminized male object found in *L'amant*. It also corroborates the undoing of the lover's exoticization as an object of desire noted by Hsieh.

In *L'amant de la Chine du Nord* the child herself is just as Asiatic as in *L'amant*, although this orientalism does not pertain particularly to her skin colour. She is said to hate France and the red meat of western steaks (p. 36), and to have the body of a 'mixed-race female' ('*métisse*'), which is what the huge majority of the girls at the boarding school actually are, having been abandoned by their white fathers (p. 173). (It is explicitly stated in *L'amant de la Chine du Nord* (p. 63) that the favours accorded to the child and Hélène at the school—e.g. being let off compulsory walks—are granted because the two girls are white.) The lover tells the child that the Asiatic quality of her body is due not just to her 'rain skin', but to the fineness of her wrists and ankles (p. 82). Only mixed-race boys ('métis'), not French boys, have admired her hitherto, a fact which, when combined with the North China lover's fair skin, conspires to make their mutual desire the 'whitest' each of them has known. In fact, racial difference is a much less significant factor in the creation of heterosexual desire in *L'amant de la Chine du Nord* than in *L'amant*, and economic difference is concomitantly more important, as is suggested by the extended plot concerning the 'prostitution' economics of the colonial system. The historical situations of the two minorities from which the child and the lover are derived are surely important here: the Chinese, although in political alliance with the Indochinese against the ruling white minority at the time of Duras's adolescence, were themselves historically colonialists in Indochina (from 111 BC to 939 AD and again in the fifteenth century), and Vietnam was still a Chinese protectorate when the French took over in the 1860s.[15] As the story of M. Jo's father in *Un barrage contre le Pacifique* and that of the lover's father in the later two autobiographical texts illustrates, the Chinese still practised a form of economic colonialism in the region in the early twentieth century, due to their skill in the building of property for natives, the strength of the Chinese stock exchange, and their dominance of key trades such as opium, gold, tea, jade and silk (*L'amant de la Chine du Nord*, pp. 213–14). (Demographic statistics about the relative size of the Chinese and the white minorities in French Indochina are revealing: in 1936 the Chinese represented 1.42% of the population (a fall from the mid-1920s because of the economic crisis), as against 0.18% of whites in 1937.)[16]

What is striking about the representation of colour in *L'amant de la Chine du Nord* is that, although the whites are the colonialists as in all Duras's 'autobiographical' and fictional texts, self-designations of whiteness and observations of the white skin colour of others seem, in a manner that deftly reverses most representations of the colonial Other, to attribute racial exoticism to whiteness rather than to the colour of the oppressed natives—yellow rather than black or brown in the case of the Indochinese. Hsieh draws in this regard on the work of Suzanne Chester, who identifies three topoi of Said-inspired 'orientalist' discourse in the first two of these texts by Duras: (1) the eroticization of the exotic, (2) the feminization of the Other, and (3) the representation of the Orient as an ontological essence.[17] As already mentioned, the feminization of the (male) Other disappears *in L'amant de la Chine du Nord*. In relation to

Chester's first topos of orientalism I would suggest not that the eroticization of the exotic disappears in the novel, but that it folds back upon the protagonists in relative *indifference* to their actual racial origin.

Duras's own spoken retellings of her autobiographical material are important and revealing where race and colour are concerned. In the 1984 'Apostrophes' interview with Pivot, as well as later and elsewhere, she designates herself as creole: 'I'm creole, you know, I was born there' ('Je suis créole, vous savez, je suis née là-bas'). In this semantically and syntactically significance-laden sentence, Duras insists on both her own racial hybridity and on her affinity with the Indochinese natives. In view of the context in which the statement was made—the first flush of Duras's 1980s media stardom—it is likely that the 'there' ('là-bas') in this sentence is at least as important—if not more so—than the 'creole', in other words, that the phrase serves just as much to position Duras as a continued 'outsider' in French society (she comes from elsewhere, 'là-bas') as it does to create proximity to the Indochinese.[18] However, her comment to Pivot on the appearance of the Chinese lover when she first saw him is also revealing, as it likens him to herself rather than racially differentiating him: 'He was in some way from the same place as me … in some way against my mother, if you like' ('Il était un petit peu du même lieu que moi … un peu contre ma mère, si vous voulez').[19] This being 'against the mother' can be linked to the racial hybridity and affinity with the natives of Cochinchine repeatedly claimed for the child and her brothers (or certainly Paulo) in *L'amant de la Chine du Nord*. In this they are distinct above all from one character, their mother. The story of the mother's exploitation by the colonial regime, told in most detail in *Un barrage contre le Pacifique*, and of her preferential love for her eldest boy-child over the younger brother and sister which keeps her aloof from the latter (although less so in *L'amant de la Chine du Nord*), puts her in a space of her own which is marked distinctively 'white': the mother is never ascribed the flexibility of body and race that characterizes the two younger siblings.

What is more striking about the mother is that her enterprising character and obstinate determination to cultivate the uncultivatable concession sold to her by the colonial regime is an excellent instance of what Dyer identifies in *White* as a specific and vital attribute of whiteness, 'white spirit'. 'White spirit' is evidently linked to European imperialism. It comprises all the characteristics of enterprise—energy, will, ambition, the ability to think and see things through—and, in the economic sphere, wealth creation, the building of nations and the organization of labour.[20] The more general constituent elements of white spirit, which is not equivalent to white 'soul' or spirituality, are 'get up and go, aspiration, awareness of the highest reaches of intellectual comprehension and aesthetic refinement'.[21] White spirit is essentially paradoxical, in that it governs the posture, movements, and some of the activities of the white body, yet although described as 'white' it 'cannot itself be seen'.[22] Dyer enlarges upon the relationship of white spirit to white body, suggesting that the white spirit 'organizes white flesh and in turn non-white flesh and other material matters'.[23] I will not rehearse Dyer's tracing of the important links between Christianity and white spirit; it is sufficient for my purposes here to establish that the mother of *Un barrage contre le Pacifique*, *L'amant* and *L'amant de la Chine du Nord* displays all its main characteristics, although unsuccessfully and then despairingly so, her spirit having proved active out of all proportion to the realities of her situation. As a teacher, however, the mother is widely known in the colony for her qualities of determination and perseverance, for having survived her exploitation, despite the high price paid for it by her health and by the lack of material benefits she is able to give her children. Dyer's whole project of exploring the category 'white' is concerned to expose it as a symbolic category, one with a history like other racial designations and constructed within a system of differences from those other designations. This does not mean that 'white' is just like other lexical markers of colour and race, far from it. The specificity of 'white' is that it has for a long time been indistinguishable, emphatically so, from the supposedly neutral marker 'human'. As Dyer puts it: 'At the level of racial representation ... whites are not of a certain race, they're just the human race'.[24] And as is perhaps obvious, but Dyer rightly and necessarily stresses it at the very beginning of his book: 'There is no more powerful position than that of being 'just' human. The claim to power is the claim to speak for the commonality of humanity. Raced people can't do that—they can only speak for their race'.[25]

In the light of this view of 'whiteness' as a non-neutral, marked, symbolic category, I would like now to discuss it as it pertains to the third of the three women under discussion. Anne-Marie Stretter. AMS is clearly white, and an emblem of whiteness, in that she moves in the very top rank of colonial white society, that of the most powerful civil servants. (Two more ranks can probably be identified between hers and that of the mother, firstly the rank of the rich colonial industrialists, and secondly, that of the liberal professions—lawyers and doctors. 'Petits fonctionnaires' such as teachers were at the bottom of the colonialist social pyramid.)[26] As a white 'lady' AMS is whiter than her male counterparts; Dyer notes that in western representations of skin colour since Greek vase-painting, 'any male lover is darker than his female beloved'.[27] My contention, in fact, is that AMS is not the kind of 'white' outlined in most of Dyer's book, the type to which the mother conforms, i.e. the neutral, passing-for-human, unmarked kind. She corresponds much more closely to another kind of whiteness Dyer that mentions only at the very end of his book, although his last chapter 'White Death' is devoted to some of its manifestations. This is the category of the 'extremely white', an 'exceptional, excessive, marked' whiteness, which, according to Dyer, is 'what whiteness aspires to and also [what] it fears'.[28] Dyer suggests that this extreme whiteness is 'even perhaps a condition of establishing whiteness as ordinary'. His examples of this deathly-white extreme whiteness come from science fiction—the *Alien* films and the Ridley Scott cult classic *Blade Runner*—and from the recent American independent film *Falling Down*. And he finds the best illustration of the association of 'extremely white' with death in Hammer Horror and non studio-produced, more avant-garde vampire films. I am not suggesting that we think of Anne-Marie Stretter as a vampire, but at least one of their paradoxes could apply to her and to her much-described deathly languour, desire and despair: vampires are themselves dead but live only in order to spread their deathliness, to contaminate life with death, in much the same way as visitors to the Embassy social coterie take on the characteristics of suffering and deathly desire emanating principally from Anne-Marie Stretter.

When, by means of the imitative sequence of dances at La Cascade in *L'amant de la Chine du Nord*, the child *becomes* AMS, she implicitly takes on all the latter's characteristics, many of which she already possessed. If Anne-Marie Stretter is 'extremely white', then her extreme, marked whiteness is one of the characteristics Duras's autobiographical persona is aspiring to. I do not wish to prejudge the type of desire at work in this apparent identification, and it is a timely moment to remember the fundamental Freudian distinction between sexual object-libido and narcissistic, or ego-libido. The latter is the type of desire at work in identification as Freud describes it, whereas in Dyer's work, 'white female' is above all the object of sexual desire. The frontispiece of his book is an 1880s *Birth of Venus* by William Bougereau, in which Venus is seen rising up out of the sea in an oyster shell, the object of the gaze of men and women, although there is nothing suggestively un-heterosexual about the picture. Where whiteness is concerned, though, it does seem extremely important to distinguish between desire directed at male and female, since 'white male' is so evidently the chief colour category responsible for identifying itself as plain, unmarked, neutral, and human. To identify with white male is much more obviously to identify as the most subject-like of subjects, whereas to identify oneself as white female may be to identify with/as the ultimate object of desire.

To insist that the desire in motion in the dancing scene at La Cascade in *L'amant de la Chine du Nord* is narcissistic and not object-libido would foreclose much suggestive material about female homoeroticism in Duras's writing. Hélène Lagonelle is still very much the object of the female protagonist's desire in *L'amant de la Chine du Nord*, and Béatrice Bonhomme points out that in this novel Hélène is paler and more frail than in *L'amant*.[29] However, if I provisionally adopt the 'identification' reading, this scene shows, in addition to the most advanced blurring of the 'autobiographical' and the fictional in any of Duras's texts set in French Indochina, a kind of pinnacle of the self-mythification that characterizes much of *L'amant de la Chine du Nord*. Duras, as we have seen and already knew, is very capable of identifying herself erotically and exotically as other-than-white, as well as nationally other-than-French, a sexual, racial and national hybrid who floats between fixed categories of identity according to the moment. But by means of this identification with the extremely white Anne-Marie Stretter, she may be revealing a desire *to be* white, extremely white, the white of colonial social elites, of the lady who is the ultimate object of desire. My analysis of race and colour in *L'amant de la Chine du Nord* is, I hope, suggestive in relation to debates about the sense in which Duras is a writer of otherness, or alterity, in so far as it indicates in whom, and where, the telos of Duras's trajectory to and through alterity may be situated, at least in one of her texts.

Notes

(N.B.: All translations from the French are my own except in the case of *L'amant* where I have used *The Lover*, trans. Barbara Bray, London, Flamingo, 1986.)

1 Anne de Gasperi in 'Ah! quels titres', programme presented by Philippe Tesson, FR3, March 1996.

2 Julia Kristeva, *Soleil noir: dépression et mélancolie*, Paris, Gallimard, 1987.

3 Emma Wilson, *Sexuality and the Reading Encounter: Identity and Desire in Proust, Duras, Tournier and Cixous*, Oxford, Clarendon Press, 1996.

4 Renate Günther, *Duras,* Le Ravissement de Lol V. Stein *and* L'Amant, London, Grant and Cutler 'Critical guides to French texts', 1993.

5 Kate Ince, 'Woman, lover, daughter, mother: female genealogies in *Le navire Night* and *Savannah Bay*', in *Duras. Lectures plurielles*, ed. Catherine Rodgers and Raynalle Udris, Amsterdam, Rodopi, 1998.

6 Panivong Norinder, '"*Errances*" and Memories in Duras's Colonial Cities', *differences*, Vol. 5, No. 3 (1993), pp. 52–78.

7 James S. Williams, *The Erotics of Passage: Pleasure, Politics, and Form in the Later Work of Marguerite Duras*, Liverpool University Press/St Martin's Press, 1997.

8 Christine Holmlund, 'Displacing Limits of Difference: Gender, Race and Colonialism in Edward Said and Homi Bhabha's Theoretical Models and Marguerite Duras's Experimental Films', *Quarterly Review of Film and Video*, Vol. 13, Nos 1–3 (1991), pp. 1–22.

9 Richard Dyer, *White*, London and New York, Routledge, 1997.
10 Leslie Hill, *Marguerite Duras: Apocalyptic Desires*, London and New York, Routledge, 1993.
11 Marguerite Duras, *L'amant de la Chine du Nord*, Paris, Gallimard, 1991, p. 35.
12 Marguerite Duras, *L'amant*, Paris, Minuit, 1984, pp. 110–11/*The Lover*, p. 95.
13 Deborah Glassman, *Marguerite Duras: Fascinating Vision and Narrative Cure*, Cranbury NJ and London, Associated University Presses, 1991.
14 See Yvonne Hsieh, 'L'évolution du discours (anti-)colonialiste dans *Un barrage contre le Pacifique, L'Amant* et *L'Amant de la Chine du Nord* de Marguerite Duras', *Dalhousie French Studies*, No. 35 (1996), pp. 55–65; p. 62.
15 Hsieh, 'L'évolution du discours', p. 61.
16 See Aimée Leon, 'Analyse Critique de *L'Amant*, *L'Amant de la Chine du Nord* et *La Douleur* dans un contexte socio-politique', unpublished dissertation, MA in Contemporary French Studies, London Guildhall University, June 1997, pp. 22, 26.
17 Hsieh, 'L'évolution du discours', p. 59. See Suzanne Chester, 'Writing the Subject: Exoticism/Eroticism in Marguerite Duras's *The Lover* and *The Sea Wall*', in *Decolonizing the Subject: The Politics of Gender in Women's Autobiography*, ed. Sidonie Smith and Julia Watson, Minneapolis, University of Minnesota Press, 1992, pp. 436–57.
18 On Duras's self-positioning as an 'outsider' in France, see Chapter 6 of Williams, *The Erotics of Passage*, esp. pp. 122–37.
19 '*Apostrophes*: Bernard Pivot rencontre Marguerite Duras', Paris, Seuil/INA, 1984.
20 Dyer, *White*, p. 31.
21 Dyer, *White*, p. 23.
22 Dyer, *White*, p. 24.
23 Dyer, *White*, p. 15.
24 Dyer, *White*, p. 3.
25 Dyer, *White*, p. 2.
26 See Leon, 'Analyse Critique', pp. 22–24.
27 Dyer, *White*, p. 57.
28 Dyer, *White*, p. 222.
29 Béatrice Bonhomme, 'L'Ecriture de Duras ou La Récriture du Livre: *L'Amant de la Chine du Nord* ou *L'Amant Recommencé*', *Revue des Lettres Modernes (Histoire des Idées et des Littératures)* (1993), pp. 121–61; p. 149.

Détruire dit-elle (1969).
Courtesy of BFI Stills,
Posters and Designs.

Nathalie Granger (1972). Courtesy of BFI Stills, Posters and Designs.

India Song (1975). Courtesy of BFI Stills, Posters and Designs.

Son nom de Venise dans Calcutta désert (1976). Courtesy of BFI Stills, Posters and Designs.

Le camion (1977). Courtesy of BFI Stills, Posters and Designs.

CHAPTER 7

'Like the French of France': Immigration and Translation in the Later Novels of Marguerite Duras

Martin Crowley

For practically the entirety of her career as a writer, Marguerite Duras displayed a determination to uphold the rights of immigrant communities and other groups facing oppression in racial terms. Examples of Duras's early journalism testify to a determination to focus attention on the problems faced by immigrant workers in Paris confronted by a racism that is both banal and institutional (see in particular 'Les Fleurs de l'Algérien', 'Racisme à Paris', and 'Les deux ghettos' in the collection *Outside: Papiers d'un jour*); one of the exhortations to be found in Duras's 1969 publicity text for her film *Détruire dit-elle* is that in favour of a general alignment with 'the last coolie'; and Duras's alignments with racially marginalized groups are constant.[1] In 1970, she took part in a protest against the death of five immigrant workers in a Foyer de solidarité franco-africaine in Aubervilliers, during which a group of 200–300 protesters seized the premises of the Conseil National du Patronat Français, and 116 (including Duras and Jean Genet) were arrested.[2] Her denunciations of the Front National during the 1980s are frequent and vociferous; at this time, she also begins to insist polemically on a vision of France as exemplarily open to a welcome flux of immigration. In Duras's literary work of the 1980s and 1990s, the figure of the immigrant accordingly becomes an important one; this figure is accompanied by a generalized interest in questions of racial difference, insistent not least in her avowedly autobiographical revisitings of her adolescence in

French Indochina, which inscribe Duras's authorial persona intimately within a complicated economy of identity and difference in terms not only of race, but also of gender and class. An emphasis on questions of racial identity is, moreover, also rehearsed formally by Duras at this time, as the texts in which these questions come to the fore (for example, *L'amant, Emily L.*, and *La pluie d'été*) begin to include noticeable elements of languages other than French, while also engaging internally with the business of translation. Typically, however, Duras's textual interventions into this field do not constitute a simple, safe, or polite consideration of the principal issues securely embedded within a liberal ethos of tolerance and solidarity, or a stable textual model of reflection or performance. We might recall, for example, that *Le camion*, which represents a crucial moment in the articulation of the beginnings of this period of Duras's work, is accompanied by texts in which Duras refuses to commit her art to any active project which would restrict its radical embrace of intransitivity, refusal, and negativity—and this includes, therefore, the rejection of an art which would be in solidarity with immigrant communities (specifically, here, immigrants from Portugal, Mali, and Senegal).[3]

While Duras does indeed generally align herself with those oppressed in racial terms, she frequently does so as part of a problematic celebration of unemployable negativity (including the loss of positive identity) which makes the notion of a positive textual commitment to such alignment at the very least uncertain. Whether meeting her immigrant characters in a shared gesture of refusal, incorporating languages other than French into her texts, or offering a delicate and idiosyncratic exploration of the nature of translation, Duras's writing in this area is consequently beset by a degree of uncertainty as it encounters particular demands of the substantive issues, which serves notably to highlight the risks of this encounter. Awkwardly, the profound lesson of Duras's textual address to questions of racial and linguistic difference is located precisely in the space of complication, error, confusion, and even possibly prejudice on to which this address opens. In this chapter, I aim to assess the role of questions of racial and linguistic identity in this period of Duras's work. I will initially present the elaboration of immigrant identity and the gesture of textual solidarity with this identity presented in one particular work, before going on to demonstrate the presence of a kind of linguistic pluralism in the texts of this period, and then, by means of a close reading of the problematic of translation in the 1987 text *Emily L.*, identifying some of the considerable and important difficulties which result from Duras's treatment of racial and linguistic difference at this time.

In the 1980s, Duras starts to express her alignment with racially oppressed communities by insisting on a vision of France as a paradigm of openness to immigration. In 1981, for example, in a text which draws attention to the geographical situation of France (as part, crucially, of northern Europe, and thus, in this context, as recipient of immigration), she interprets the nation as having just voted 'for El Salvador, for Nicaragua, and for the colonial proletariat come to her as emigrants, these people from Africa and from the poor parts of Europe who for thirty years have built her motorways, her car parks, the shell of her environment'.[4] In 1985, moreover, she celebrates what she calls 'the internationalism of the idea of France'.[5] Praising Simone Signoret on the event of her death in the same year, Duras highlights what she sees as Signoret's creation of just such an open, international dimension: 'She made France fly off the handle, she made it international. She proclaimed human rights everywhere. Signoret will never be replaced.'[6] And denouncing the Front National in 1992, Duras repeats this vision of an open France in terms which recall her disgust in *La douleur* at what she saw as De Gaulle's elision of grief after the Holocaust: 'They have made France dirty, France which is the holy land of Europe, the land of welcome and of freedom, which wept for the Jews'.[7] These interventions in the press may be taken as indicative of the position Duras adopts at this time: namely, an increasingly explicit emphasis on the solidarity with immigrant communities which had, by now, marked her journalistic presence for three decades. Clearly, what Duras adds to this solidarity in the 1980s as its particularly provocative ingredient is a bold reversal: France comes to be defined reactively, in terms of its attitude to immigration, and so straightforward polarities of identity and difference are inverted, the 'home' nation radically opened out by what Duras presents as its gesture of unconditional welcome. What is perhaps lost, on the other hand, is an attention to specificity. Whereas Duras's pieces from the 1950s focus principally on tiny but significant individual stories (represented best by 'Les Fleurs de l'Algérien'), her declarations of the 1980s and 1990s, while they may be offered as responses to particular events, take the form of generalized and often programmatic statements.[8] This, then, is the particular context of polemic and engagement within which Duras's contemporary literary address to the question of immigration needs to be discussed.

It is in 1990 that Duras offers her principal literary intervention into this context, in the (typically both tangential and blunt) form of *La pluie d'été*. Featuring an immigrant family living in a Paris suburb, the text is concerned with a range of issues which are present in much of Duras's work of this period, most notably the Holocaust and (Duras's own interpretation of) Jewish identity; childhood; incest; a generalized notion of identity as residue; and a kind of quasi-mysticism, marked here notably as a subversion of order and reason. As the text is set explicitly within a suburb—Vitry—which Duras declares (in her coda to the text) to be insurmountably real, these issues are situated firmly within their contemporary political context—and are all, therefore, enmeshed in the text's overall concern, namely immigration. Duras's stress in this declaration is on the fact that her Vitry is at once utterly real, profoundly unliterary, and therefore, as she puts it, the product of her invention. It not only aligns her own writing with the refusal of logic offered by the text's central figure, Ernesto, but it also announces (retrospectively) that this text demands to be read against its real context, while also reserving the right to a kind of quasi-transcendent intransitivity which, as suggested above, Duras during this later period of her work champions as the essence of the literary. It is in this way, then, that Duras here negotiates the double demand of writing into a specific, real context while also maintaining a certain textual autonomy (which, as will shall see shortly, articulates the refusal that will represent the text's ultimate gesture of solidarity): 'Vitry is a terrifying suburb, hard to locate and ill-defined, but I started to get fond of it. It's the least literary place imaginable, the least definite. So I invented it.'[9]

In order to sketch the alignment which exists between the text of *La pluie d'été* and its immigrant characters, we will need first to define the terms in which this immigrant identity is elaborated in the text. We might note initially that Ernesto, Jeanne, their mother and father and numerous brothers and sisters, represent a poor but ungraspable irritant within Vitry, both for the municipal authorities, to whom they are defined by what is described in Duras's French as an 'obstination *étrange*' (*La pluie d'été*, p. 12) marked by the strangeness of the foreign, and for the general population, of whom they are the object of so much resentful gossip that focuses on the clichés of their supposed exploitation of welfare, their failure to educate their children (who nevertheless are particularly beautiful), and so on. This status combines poverty and a certain, ill-defined sense of resistance, evident less in any active stance than in the general frustration evinced by all those (from the schoolmaster to the journalist) who come into contact with them. Immigrant identity is clearly connected by Duras in this text to a bewildering avoidance of fixity, a displaced and fragmented residue which both outstrips and infuriates those by whom it is confronted. This confusion of identity is apparent in the multiplication of names within the text (affecting the father, Ernesto, Jeanne, and most especially the mother), and also in the lack of clarity about the mother's origins; its implicit connection to notions of residuality is rendered explicit in the relation of both the mother and the father to their native tongues. The mother has forgotten this language but hauntingly, ungraspably, it remains:

> The mother has forgotten the language of her youth. She speaks like all the other people in Vitry, and without an accent. She only makes mistakes in the conjugations of the verbs. But there survive from her past certain ineffaceable sounds, soft words that she seems to be paying out slowly, chanting sounds that moisten the inside of her voice and sometimes make the words emerge from her body without her realizing it, as if she were being visited by the memory of a language long forsaken. (*Summer Rain*, p. 24)

The father is also at times traversed by the remnants of his lost identity, again in a language experienced physically as its last, poor residue:

> And then all of a sudden he'd start speaking Italian, but an Italian the children didn't recognize, extremely fast and garbled, very ugly and dirty and coarse, and it poured out of him as if his last hour had come and he was ridding himself of all that remained of the other life he'd had before he was buried by this avalanche of children. (p. 65)

It is, thus, linguistically that Duras chooses to emphasize the residuality by which immigrant identity is, for her, marked. This residuality is ultimately what allows the family to escape the grasp of their inhospitable surroundings, since their drunken, late-night song, *La Neva*—the forgotten and eroded evocation of a mysterious Russian point of departure—comes to flow through Vitry in such a way as to confound all attempts to bolt questions of identity firmly to notional origins:

> A lot of the people who lived in the villas along the way to Vitry town centre knew the wordless *Neva*, but couldn't remember where they'd heard it, whether on television or sung by immigrant children in the streets of Vitry. But plenty of non-immigrant children sang *La Neva* too. So they couldn't tell where it came from. (p. 103)[10]

The resisting force of this poor residuality implicit in this free-floating song is clearest in this text in the figure of Ernesto. With an apparently paradoxical declaration which soon makes him famous, Ernesto refuses to go to school 'because at school they teach me things I don't know' (p. 19). As Ernesto's extraordinary intelligence takes him quite independently through such academic disciplines as sociology and most of German philosophy (to the extent that it is suggested towards the end of the text that he became first a 'brilliant young professor of mathematics and then a scientist' (p. 141)), his declaration will not be reduced journalistically to a mere stance, to any available cliché of active, oppositional rebellion, as his sister makes clear:

> *Reporter*: Forgive me … I may have got it wrong … In which case it might be a kind of protest … about injustice … immanent injustice … the state of society or something …
> *Jeanne*: I don't think my brother's interested in all that.
> *Reporter*: I'm sorry … But … these things have to be said … Can you at one and the same time live off this society and expose it … the way it works?
> She's beautiful, Jeanne. And she's not shy. She likes to laugh, and she likes to cry.
> She's lucid, too. Like amber, the mother says. She says, politely still:
> *Jeanne*: If that's what you've come for it's not worth waiting, we have no opinion about that sort of thing here. (pp. 109–10)

If the journalist's terminology of critique and denunciation fails to grasp Ernesto's refusal of his education and collapses into faltering inadequacy, this is because Ernesto's declaration has nothing to do with a contestation of the world as it is, but rather represents an opening onto the mystical and residual beyond of knowledge, or whatever would be left after the completion of the Hegelian dialectic, which Ernesto suggests might consist of '[a]ll of a sudden the inexplicable … Music, for example …' (p. 108). Thus aligned at once with a kind of quasi-Bataillean unemployable negativity and some sort of mysticism, Ernesto's refusal points beyond the here and now in two directions: both to the intimation of an ineffable beyond, and to a specific historical dimension figured by Duras in characteristically mythical terms. This refusal, which Duras links metonymically to a resistant residuality, will ultimately prove the sign under which the text of *La pluie d'été* aligns itself with its immigrant characters. To grasp the terms of this alignment, we must first consider the object in which these two directions meet, namely, a sacred text.

Elaborating his own particular creation story, Ernesto stresses the originary presence of a certain, essential lacuna:

> *Ernesto*: It's something … you think you ought to be able to say what it was … but at the same time you know it's impossible to express … It's personal … you think you could … should be able to … but no … (p. 34)

Ernesto thus becomes the source of a kind of negative theology, in his mother's interpretation at least:

> Ernesto was the only one of her children who was interested in God. Ernesto had never uttered the word God, and it was through the omission that the mother guessed something of the sort. (p. 43)

Ernesto's interest is not, however, ultimately in God—whom he describes as 'my stupid mother's rigmaroles' (p. 73)—but rather, as his mother realizes, in the term which, along with 'refusal', is the key Durassian marker of negativity—despair:

> God, for Ernesto, was the despair he always felt when he looked at his brothers and sisters, his mother and father, the spring, or Jeanne, or nothing. The mother discovered Ernesto's despair by accident, so to speak, when she saw him standing one evening looking at her with that look of his, always anguished and sometimes blank. That evening the mother realized that Ernesto's silence was at once God and not God, a passion for living and a passion for dying. (pp. 43–44)

It is to this affective puncture that Ernesto's refusal leads. His concentration on its essential ineffability is increasingly articulated through the text of what is referred to as 'the burned book' (p. 11 and passim), a leather-bound volume which has somehow escaped an inexplicable ordeal by which it is still marked, and which is gradually revealed to be the Bible (or at least the Old Testament). It is, crucially, this volume which links Ernesto's mysticism to a historical dimension which extends from ancient Jerusalem to contemporary Vitry. As Ernesto speaks in the voice of the preacher of Ecclesiastes (to which Duras will return in *C'est tout*), he initially makes the link between the stories of the burned book and the Holocaust:

> Then I looked on all the works that my hands had wrought, and on the labour that I had laboured to do: and behold, all was vanity and vexation of spirit. Vanity of Vanities. Chasing the wind.
> The children listened eagerly to what the King of Israel had done. They asked where they were now, these people, the Kings of Israel.
> Ernesto said they were dead.
> How? asked the children.
> Gassed and burned, Ernesto said. (pp. 51–52)

And at the end of this scene, the connection to Vitry is made clear: 'Then Ernesto asked them not to forget that the last Kings of Israel, in Vitry, were their parents' (p. 53). It is, of course, Jewish identity that serves most insistently to figure Duras's notion of an eroded identity which would be at once residual and resistant. Its invocation in this context provides an intense tying-together of the threads of immigrant identity, residuality, and, crucially (via the 'burned book') writing.[11] And it is to this final, key term that we may now turn.

In *La pluie d'été*, Duras offers a chain of association constructed as follows: the residual identity of the immigrant family positions them in part as resistant to the order of their surroundings; this resistance is elevated by Ernesto into a radical refusal of this order; this refusal leads to a kind of mysticism, articulated primarily through a biblical voice which connects this chain to an historical continuum, to 1990s Vitry, and ultimately to a gesture of textual solidarity. For there is a constant thematization throughout *La pluie d'été* of books and writing as aligned with immigrant identity in a shared status as poor, residual, surviving. The opening lines of the text establish this alignment immediately, as the father finds the odd leftovers that books have here become in a manner which urgently evokes poverty:

> Books—the father used to find them on suburban trains. Or piled up separately, as if they were being given away as presents, beside garbage bins after someone had died or moved house. (p. 7)

Next, we learn that Ernesto's brothers and sisters spend their time browsing through books at the supermarket, which presents texts (even of the supposedly luxurious variety) and their reading as something wonderfully cheap and chaotic (the children are, as it were picking up the scraps of the publishing industry):

> *Ernesto*: Where are my brothers and sisters?
> *Mother*: Where do you think? At the Prisu, of course …
> *Ernesto*, laughing: Sitting on the floor by the bookshelves … reading coffee-table books. (p. 21)

Most powerfully, of course, this alignment (between writing, poverty, residuality, and survival) is suggested by the 'burned book', which (evoking by opposition—fire rather than flood—the supposed survival of the diary section of *La douleur*) both symbolizes a residual force of survival and allows reference to the event in relation to which these questions are most often considered by Duras, namely the Holocaust. This residuality produces a mystical force, evident in a mystical experience of language which adumbrates Ernesto's fascination with the originary absence that is, for him, fundamental:

> *Ernesto*, trying to find a way to put it: Exactly … with that book … it was as if knowledge took on a new aspect, Monsieur … Ever since entering into the kind of light that issues from the book … it's been like living in a state of wonder … (Ernesto smiles.) I'm sorry … it's hard to express … Words don't change their shape, they change their meaning, their function … They don't have a meaning of their own any more, they refer to other words that you don't know, that you've never read or heard … you've never seen their shape, but you feel … you suspect … they correspond to … an empty space inside you … or in the universe … I don't know … (pp. 100–01)

It is, moreover, in connection with the 'burned book' that Ernesto describes his own experience of reading and writing, which bypasses logic and lands, again, to the mystical:

> *Ernesto*: I'm sorry, Monsieur, but ... no ... I could read ... without knowing how ... before ... So you see ...
> *Teacher*: But how ... I don't want to bother you, but ...
> *Ernesto*: Well, I just opened the book and read ... You remember, don't you, Monsieur. The burned book ... so you could check that I hadn't got it wrong?
> *Teacher*: What about writing, Monsieur Ernesto?
> *Ernesto*: That was the same, Monsieur. I picked up a pencil stub and just wrote. How do you explain that, Monsieur?
> Silence.
> *Teacher*: It's inexplicable. I can't understand it. How do you explain it, Monsieur Ernesto?
> *Ernesto*: I couldn't care less about explanations, Monsieur. (pp. 97–98)

So, the words of the 'burned book' resound with an originary absence which can never be filled; Ernesto read this sacred text before he could read. It is, ultimately, in this negatively charged mysticism that Duras's gesture of textual solidarity with her immigrant characters is to be found. For it is with the culmination of this chain of reference in the mystical volume that Duras's particular, oblique textual engagement with immigrant identity in this text becomes clear. Rather than taking the way of critique or denunciation (and thus violating what she at this time celebrates as the radical intransitivity of writing), Duras builds up a string of associations which allow her both to invoke the concrete realities of contemporary France and (self-consciously and implicitly) to inscribe her writing, qua writing, into the demands of these realities, without it thereby being reducible to mere description or manifesto. Bound up with the milieu it describes, Duras's writing thus continues to embrace radical negativity and refusal (refusing a *useful* attack on the situation of immigrant communities in modern France), and thereby aligning itself (thanks notably to Ernesto) with the immigrant figures it presents. While this alignment might be criticized for privileging the aesthetic citation of specific details of *banlieue* scenery over a detailed engagement of the aesthetic in the specific, and while it certainly takes place entirely on Duras's terms (it works, that is, only on condition that one accept her notions of immigrant identity as a matter of residuality, resistance, and refusal as well as recognize her implicit claim via the symbol of the 'burned book' for the quasi-mystical association of writing with these terms), it is nevertheless by this self-conscious process of intransitive self-implication that Duras keeps the would-be autonomous writing of *La pluie d'été* at least involved in the urgent question of contemporary immigration. This involvement is never more than implicit, and hence tenuous; nor can it be otherwise, since Duras is seeking to avoid a more active, prosaic sort of engagement with her subject (say, 'polemic', or 'critique'). But this technique means that her writing here aligns itself with the immigrant group it (in its way) describes by means of general implication and suggestion rather than specific commitment, while nonetheless insisting that the specifics of 1990s Vitry *are* present within its weave. As we will now see, this kind of tenuous lack of resolution is entirely typical of Duras's writing in the face of questions of racial identity at this time, and it may, indeed, not be without its own, important point.

As noted above in the figures of the mother and the father, in *La pluie d'été* the residual identity which Duras problematically celebrates in the figure of the immigrant is also suggested linguistically. This technique begins to suggest that, even as it risks fetishizing the oppression of the immigrant by aestheticizing the vulnerability of this figure, Duras's writing might, beyond an implicit solidarity with the refusal which she associates with this residuality, also become the space of an exemplary openness to racial otherness by embracing a kind of linguistic immigration within itself. And it is to this aspect of Duras's textual practice in the 1980s and 1990s that I now propose to turn. At this time, Duras presents her texts as exemplary international spaces in which locations become mutually impacted in a refusal of political separation. *L'été 80*, for example, includes, in the course of only 102 pages, references to at least the following locations: Moscow, Gdansk, Trouville, Czechoslovakia, Afghanistan, Munich, Bologna, Long Island, Nantucket, Germany, Uganda, Vietnam, the Golan Heights, Cairo, China, Hiroshima, Iran, Guatemala, Melbourne, Vancouver, Paris, Caen, Bordeaux, Helsinki, Le Havre, the Ukraine, Silesia and Siam. Of greater interest, however, is the way in which this internationalism is also performed by Duras's texts in their linguistic constitution. Accordingly, I will now present the linguistic weave of certain of Duras's later texts and will argue that this texture offers a view of these texts as exemplarily open to the call of otherness within the field of national identity, before examining how this exemplary openness may also fail always to achieve a stability of performance.

Bakhtin's notion of *heteroglossia* presents language as always already overdetermined, shot through with the discourses of its inhabitants. 'At any given moment of its historical existence,' he writes, 'language is heteroglot from top to bottom: it represents the coexistence of socio-ideological contradictions between the present and the past, between differing epochs of the past, between different socio-ideological groups in the present, between tendencies, schools, circles and so forth, all given a bodily form.'[12] Of the 'different socio-ideological groups' to which Bakhtin refers, we may perhaps isolate, in the context of this discussion, different national identities inasmuch as these may be represented in different languages. The model of heteroglossia then indicates that a national language may represent an agglomeration of different languages, and may, therefore, be already traversed by linguistic difference. As Bakhtin puts it, using the image of a national frontier: 'Discourse lives, as it were, on the boundary between its own context and another, alien context.'[13] Within a language thought of as unitary, certain immigrant words may nonetheless figure, and their status may vary, from illegal alien to assimilated resident. Duras's texts display such terms in abundance, and, by placing them in a context already sensitized in the manner described above to questions of national identity, manage to foreground the residue of immigrant status that attaches to even relatively well-established imports. This insistent opening of French to the residual otherness within (i.e. the otherness of the residual immigrant term) may, then, be interpreted as the linguistic counterpart of Duras's political insistence during this period on the significance of France as an open space. Such a space develops out of those of her novels of the 1950s and early 1960s (*Le marin de Gibraltar*, *Les petits chevaux de Tarquinia*, *Dix heures et demie du soir en été*) which, set in and around Italy and Spain, include and make play with elements of those and other languages.

L'amant de la Chine du Nord, set in a colony, is inscribed explicitly within an area of linguistic plurality. The young girl whose story it tells is bilingual, and is also able to mimic usage of the Chinese of the colony:

> 'I'm still small.'
> 'How many years?'
> She answers the way a Chinese would:
> 'Sixteen years'.[14]

The text is thus already marked by an openness to a certain linguistic difference, quoting the displaced French that marks its setting. In this context, the reader may become sensitized to signs of linguistic difference in the text as a whole—and they are certainly there to be found. Items such as 'boycottée' (*L'amant de la Chine du Nord*, p. 120) and 'boy' (p. 13), both nineteenth century imports into French, are as it were subjected to the X-ray of the reader's enhanced sensitivity, and their ambiguous nationality begins to show through.[15] (This is especially true in the case of 'boy', of course, since its doubly displaced origin—not only as an anglicism, but as redolent of colonialism—already repeats the context in which it is set.) Similarly, the appearance in *La pluie d'été* of imported terms such as 'buildings' (*La pluie d'été*, p. 41) and 'bulldozers' (p. 119) in a context explicitly concerned with the status of the immigrant self, signals the language in which this concern is elaborated as itself already harbouring a residually immigrant population, and so gently tilts the text's ethos in favour of a generous welcome.

Such signalling may also be achieved by the alterations undergone by certain terms during their passage from one language into another. This shift may be semantic, for example, as in the case of 'dancing' (*L'amant de la Chine du Nord*, p. 168), which enters French in 1919 as an ellipsis of 'dancing-house', and so remains suspended between its origin and its new context, neither foreign nor simply assimilated. Alternatively, a term may have its residual alterity marked by the difference between its behaviour in its two linguistic homes. The pluralization of anglicisms in French is a case in point here: 'chewing-gum', for example, becomes countable on its entry into French, and so the form 'des chewing-gums' (referring to sticks, not varieties) emerges (*La pluie d'été*, p. 80; p. 109); conversely, 'tee-shirt' drops its plural 's', and so Ernesto's family's clothing allowance includes 'beaucoup de lainages, de tee-shirt' ('a lot of sweaters and T-shirts') (*La pluie d'été*, p. 26; *Summer Rain*, p. 24). Such slippages create a twilight zone between languages folded back within a language, calling attention to the residual foreign presence which may inhabit a national language, and, by implication, a national identity.

Not necessarily tied to immigration which has already taken place, a text may itself import terms which remain marked as entirely foreign within their new context. Thus, the eponymous heroine of *Emily L.*, for example, briefly speaks Italian ('una cosa mentale'), and *L'amant* slips into English ('l'*experiment*').[16] More dramatically, however, such terms may be smuggled in, passed off as assimilated and no longer declared typographically as alien. Thus *L'amant de la Chine du Nord* refers to 'Asia' (Duras, *L'amant de la Chine du Nord*, p. 219), 'chettys' (p. 194), and 'choum' (p. 88; p. 121), with neither italics nor a translation to provide a residence permit; and *La pluie d'été* has its gang of 'brothers et sisters' (Duras, *La pluie d'été*, p. 13, p. 18, and passim) inhabit 'la casa' (p. 17; p. 19; p. 21) while refusing to mark these as foreign. The identity of the dominant language is thus challenged, its mythic hegemony fractured, and the linguistic immigrant opens the text on to a plural, international space. Still more surreptitiously, the language of a text may itself become distorted in such a way as to suggest the subterranean presence of another language, the side effects of whose hidden working again displace a unitary linguistic nationality. Taking English as our example of a subtle, silent difference refusing to allow Duras's French to coincide with itself, we find, as the most condensed instance of this phenomenon, the distorted pun which splits the title of *L'été 80*. Alerted by this, we may hear a similar silent play within the phrase 'fleur de farine', used to describe Hélène Lagonelle's breasts in *L'amant* (p. 91) (which, beyond its literal meaning of 'fine wheaten flour', one might whimsically translate as 'flour flower'), in which the status of the pun as both aural and dependent upon a translation renders it doubly silent.[17] Finally, the simple inversion of the compound adjective 'ciel bleu' (*La pluie d'été*, p. 58) again mimes the operation of another language, and produces a form of French haunted by a silent English which leaves its subtle traces as challenges to the national identity of the text.[18] Linguistically, national identity may also be a matter of residues, as a shadowy other language displaces the identity of its host into something rather more fragile.

In *Emily L.*, the encounter between Duras's French and other languages is far from shadowy; it takes the form of an explicit and extended dialogue. The dialogue in question is almost exclusively with English, and arises from the presence in the text of the enigmatic English couple whose hypothetical history it reconstructs. Like *L'été 80*, the text establishes itself as an international space with a range of geographical references, for example, to the Strait of Malacca, the Sunda Islands, and Singapore, while its cross-Channel axis is indicated by references to Southampton, Newport, and even Buckingham Palace. Although English is also smuggled into this nautical text in the unmarked name of the 'Captain' figure, the text's most important linguistic work is transactional rather than contraband, for it is in this text that Duras's technique of incorporation of other languages into the French of her writing develops into a detailed exploration of the various possibilities of translation within a literary text, and of the effect of these possibilities on the production of meaning. As this exploration develops, the model of a textual performance of linguistic national identity open to residual otherness begins to show its risks. Its generosity is sustained by no happy liberality. Rather, as the performance of the gap of difference, this textual enactment presents the uncertainty attendant upon the embrace of otherness, risking the annihilation of both the other and the self. The optimism which simply urges an openness to otherness, while indispensable, is nonetheless given encouragement by this uncertain enactment to consider its own awkward location between fragility and brutality. A consideration of the operation of translation within this text may provide a position from which to assess Duras's treatment of linguistic and racial difference in general.[19]

In its most straightforward form, English features in *Emily L.* as the words of the English couple, accompanied by their French translation. The most common version of this has the French translation first, followed by the italicized English original (and even in this most straightforward form, the status of an original meaning is already questioned, making the original a translation of its supposed translation):

> Le Captain a dit: C'est ça. C'est le mot. *That's it.* (*Emily L.* (Fr), p. 39)
> Elle change d'idée toujours. *She's always changing her mind ...* (p. 73)
> La dernière, il avait dit: *The last one.* (p. 128)

This relation of translation is prone to slippage, however. The symmetry of the arrangement is not always maintained, and information may slip out of one side into another until the translation becomes more impressionistic, more approximate:

> Chaque été je vous voyais quand vous reveniez de voyage. *When I was little … Every year, every summer … I used to see you …* (p. 36)
>
> (Every summer I used to see you when you came back from your journeys. *When I was little … Every year, every summer … I used to see you …*)
> (My translation)

Translations become more like sketches, drafts for possible versions; the subtle semantic disjunctions between the two sides of the encounter gradually fade the meaning out of both, and the hierarchy of the relation (original/translation) becomes irredeemably complicated. Indeed, at times one half of the pairing disappears altogether. With no French translation to smooth its passage, the text's English becomes curiously like a series of textual blockages in which an opaque original sets up the expectation of supplementary clarification which never arrives:

> Le Captain a un gémissement de douleur. Comme un cri sourd, tragique. Il dit*: Oh … It's too sad … too much …* (p. 34)
>
> (The Captain moans with pain. It's like a dull, tragic cry. He says*: Oh … It's too sad … too much …*) (My translation)[20]

This frustration of expectation produces a hole in the original, as its full meaning is somehow felt to be missing in the absence of its (prior) translation. Or, conversely, the original seems too full, too evocative of a meaning which remains opaque. This opacity is increased by the tendency of the French translation to absent itself at moments of emotional intensity, which empties semantics out into a haunting affectivity:

> Une fois, ça ne tarderait plus maintenant, quand il se retournerait vers elle, il le savait, le Captain, elle aurait glissé sur le sol. *Darling … Darling …*
>
> Que ça s'approchait de lui comme une terre invisible dans la nuit des océans, il le savait aussi, le captain. *Darling … My poor little girl …* (p. 98)
>
> (Someday, he knew it couldn't be long now, he would turn to her and find she'd fallen down on the floor. *Darling … Darling …*
>
> He knew it was coming closer, like an invisible landfall in the darkness of the oceans. *Darling … My poor little girl …* (*Emily L.* (Eng), pp. 70–71.))[21]

Such moments may, moreover, introduce an ironic, self-referential lament at their own opacity, as their English expresses the difficulty of expression:

> Le Captain a ri. Il a dit: *God … How can I possibly tell you …* (p. 38)
>
> (He laughed and said, God! *How can I possibly tell you?* (p. 25))
>
> Merci de le boire à sa place, parce que à elle ça fait tellement de mal, c'est terrible, vous ne pouvez pas imaginer … *It's difficult to explain …* (p. 96)
>
> (Thank you for drinking it for her. It does her so much harm, it's terrible. *It's difficult to explain …* (p. 69))

The tendency of the text's English is, in fact, to become increasingly free-floating, to liberate itself from both translation and dependence on a particular voice. The last example quoted above actually represents part of an extended hypothesis on the part of the narrator, and the text's 'you', the narrator's interlocutor, appears to break into English at one point (although the text may be repeating a fragment of speech from elsewhere):

> Vous, l'homme aux yeux rieurs, vous avez dit: Elle veut mourir. *That's the point.* C'est ça qu'elle demande, un caprice comme un autre. (p. 107)
>
> (You, the man with laughing eyes, said, 'She wants to die. *That's the point.* Another of her whims.' (p. 77))

A space opens up within the linguistic text, neither simply English nor simply French, its meaning emerging in a strangely elegiac tone, somewhere between the two. Even as it describes a sense of isolation on the part of the Captain amongst the clientele of a French bar, the text embraces this position in a kind of momentary, bilingual 'free indirect discourse', and denies this separation even as it is evoked:

> Il regarde les French avec antipathie. Il n'en veut plus, on dirait. Il grogne. Qu'est-ce qu'il ferait avec les French. Il ne cherche plus à s'intéresser, le Captain, il ne cherche pas à entendre ce que les French disent autour du bar. Il se sent ficelé parmi les French, le corps saucissonné, là, parmi les French. (p. 99)
>
> (He looks at *the French* with dislike. As if he's fed up with them. He groans. What are the French to him? He's given up trying to take an interest, given up listening to what they're saying as they stand around the bar. He feels awkward among them, trussed up. (p. 71))

This generosity is paradoxically grounded in instability, however; the price for the incorporation of linguistic difference may, as we have seen, be paid in the fading of meaning, which implies also the complication of interpretation. When the text's bilingualism appears to go awry, for example, the limits of interpretation are exposed as extremely uncertain. Encountering '*Manilia*'

(*Emily L.* (Fr), p. 40), or *'The nicest one we ever have'* (*Emily L.* (Fr), p. 140), the temptation to class the usage in question as erroneous appears both rather churlish, given the linguistic generosity of the text, and possibly inappropriate, given the text's work to destabilize security of meaning across a bilingual gulf.[22] Are such examples mistakes, or further instances of the dismantling of secure linguistic identity? This question must remain undecided, to trouble in particular the Anglophone reader, whose language is deprived of its internal regulation even as s/he reads. It has become impossible to distinguish between the disruptive and the simply incorrect. Generous, nuanced, subtle in its embrace of linguistic alterity and its exploration of the residual echoes produced by this alterity in its context, *Emily L.* is perhaps also simply wrong—and hence wise enough to indicate that the destabilization of linguistic identity, while perhaps offering a paradigmatic openness to otherness, does so at the risk of error, which necessarily questions the confidence of the generous gesture with the suggestion of mere accident.[23]

And the text is also prepared to implicate itself in this risk, by providing a *mise en abyme* of the possible loss of meaning of a literary work across the chasm of translation in the story of Emily L.'s lost poem, 'Winter Afternoons'.[24] As the narrator and her companion reconstruct the history of the Captain and his wife, the latter emerges as a writer, albeit one whose work is published without her knowledge. In accordance with this position (and perhaps further to underline the teasing parallels between herself and the figure of Duras), Emily L. offers a model of the business of writing. This model is relatively secure, and claims that any actual poem is but a contingent, culturally-inflected translation of an ideal Poem:

> She was one of those who incline to believe the same poem is written everywhere, but in different forms. That there's only one poem to be sought for through every language and all civilizations. (pp. 57–58)

The security of the translation on which this model depends is already threatened by its opacity, however, inasmuch as the absolute Poem remains veiled, 'to be sought for', beyond any of its actual manifestations. And the example of literary creation offered by the text incorporates an act of translation that brings to a head the uncertainty of the bilingualism displayed in the text in general.

As mere approaches to an ideal Poem, actual poems are presented in *Emily L.* as rather delicate affairs. Emily L.'s works are disseminated without her knowledge, via the Captain and her father, and it is in part the apparent mystery of this unwilled circulation that convinces her of the irresistible translatability of any poem:

> She believed poems written in one country soon spread to others, breaking down by their own mere existence and self-evidence the barriers of seas, skies, continents, political systems, and prejudice. (p. 57)

The distance that constitutes the articulating space across which the poem travels in its translation may, however, become folded back on to the poem itself. Some months after her poems have been collected and published, and after she has lost a stillborn daughter, Emily L. writes one more poem, a departure from her previous work ('a different kind of poem' (p. 63)) and whose centre is incomplete ('The middle of the poem, with its variants, took up half the page. It was full of crosscuts' (p. 60)). The Captain, who has always experienced his wife's poetry as a kind of infidelity, is devastated by this return of a practice he had thought was finished, and burns the poem. This missing poem then becomes central to her oeuvre: it would, for example, have provided the title for the published collection of her work (p. 81). The figure of the absent centre is coming to characterize this key work, whose middle lines are crossed out and whose destruction punctures the heart of Emily L.'s corpus. And the subject of this missing piece is, precisely, the piercing of the heart by rays of winter sunlight:

> I said the rays of the sun wounded like heavenly swords, piercing the heart ... but without leaving any scar, any trace, except ... except ... I forget, and yet it was the most important thing of all. (p. 82)

Again, the centre ('the most important thing of all') is absent. When it returns, it appears as the motto for precisely this phenomenon of the broken middle: no traces of the heart's piercing remain, '[b]ut for an internal difference in the heart of meanings' (my translation; Duras's French reads 'Sauf celle d'une différence interne au coeur des significations' (*Emily L.* (Fr), p. 114)—for reasons that will soon become apparent, it is vital that this line be translated literally). This central piercing is thus performed in the repetitions of internal aporia within its poetic elaboration. With a hole in its heart, 'Winter Afternoons' provides a stable enactment of its central—absent—concern.

Until it is translated, that is. For the stable enactment of this internal difference in fact opens up a deal of paradox and uncertainty. The paradox of the stable enactment of an irruptive hole means that 'une différence interne au coeur des significations' is converted by this enactment into its opposite, becomes whole, meaningful—as is also the case when the line is more or less returned to Dickinson's original English, as: '*But internal difference, Where the Meanings are*' (*Emily L.* (Fr), p. 114; Duras's version misses Dickinson's comma before 'are'). From meaning being holed by internal difference, internal difference becomes (in its good enactment, and then its translation-cum-original) the hole in which whole meanings (signalled by their capitalization) dwell. Stable enactment collapses into the gap it performs, as translation performs two incompatible meanings. The gap between the original French line and its English version (more or less its original) locates the whole Meaning—that meanings are holed—within the internal difference of translation, and so confirms both that meaning is holed (the two lines are incompatible) and that it is whole (as the incompatibility between the two lines performs securely the 'différence interne'). And so the gap of translation enacts at the same time the two incompatible lines, which is impossible. Translation thus offers the dizzying spectacle of an impossible enactment. Internal difference, where the Meanings are *and* aren't.[25]

This might all just be a mistake, a mistranslation. But, as discussed above, *Emily L.* renders undecidable the question of whether an apparently erroneous piece of English is to be considered a mistake, or the staging of a mistake. In this case, would the correct version be the French (encountered first, but a translation), or the English (encountered second, the original, but a translation of sorts)? Even simple error resolves nothing. Writing to the Assises de la Traduction Littéraire in Arles in November 1987, Duras gives some of her views on translation. She emphasizes that a literary translation should not be governed by substantive accuracy, but by a more subtle fidelity:

> Everybody knows perfectly well that translation does not consist in the literal accuracy of a text, but perhaps we ought to go further: and say that it consists, rather, in a musical kind of approach, rigorously personal and even, if necessary, aberrant.[26]

Perhaps the aberrant space between the two versions of *Emily L.*'s key line reveals this missed encounter to be the perfect translation? As a *mise en abyme* of the problematic of translation in the text as a whole, the hole in the heart of (the meaning of) *Emily L.* allows an uncertain linguistic self-sacrifice, as the identity of the text is traversed by the unstable presence of an otherness which questions the security of its meanings, without allowing this questioning itself to become securely meaningful. Perhaps, then, we should read Duras's presentation of the slippages produced within the heteroglot text as the textual elaboration of a call for an openness to otherness in the field of national identity which must, nonetheless, also disrupt itself to present the disturbances produced as the residual effects of difficult and necessarily incomplete assimilation? For Duras's exploration of the nature of racial and linguistic identity is not without its problems. Having traced this exploration from the figure of the immigrant self via Duras's sometimes confusing use of translation within her texts, we may now move back to the implications of this Durassian encounter with racial otherness, taking the difficulties seen in Durassian translation as a guide to her approach to racial identity in general.

As far as racial identity is concerned, Duras's key figures often seem poised between stereotype and uncertainty, on the line between the reconfirmation and the refusal of racist discourses. Examples of the use of racial stereotypes are not hard to come by in Duras's texts. In *L'amant de la Chine du Nord*, for example, the young girl's elder brother refers to her Chinese lover as 'Filthy chink' (*The North China Lover*, p. 156). Such examples imply no espousal by the text's narrative voice of the position in question, and can be read straightforwardly as its critical staging. It is not always thus, however. In *Emily L.*, the couple from the Isle of Wight whose story is reconstructed in hypothesis by the text's 'I' and 'you' figures are said to drink 'the sort of drinks hard drinkers from England and America go in for: a dark Pilsen for him, a double bourbon for her' (*Emily L.* (Eng), p. 9). In this case, there is no safe distance between simplistic position and narrative voice. When other, more serious, racial stereotypes are invoked elsewhere in Duras's work, this unstable critical frame can become disturbing. Such images are in plentiful supply in *Emily L.*, in the narrator's perceptions of a group of Koreans who have inexplicably appeared in Quillebeuf. On their first, enigmatic appearance, the group all look alike:

> I look around and suddenly there are people on the other side of the square, at the entrance to the disused path, where there shouldn't be anybody at all. They've stopped and are looking at us. About fifteen of them, all dressed alike, in white. The same person multiplied indefinitely. I look away. (pp. 4–5)

Her presentation of these figures appears relatively content to dehumanize or at least patronize them:

> Some of them had started playing, running about and chasing each other. More of them had arrived from along the disused path by the river; they were just the same as the rest chubby men, prematurely obese. When they ran they bounced along like balls, like big babies. (p. 33)

And the terror inspired in the narrator by these figures is linked, apparently, to a visceral conviction of their innate cruelty:

> I point to the Koreans. 'Look at them. Just now I thought they were going to surround the café and exterminate us. As I said, they're very cruel. The most cruel people on earth.' (p. 38)

Such crude generalizations are justified by the narrator on two grounds. First, she invokes a model of scandal, according to which offensiveness may serve as a mark of truthfulness. As in Duras's infamous 1985 piece on Christine Villemin, refrains such as 'I'd said what I think' (p. 7) ('j'ai dit ce que je crois' (*Emily L.* (Fr.), p. 14)) affirm the blunt nature of the belief in question as evidence of its supposed value. More subtly, perhaps, the narrator also justifies her feelings by reference to her colonial past, which, she claims, has afforded her insights into an 'Asiatic' mentality:

> I said I knew Asiatics: they were cruel, they used to amuse themselves on the plain of Kampot by driving their cars over dying dogs. (p. 32)

> I talked some more about the Asiatics. I said they were cruel, and gamblers and thieves and hypocrites and madmen, and I had vivid memories of the animals in Indochina, all gaunt and mangy as in southern Spain and black Africa. (p. 45)[27]

In such pronouncements, the fragile self resisting racist aggressions by means of this very fragility (seen above in *La pluie d'été*) seems to have been reduced merely to the status of the binary other of a discourse of racial certainty. Not all immigrants, apparently, are equally valorized. With the second of these examples, however, the invocation of a colonial past that serves primarily to justify a position based on the fixity of national and racial identity begins to tip over into the complication of just such a position. The comparison with other geographical contexts inevitably destabilizes the claim being made for the particular cruelty of the 'Asiatics' (although it remains within the prejudices of northern Europe). Elsewhere, the narrator's colonial past is also invoked in order to provide evidence of her own complicated national identity. Even as she is describing more examples of Indochinese cruelty, the narrator concludes in a phrase which necessarily complicates the simplistic model she is espousing:

> While they clubbed dogs to death on the plain of Kampot they went on smiling like children. They laughed without a qualm, they enjoyed watching the dying contortions of those fleshless skeletons. I say I can't be like the French of France after a childhood like that. (p. 36)

This represents no stable qualification, however. The narrator may be claiming that her childhood has removed her from perhaps the more liberal presuppositions of 'the French of France', but the distinction certainly introduces a slippage within national identity, with the narrator claiming for herself a residual immigrant identity.[28]

Where there may be simple espousal of a fixity of national/racial identity, there may also be the qualification of this fixity. So, while the narrative adopts the narrator's ignorance of the identity of the Koreans on their first appearance, and so enforces an alignment (however temporary) with her position, it also incorporates the dismissive criticism of this position by her companion: 'Lousy racist' (p. 7). Moreover, the narrator herself presents her fear of the Koreans as a kind of pathological condition ('I've been told it was probably the colonies—living there as a child—and drink' (p. 34)) and as pathetic, this judgement itself presented as a prophecy fulfilled in its writing: 'And you knew it was no use arguing, and that, as I'd admit later on in a book, I was as hopeless an idiot as ever' (p. 7). There is, then, also a displacing frame around the narrator's racism; and the self-fulfilling *Emily L.* explicitly asks to be read as a critical staging of her position. The frame is not safe, however, and the position in question is not simply denounced by its staging. Rather, a potential frame is juxtaposed with material it may, or may not, qualify. The unease created by this (un)framed material will not quite be removed by its possible framing. The text presents both the stereotype and its critique, without allowing the latter quite to qualify the former. Ambiguity may, then, operate here to propagate rather than to refuse a racist position; but necessarily double, it may also operate in the opposite direction. There are racist positions here; and there is their possible qualification.

And here we have a clear encapsulation of the problematic encounter with linguistic and racial otherness to be found in this period of Duras's writing. The prejudice of the narrator of *Emily L.* is both espoused and qualified. The figure of the immigrant is celebrated in terms of a fragility that also repeats the racist denial of selfhood. The textual gesture of solidarity with this immigrant identity appears bound to remain uncertain, never to progress beyond the implicit and the intransitive. Duras's writings even appear to remain on the difficult line between a positive, affirmatory response to racial difference and the reduction of this difference to prejudice and platitude. And when the textual elaboration of this difference in the texts of this period is examined, a similar tension may be remarked. While many of Duras's texts may be read as enacting in their linguistic pluralism an openness to cultural otherness, the most sustained instance of this technique, *Emily L.*, offers a version of this openness which, collapsing into paradox, declares little more than the difficulties of such an encounter. Duras's texts encounter racial and linguistic difference as a matter of difficult and incomplete assimilation, immigrant self and word representing an 'internal difference' whose force and meaning are clearly unstable.[29]

In conclusion, then, we might read Duras's work in this area as a useful reminder that an openness to otherness might not represent simply happy, liberal tolerance, but may, if this otherness is embraced in its true difference, entail a deal of difficulty as the price of avoiding the erasure of difference which straightforward tolerance or assimilation might imply. Such a reading would, however, do Duras's work in this area rather too much credit, or, alternatively, would reduce the complexities of her approach. For this interpretation effaces the fact that Duras's writing shows this difficulty precisely by failing safely to stage it for critical inspection, by falling into it or becoming, potentially at least, complicit with it. While both her literary work and her political activity show a constant concern to oppose racist aggression, the details of this work demonstrate that, for Duras, such an opposition takes place by means which, by their very nature, always risk the reduction of this contestation either to the merely implicit, or even to a possible repetition of the position opposed. In some respects an exemplary encounter with the demands of otherness, Duras's work attains this status in part by failing to sustain the generosity by which it is sometimes impressively marked.

Notes

1 For Duras's expression of solidarity with 'le dernier coolie', see Jacques Rivette and Jean Narboni, 'La destruction, la parole', *Cahiers du Cinéma*, No. 217 (November 1969), pp. 45–57; p. 51.

2 See Jean Genet, *L'ennemi déclaré, Oeuvres complètes*, Vol. 4, Paris, Gallimard, 1991, p. 338.

3 See Marguerite Duras, *Le camion, suivi de Entretien avec Michelle Porte*, Paris, Minuit, 1977, p. 73.

4 '[P]our le Salvador, pour le Nicaragua, et pour le prolétariat colonial chez elle émigrés, ces gens de l'Afrique et de l'Europe pauvre qui depuis trente ans construisent ses autoroutes, ses parkings, le gros oeuvre de son habitat' (Marguerite Duras, 'Un Pays du Nord', *Des femmes en mouvements (hebdo)*, No. 48 (3–10 July 1981); p. 25). This chapter on translation necessarily has its own translation protocol which is as follows: when using my own translations, I will provide the original French in a note, as here; when quoting from published translations, I will generally for the sake of economy cite the English text only, with reference to the original where necessary (for example, when discussing the presence of other languages within Duras's French).

5 See Marguerite Duras, 'L'Internationalisme de l'idée française', *Globe*, No. 23 (December 1987), p. 36.

6 'Elle a sorti la France de ses gonds, elle l'a faite internationale. Elle a crié les droits de l'homme partout. Impossible de remplacer Signoret' (Marguerite Duras, 'Elle a sorti la France de ses gonds', *Le Quotidien de Paris*, 1 October 1985, p. 25).

7 'Ils ont souillé la France, qui est la terre sainte de l'Europe, la terre de l'accueil et de la liberté, qui a pleuré pour les Juifs' (Marguerite Duras, 'Vive Cresson et la lutte des classes!' (interview with Jean-Louis Ezine), *Le Nouvel Observateur*, 2–8 April 1992, p. 65).

8 In the context of his detailed discussion of the relationship between racial difference and formal rhetoric in *Les mains négatives*, James S. Williams also draws attention to this feature of Duras's media interventions, citing an article from *Le Monde* in 1985 entitled 'Une certaine idée de la France' in which she claimed 'that the attempt in France over the last forty years at "assimilation" was false and misguided, although she offered no alternative solutions, declaring only her pride in the fact that France's open borders made her a world model for democracy!' (James S. Williams, *The Erotics of Passage: Pleasure, Politics, and Form in The Later Work of Marguetite Duras*, Liverpool University Press/St Martin's Press, 1997, p. 127).

9 Marguerite Duras, *Summer Rain*, trans. Barbara Bray, London, Flamingo, 1993, p. 143 (originally published as *La pluie d'été*, Paris, POL, 1990) (references to the French text will here be made to the edition published in 1994 by Gallimard in the 'Folio' collection). This paradox also recalls significantly (if in rather truncated form) the dialectical relationship between truth and artifice found in Robert Antelme's *L'espèce humaine*, where the testimonial authenticity of the text is assured precisely, in part, by its passage through a kind of imaginative reconstruction necessary for the communication of what Antelme calls the unimaginable. See Robert Antelme, *L'espèce humaine* (1947), Paris, Gallimard, 1957; édition revue et corrigée, coll. 'Tel', 1978. This echo supports the idea that the notion of an irreducibly resistant residue of identity, crucial to Antelme's genuinely extraordinary testimony, is also—as I will argue—of some importance *to La pluie d'été.*

10 Producing a disturbance in the field of identity which extends beyond its own limits, the Durassian figure of the immigrant self offers, in *La pluie d'été*, an exploration of the self as residual that is intimately linked to a contemporary identity politics. The valorization of the figure of the immigrant self against the platitudes of racism represents not (simply) the celebration of a different identity, but rather the elaboration of a different model altogether, in which the self is presented and embraced as fragile, residual and resistant. In relation to the identity of the oppressed, this is in fact Duras's characteristic move: she embraces the oppressed identity precisely in the terms of its oppression, as different, other, displaced. The danger of this technique is obvious: in celebrating the oppressed term of a hierarchy in the very terms in which it is oppressed, Duras clearly risks the repetition of this oppression rather than its displacement. For Duras, the force of disturbance which she identifies in the figure of the immigrant will always outstrip the racist response to this disturbance. Politically, however, it remains at least questionable whether the celebration of immigrant identity in the name of a loss of fixed identity allows any necessarily collective position from which to resist aggression. While Duras's biography is full of instances of such resistance, then, it is by no means certain that her literary treatment of the identity of the immigrant may not, in fact, undermine assumptions about identity necessary to the struggles of oppressed groups.

11 Jewishness is, in fact, Duras's most frequently-used, and most problematic, figure of complication within the field of identity. I do not have room here to discuss

this in detail as its importance in Duras's work deserves more focused treatment. For discussions of the issue, see in particular Charlotte Wardi, 'L'oubli du génocide dans le roman français de 1945 à 1970', *Les Nouveaux Cahiers*, No. 58 (Autumn 1979), pp. 4–9, which includes a strong denunciation of Duras's treatment of Jewishness; and Leslie Hill, *Marguerite Duras: Apocalyptic Desires*, London and New York, Routledge, 1993, esp. pp. 132–36. With reference to Duras's treatment of Jewishness, Marilyn R. Schuster raises a point of considerable significance to her celebratory use of the figure of the immigrant as impoverished, weak, vulnerable and worn out (the dangers of which are discussed in note 10 above). Schuster writes that Duras 'still encloses Jewish identity within terms set by the oppressor. Victim, wanderer, isolated in a foreign land, the Jew in Duras's work resists only by crying out or, perhaps, by writing. Again, the line between sympathy with an oppressed group and appropriation of their story, between empathetic representation and fatalism, remains problematic' (Marilyn R. Schuster, *Revisiting Duras*, New York, Twayne, 1993, p. 103).

12 Mikhail Bakhtin, 'Discourse in the Novel', in *The Dialogic Imagination*, ed. Michael Holquist, trans. Caryl Emerson and Michael Holquist, Austin TX, University of Texas Press, 1981, p. 291.

13 Bakhtin, 'Discourse in the Novel', p. 284.

14 Marguerite Duras, *The North China Lover*, trans. Leigh Hafrey, New York, The New Press, 1992, p. 38 (originally published as *L'amant de la Chine du Nord*, Paris, Gallimard, 1991). Since the text also presents itself as autobiographical, we should no doubt recall in relation to this example that Duras took her baccalauréat in Vietnamese. See Marguerite Duras and Michelle Porte, *Les lieux de Marguerite Duras*, Paris, Minuit, 1977, p. 60.

15 All references to the provenance of particular words taken from *Le Grand Robert de la langue française* (second edition).

16 See Marguerite Duras, *Emily L.*, Paris, Minuit, 1987, p. 51, and *L'amant*, Paris, Minuit, 1984, pp. 16 and 28.

17 Barbara Bray translates this phrase as 'flour-white'. See Marguerite Duras, *The Lover*, trans. Barbara Bray, London, Flamingo, 1986, p. 78.

18 Similar torsions may be found within Duras's grammar, which (amongst its many liberties) occasionally seems to mimic English construction. See on this point Christiane P. Makward, 'For a Stylistics of Marguerite Duras', *L'Esprit Créateur*, Vol. 30, No. 1 (Spring 1990), pp. 28–39. Pointing to what she terms 'pseudo-anglicisms' in Duras's writing, Makward argues that '[t]hese examples are merely *gauchissements* or mild distortions of syntax that do not affect signification' (p. 33). My argument here, however, is that at the broader level of the identity of the text, and especially in texts which are explicitly concerned with questions of national identity, an accumulation of such examples can have a symbolic significance, representing a key part of the text's often problematic self-implication in the questions it raises.

19 I ought to add at this point that the awkwardness highlighted in this operation will only be exaggerated in what follows, as it ironically becomes impossible to demonstrate in translation the twists of translation within *Emily L.* I will,

therefore, present in the following section Duras's original French, supplemented where necessary by the relevant—but, as will soon become apparent, inevitably incomplete—translation. Where translations would be otiose, they have been omitted; where the detail of Duras's intra-textual translations is lost in the published English translation of *Emily L.*, I will provide my own translation, and will signal this fact in the text. Where English text from *Emily L.* appears without such indication, it is taken from the published translation. The French text of *Emily L.* has already been cited; the English translation to which I will be referring is Marguerite Duras, *Emily L.*, trans. Barbara Bray, London, Collins, 1989. It will largely be apparent which edition is being cited, although where necessary, the two texts will be distinguished as *Emily L.* (Fr) and *Emily L.* (Eng). Significant differences between the English and French versions of *Emily L.* will be indicated in subsequent notes.

20 Barbara Bray translates the Captain's words—from English into English, intriguingly—as 'Oh, how sad! How very sad!' (*Emily L.* (Eng), p. 22).

21 In Bray's translation, elements of the text which are in English in the original are italicized (as in the original).

22 Both of these examples are corrected in the English translation of the text, to 'Manila' (p. 26) (no italics) and '*the nicest one we ever had*' (p. 102) (italicized).

23 Williams, who (significantly, in this context) describes part of *Emily L.* as 'knowingly false', highlights this instability by referring to 'the seam of (mis)translation in the text, specifically in its title, "*Emily eLle.*"' (see Williams, *The Erotics of Passage*, pp. 78–79).

24 As Williams and others have pointed out, the poem is, in fact, by Emily Dickinson, and runs as follows:

> There's a certain Slant of light,
> Winter Afternoons—
> That oppresses, like the Heft
> Of Cathedral Tunes—
>
> Heavenly Hurt, it gives us—
> We can find no scar,
> But internal difference,
> Where the Meanings, are—
>
> None may teach it—Any—
> 'Tis the Seal Despair—
> An imperial affliction
> Sent us of the Air—
>
> When it comes, the Landscape listens—
> Shadows—hold their breath—
> When it goes, 'tis like the Distance
> On the look of Death—

(from *The Complete Poems of Emily Dickinson*, ed. Thomas H. Johnson, London, Faber and Faber, 1975, pp. 118–19).

25 In translation, these swirling effects are inevitably lost, as the line—in both its versions—becomes 'But internal difference where the meanings are' (*Emily L.* (Eng), pp. 82–83). Curiously, this translation responds to its dilemma by refusing to translate 'Sauf celle d'une différence interne au coeur des significations', substituting for it the contradictory 'translation' given in the original as well as effacing Duras's echo of Dickinson's capitalization, thus placing the line in a kind of limbo between Dickinson's original and Duras's version. In his reading of *Emily L.*, Williams also discusses briefly the 'rewriting' of this line (see Williams, *The Erotics of Passage*, p. 79).

26 'Tout le monde sait bien que la traduction n'est pas dans l'exactitude littérale d'un texte, mais peut-être faudrait-il aller plus loin: et dire qu'elle est davantage dans une approche d'ordre musical, rigoureusement personnelle et même, s'il le faut, aberrante' (Marguerite Duras, *Le monde extérieur: Outside II*, Paris, POL, 1993, pp. 131–32).

27 These references to a supposedly 'Asiatic' cruelty are, as it were, backed up by the figure of the lover in *The North China Lover*: asked twice by his young lover how he would have murdered her, he replies: 'Like a Chinese. With cruelty on top of the killing' (*The North China Lover*, p. 101).

28 Again, *L'amant de la Chine du Nord* provides interesting echoes here, as the figure of the young girl (in a sense the younger self) is said—briefly, and in *a style indirect libre* that embraces the perception of her Chinese lover—to resemble a 'half-caste' (*The North China Lover*, p. 29); she carries a '"native" suitcase made of pasteboard' (p. 31); and her mother tells the children that 'this land of Indochina was their true homeland' (p. 23). For an evocative description by Duras of her displaced national identity and her Vietnamese childhood, see *Les lieux de Marguerite Duras*, pp. 60–61. Elsewhere, Duras presents her displacement from Indochina as a liberation from the baggage of national identity: 'At the age of seventeen, when I went to Paris to go to university, I was definitively cleansed of belonging to any homeland' (Marguerite Duras, 'The Thing' (interview with Rolland Thélu), *Le Gai Pied*, No. 20 (November 1980), p. 16) ('A dix-sept ans, quand je suis allée à Paris pour faire l'université, j'ai été définitivement nettoyé de l'appartenance à une quelconque patrie'). This then enables the provocative statement, 'I am creole' ('Je suis créole').

29 Some of the difficulties raised by Duras's encounter with racial difference during this period are discussed in critical detail in Williams, *The Erotics of Passage*, pp. 125–32.

Part III
Sex

CHAPTER 8

Female Homoerotics and Lesbian Textuality in the Work of Marguerite Duras

Renate Günther

It is probably true to say that most critics of Duras have interpreted the importance of love and desire in her work from a largely heterosexual perspective.[1] A different reading of her texts, however, informed by contemporary lesbian theory, shows that the overtly heterosexual Durassian scenario is infused with an underlying lesbian subtext, creating a sense of sexual and textual ambivalence in a number of her key works. A constant feature of this subtext is the presence of female couples and the figure of the female double in texts such as *Moderato cantabile*, *Le ravissement de Lol V. Stein*, *Détruire dit-elle*, *La femme du Gange*, *L'amant* and, more recently, *L'amant de la Chine du Nord*. Whereas in some of these texts lesbian desire figures in explicitly sexual terms, female homoeroticism in Duras's work as a whole appears to be more diffuse and fluid. For the purposes of this chapter, therefore, I will use the term 'eroticism', following Adrienne Rich's definition, as 'a diffuse and omnipresent energy unconfined to any single part of the body or solely to the body itself'.[2] Similarly, Rich has challenged the narrow interpretation of lesbian desire as being confined to sexual activity between women. Instead, she understands lesbianism as a 'primary intensity between and among women'.[3] This broader definition is certainly appropriate to an analysis of Durassian representations of female same-sex relationships which question socially produced boundaries between friendship, love and desire. The aim of this chapter is to provide a detailed examination of the lesbian aspects of three texts by Duras, *Détruire dit-elle*, *La femme du Gange* and *L'amant de la Chine du Nord*. My reading focuses both on the representations of love between women in these texts and on the presence of certain textual patterns as indicative of lesbian textuality in Duras.

Recent work in lesbian theory points to the existence of two apparently distinct approaches to the question of lesbian textuality. The first, which presupposes fixed categories of sex and sexuality, is concerned mainly with a thematics of desire between female figures in literary texts. The second, informed by a poststructuralist questioning of such categories, defines lesbian textuality more generally as any narrative space which disrupts the binary structures of patriarchal heterosexuality. If gender dualisms are intrinsic to constructions of sexual difference, a lesbian text, on the contrary, produces what Marilyn Farwell has called a 'disruptive space of sameness'.[4] In this context, however, 'sameness' becomes a metaphor for the absence of gendered subject positions, so that the term 'lesbian' no longer refers specifically or exclusively to women's relationships with other women. In the following section of this chapter I will argue that this apparent contradiction between 'the real' and 'the metaphorical' lesbian[5] is, to some extent at least, resolved in Duras's text *Détruire dit-elle*, for in this text the relationship between the two women characters, Alissa and Elisabeth, implies both the specificity of lesbian desire as female and the dissolution of patriarchal gender categories. What is destroyed in this text is the dominant construction of sexual difference which assigns to women the position of the 'object-other'. Indeed, it is primarily through the central female relationship that this position can be questioned and abandoned in favour of female subjectivity.

An initial reading of *Détruire dit-elle* shows that, in the early sections of the text, the relationship between Alissa and Elisabeth is cast in terms of differences, rather than similarities, between the two women. These differences are structured through a series of metaphors opposing speech and silence, presence and absence, the destroyer and the destroyed, knowledge and the inability to understand. Whilst Alissa takes up the position of the active subject in this dualistic framework, Elisabeth plays the role of the passive object. Like Lol V. Stein, 'asleep on her feet', Elisabeth recalls the feminine archetype of 'sleeping beauty'. In terms of gender positions it could be argued that, regardless of their biological femaleness, these characters can be slotted into the masculine/feminine binarism underlying patriarchal constructions of sexual relations. Seen in this light, the relationship between Alissa and Elisabeth merely replicates heterosexual models, represented in the text through the two male characters' objectifying fascination with Elisabeth. In an article on *Détruire dit-elle* Agnes Porter-Beaudry pursues this line of argument when she suggests that Alissa's attraction towards Elisabeth springs from her identification with

Max Thor and Stein.[6] Lesbian desire as a female experience is thus dismissed, as the latter is reincorporated into a heterosexual framework.

A closer examination of the text demonstrates, however, that this miming of dominant gender oppositions is, in fact, undercut by textual patterns which increasingly foreground similarity and reciprocity as the privileged aspects of the female relationship. This difference can be illustrated with reference to the scene which stages the first encounter between Alissa and Elisabeth. Like Max Thor in the opening section of the text, Alissa looks at Elisabeth who remains oblivious to the fact that she is the object of that look. Michèle Druon, in her article on 'The Figure of the Double' in *Détruire dit-elle*, comments on this scene as an illustration of her overall interpretation of Alissa as a totalitarian sadist, bent on destroying Elisabeth's 'otherness'. Druon argues that Alissa's gaze represents a metaphorical rape of the other woman's identity.[7] Such a reading of the female gaze in *Détruire dit-elle* merely reflects dominant assumptions about lesbian desire and cannot be substantiated by reference to the text itself, for, whilst Max Thor's gaze places Elisabeth into the fantasized position of the obscure female object of desire, Alissa's perception of Elisabeth emphasizes the latter's physical strength and vitality.[8] The female gaze here sees the other woman's body as inseparable from her potential status as an active female subject and thus disrupts the subject/object dichotomy of the heterosexual look. From the outset, the relationship between the two female figures is characterized by a sense of proximity and mutual involvement with each other. Thus, for instance, Alissa's initial gaze at Elisabeth is mirrored in the latter's 'discovery' of Alissa's face:

> Elisabeth brings her deckchair closer to Alissa and sits down again. They are close. Elisabeth Alione's eyes are very light. The strain of looking at Alissa is very visible. That's it: Elisabeth Alione is discovering Alissa's face.[9]

At a textual level, this pattern of reciprocity is inscribed through a variety of stylistic features. The repeated use of reflexive constructions, such as 'they look at each other' or 'they smile at each other', implies a relationship of mutual exchange in which the two women are simultaneously active and passive, perceiver and perceived. Similarly, the repetition of sentences attributing the same gestures to both women[10] contributes to the process of identification which ultimately transforms Alissa as well as Elisabeth: while their relationship enables Elisabeth to awaken from her mental and physical paralysis, it allows Alissa to transcend the boundaries of her own identity and to experience herself, at least temporarily, as part of the other woman. This receptiveness to the other is underscored by the interchangeable use of personal pronouns, particularly effective in the scene where Alissa speaks to Max Thor *as if* she were

Elisabeth, directly identifying with the other's suffering by adopting the first person pronoun.[11] The foregrounding of these textual devices recalls Bonnie Zimmerman's model for a lesbian critical reading which 'proposes the blurring of boundaries, between self and other, subject and object ... as the lesbian moment in any text.'[12]

Such a blurring of boundaries is highlighted in one of the most crucial scenes towards the end of *Détruire dit-elle* which shows Alissa and Elisabeth in front of a mirror. The mirror here becomes a central figure for female intersubjectivity and lesbian desire. As such it subverts the conventional functions of the mirror metaphor in patriarchal discourses. If the woman as 'other' has been represented in such discourses as a mirror for the male 'self', in Duras's text the mirror sets up the possibility of the mutual recognition between women as female subjects. Their relationship, moreover, calls into question dominant representations of the mirror as symbolic of female narcissism, for the construct of the narcissistic woman, gazing at herself or her female double, presupposes a subject/object split between the perceiver and the perceived. It assumes, furthermore, that the object is merely an imaginary projection of the subject and thus deprived of any independent existence. Neither of these assumptions is applicable to *Détruire dit-elle*: any initial subject/object divisions between the female characters are gradually broken down so that, during the mirror scene, both women are located in the subject position. This is underlined by the repeated use of the plural subject pronoun 'we' to denote their shared identity as women.[13] Duras's text creates a web of resemblances between Alissa and Elisabeth which suggest a crossing of boundaries between 'self' and 'other', and not a denial of the 'other' in favour of the narcissistic 'self'. Thus, Elisabeth's progressive identification with Alissa is reflected in the latter's gesture of cutting her hair so as to resemble Elisabeth even further. If, in heterosexual relations, desire is seen to depend on the construction of gendered oppositions, Alissa's love for Elisabeth is based on similarity and proximity. By defining herself and Elisabeth as women and by expressing her love for Elisabeth, Alissa confirms that her desire is, by definition, lesbian and counters the heterosexual assumption that being a woman and loving women is a contradiction in terms.

Despite the reciprocal dimension of their relationship, Elisabeth's feelings towards Alissa are ambiguous, as her growing affinity with the other woman is accompanied by an all-pervasive sense of fear. This becomes particularly evident in relation to the figure of the forest which, linked with the breaking of taboos, is like an imaginary place beyond the patriarchal law that prohibits sexual desire between women. It is interesting to note here that Duras has described the forest as representing a specifically female space 'that men are afraid of and which they massacre'.[14] Whilst Alissa, who is already 'marginal' to the law, repeatedly invites the other woman to go to the forest, Elisabeth confesses that it terrifies her.[15] This phobia is then projected on to Alissa herself: 'I'm afraid, says Elisabeth Alione. I'm afraid of Alissa. Where is she?'[16] As Marcelle Marini has suggested, desire between women in Duras can be seen as a form of resistance to the patriarchal order and signals a return to what Marini calls 'the territory of the feminine'. This return is often prevented, however, by woman's fear of transgressing social and sexual norms and by the ensuing feelings of guilt: 'A guilt that is always inscribed within this return to the feminine territory from which she feels exiled, a guilt to which she always subscribes at some point'.[17] If the female relationship in *Détruire dit-elle* subverts dominant configurations of gender and sexuality by introducing a lesbian element into the text, Elisabeth's self-imposed separation from Alissa and her hasty departure with her husband might suggest that the closing sections affirm the repression of homosexuality. And yet, whilst Elisabeth's fear of lesbian desire is allied with her perception that Alissa must be 'mad',[18] during the penultimate scene of the text Elisabeth herself now claims that she is becoming mad.[19] Furthermore, she now takes part in Alissa's simultaneously destructive and liberatory role by 'vomiting' and thus effectively expelling the repressive forces of her previous existence. Through a series of metonymic associations, Elisabeth becomes increasingly identified with precisely those aspects of Alissa which signal the latter's transgressive function in the text. If Elisabeth is unable as yet to face the consequences of her transformation, her encounter with the other woman has at least enabled her to envisage her own subjectivity.

While the female couple in *Détruire dit-elle* contributes to the dismantling of dominant constructions of sexual difference, this subversive function is also attributed to the two male figures, as well as to the relationship between Alissa and Stein. The same textual devices which highlight the similarities between the two women are deployed in the construction of the relationship between Stein and Max Thor, the use of mirrors, interchangeable subject pronouns and speaking positions creating a similarly powerful bond. This sense of empathy between men disrupts the dominant gender paradigm and, as Philippe Sollers has pointed out, lends a certain homoerotic dimension to the central male relationship in the text.[20] A similar complicity is apparent between Stein and Alissa who also undermine gender distinctions. Both characters are so complex and ambiguous that the concept of 'gender' itself is rendered meaningless. The name Stein, reminiscent of Lol V. Stein, adds to this ambiguity. Throughout the text, Stein is seen to oppose the notion of masculine rationality by sharing Alissa's uncanny intuitive perceptions. As their identities become increasingly indistinct, it is impossible to define either character as active or passive, masculine or feminine, subject or object. In *Les parleuses* Marguerite Duras referred to this 'androgynous' quality that emanates from Stein and Alissa, saying that she nearly chose a woman to play the role of Stein in the film version of *Détruire dit-elle*.[21] The mirror structures which operate throughout this text effectively destroy the binary oppositions underlying dominant definitions of heterosexuality as radical difference. Regardless of the assumed biological sex of the protagonists, *Détruire* ultimately privileges an 'erotics of sameness', to use James Williams's term, by dismantling patriarchal power structures which rely on the positioning of women as 'Other'. Therefore, Duras's text not only deconstructs 'gender', but also discrete categories of 'sexuality', as the boundaries between heterosexuality and homosexuality become blurred. The ending of *Détruire dit-elle* seems to point to a future world devoid of all identities, reminiscent of the indifferentiation of Monique Wittig's utopian fiction. Lesbian eroticism plays a crucial role in this revolutionary project, for the disintegration of asymmetrical gender categories is an essential precondition for the emergence of a female desiring subject and hence the possibility of love between women. The importance of androgyny and bisexuality in *Détruire dit-elle* indicates that, in this text at least, Duras is moving beyond any fixed binary divisions of gender, sex and sexuality. Therefore, lesbian textuality in *Détruire dit-elle* can be understood both literally, as textual patterns representing female homoeroticism, and figuratively, as a metaphor for the transgression in this text of the dualistic structures of gendered narratives.

A similarly ambiguous conjunction of identity and non-identity reappears in the scenario of the film *La femme du Gange*. This text can perhaps best be described as a sequel to *L'amour* and includes a combination of elements from *Le ravissement de Lol V. Stein*, *Le vice-consul* and *Détruire dit-elle*. Moreover, the prominent use of two female voices anticipates the film *India Song*. Like *India Song*, *La femme du Gange* is composed of two dissociated and autonomous scripts, 'the film of the image' and 'the film of the Voices'. Contrary to dominant cinematographic conventions which tend to privilege image over sound, there are several indications that Duras attaches particular importance to the interplay between the two female voices. First, the noun 'Voices' is consistently emphasized by the use of capitalisation, whereas 'image' is not. Secondly, the women's voices, far from simply fulfilling the subordinate function of providing a reassuring commentary on the images, subvert the stability of representational categories themselves. It is in these terms that Duras described the role of the voices in the preface of the script: 'They are not off-screen Voices either, in the usual sense of the term: they do not facilitate the progress of the film. On the contrary, they obstruct, disrupt it'.[22] This disturbing aspect of the female voices is highlighted, furthermore, by Duras's contrasting commentaries on the two 'films'. Whereas 'the film of the image' is described as planned, structured and coherent, 'the film of the Voices' conveys something elusive, of an unknown or buried origin, and which exceeds concious control.[23] The use of voices instead of visual representations of women effectively destroys the voyeuristic apparatus inherent in the construction of filmic images of women in mainstream patriarchal cinema. If the latter positions women as objects of the controlling gaze of the spectator, in Duras's film the women are neither visible to the spectator nor aware of his/her presence: THEY ARE TALKING TO EACH OTHER. THEY ARE UNAWARE OF THE SPECTATOR'S PRESENCE.[24]

The self-contained quality of the female voices in *La femme du Gange* is reminiscent of the relationship between Alissa and Elisabeth in *Détruire dit-elle* who, in several key scenes in the text/film, talk to each other without intervention from the male characters. The links between the two texts are reinforced, moreover, in so far as the repeated declaration of love and desire addressed by 'Voice 2' to 'Voice 1' echoes that of Alissa to Elisabeth.[25] However, unlike the earlier text, *La femme du Gange* explicitly inscribes lesbian desire as mutual:

> The Voices: the other film. WOMEN'S VOICES. Very young, twins, one burnt, the other still alive. Intertwined, they resemble each other. They come from a nocturnal space that seems high up, a balcony above the emptiness, above everything. They are joined together by desire. Desire each other.[26]

The fact that the two 'twin' voices are said to come from a 'nocturnal space' echoes the earlier comment on the unknown origin of 'the film of the Voices'. This sense of mystery and obscurity surrounding relationships between women is a recurring feature in Duras's works, appearing not only in *La femme du Gange*, but also in *Détruire dit-elle* and *L'amant de la Chine du Nord*. From a psychoanalytic perspective, the consistency of this pattern may be understood as an indication of the patriarchal repression of the pre-oedipal mother/daughter relationship and, by extension, of all female relationships. Thus, Freud described the original female bond as 'so grey with age and shadowy and almost impossible to revivify that it was as if it had succumbed to an especially inexorable repression'.[27] In *La femme du Gange*, then, the disturbing force of the voices might signal the return of this repression through the expression of lesbian desire which undermines the stability of the fixed subject/object positions of the patriarchal Symbolic. The figure of the female 'twins' in *La femme du Gange* provides a homoerotic variation on the Durassian theme of incest and adds further substance to a configuration of desire which derives more from the recognition of resemblances than the construction of oppositions. While it is true that the figure of the twin breaks down boundaries between separate identities, in *La femme du Gange* this process of deconstruction is taken one step further, for if twins are usually seen as reflections of each other, in Duras's 'film of the Voices' the mirror image itself as the basis for identification has been replaced by the more archaic echo of the intertwined female voices. Indeed, the 'film of the Voices', with its diffuse quality and its emphasis on sound rather than on vision, precedes the categories of representation and identity. In this context the voice in *La femme du Gange* recalls the music in the closing section of *Détruire dit-elle* which dissolves patterns of sameness and difference in an undifferentiated flow of sound. As in *Détruire dit-elle*, furthermore, the interchangeability of subject positions in *La femme du Gange* means that neither of the women can be slotted into fixed categories of identity. Thus, whereas the early sections of the text cast 'Voice 2' as possessing knowledge and memory and 'Voice 1' as lacking them, these positions are quickly reversed, as the two voices become interchangeable: 'Voices. They are reversed: The one who knew no longer knows. The one who asked questions informs.'[28]

The exchanges between the voices take place in the post-apocalyptic world which follows the fire at S. Thala in *L'amour*. Whereas some of the figures in the 'film of the image' already appeared in *L'amour*, 'the film of the Voices' begins by retelling the scene at the ball, central to *Le ravissement de Lol V. Stein*. In *La femme du Gange*, however, the story of the three lovers seems to function primarily as a mediating force which facilitates communication between the Voices. Talking about the triangle of desire between Lol, Michael Richardson and Anne-Marie Stretter gradually leads them to speak of their own desire. Even though the 'film of the Voices' echoes and reassembles textual elements from both *Le ravissement* and *Le vice-consul*, it is not possible to link *La femme du Gange* directly with either of these two novels. Certain details, particularly concerning the central characters, are similar but not identical. Through the Voices and their dialogue, therefore, Duras foregrounds the ambiguity of resemblances which cannot be accommodated in a conceptual framework where phenomena are either identical to, or radically different from, each other. Such ambiguity is reinforced by the alternation in the text between the presence and absence of the feminine plural pronoun to designate the voices who are, paradoxically, both female and genderless.

To what extent, then, are the Voices in *La femme du Gange* still associated with 'women'? And if they are not endowed with any gendered identity, how could their desire be described as 'lesbian'? The very fact that this central female presence appears in the disembodied form of the voice militates against any interpretation of either 'woman' or 'lesbian' in Duras's text as being primarily predicated on the body. Duras herself further reinforced this paradox with her comments on *La Femme du Gange* in *Les parleuses*. Whereas, on the one hand, she claimed that the two voices were *not* women,[29] on the other hand, in response to Xavière Gauthier's question as to why she chose female rather than male voices, she replied that the latter would play a role and that they would not be immersed in the same 'passivity' as female voices.[30] As Duras explains in a subsequent passage in *Les parleuses*, 'passivity', like 'silence', is to be understood in a political sense, as an expression of opposition to all forms of power, including patriarchal power. The choice of female rather than male voices to convey such resistance suggests, therefore, that in *La femme du Gange* gender distinctions have become dissociated from anatomical sex categories and function primarily to represent historical and political, rather than biological, differences. However, such gendered identities are merely provisional, as ultimately all identities are dissolved in an undifferentiated circulation of desire which is described as 'whole, deadly'[31] and annihilates the individual 'self'. Thus, the 'murder' of 'voice 1' by 'voice 2' corresponds to the reduction of Lol V. Stein's identity to the letters LVS as well as to the breakdown of self-boundaries which characterizes the group of figures referred to as 'the madmen'. Like the voices, this group belongs to an archaic, pre-symbolic universe where dualistic concepts giving rise to the construction of identities do not as yet exist: 'An animal-like compassion that stems from a state of loving—the first automatism—when the impulse to think oneself is not yet possible'.[32]

The two voices in *La femme du Gange*, although still recognizable as female, contribute to the disintegration in this text of all fixed definitions of being. As in *Détruire dit-elle*, lesbian desire and textuality blur the borderlines between separate categories of identity, in particular the male/female, self/other oppositions of the patriarchal Symbolic order. At the same time, if 'sex' and 'gender' merge into an undifferentiated 'androgyny', then the boundaries between heterosexuality and homosexuality also become destabilised. Historically speaking, this particular representation of lesbian desire in Durassian texts of the late 1960s and early 1970s could be seen to coincide with the radical feminist current dominant within French feminism at that time which also sought to undermine fixed patriarchal notions of gender and sexuality. Furthermore, by breaking down oppositional categories of sexuality in these texts, Duras indirectly questions the privileged position of heterosexuality over homosexuality. On the other hand, her representations of lesbianism as a preliminary step towards androgyny and bisexuality ignore the historical dimensions of lesbian relationships as sexual, emotional and political experiences specific to women. Since this specificity is itself put into question, lesbian desire is in danger of becoming simply reabsorbed into existing heterosexual structures.

Indeed, over the ten-year period following *La femme du Gange*, heterosexuality predominates in the work of Duras, virtually eclipsing any possibility of female couples. It is not until the publication of *L'amant* in 1984 and *L'amant de la Chine du Nord* in 1991 that female homoeroticism reappears through the relationship between the narrator and Hélène Lagonelle. But whereas in *L'amant* the memory of Hélène is condensed into a few pages, in the 1991 text it is evoked much more extensively. The two versions also differ in so far as the relationship in the latter is dramatized through the dialogues between the two girls, whilst in the former it is merely recounted by the dominant first-person narrative voice. If in *L'amant* Hélène appears as the passive object both of the narrative and of the narrator's desire, in *L'amant de la Chine du Nord* this desire is clearly mutual. And whereas in the earlier version the relationship seems to be largely a fantasmatic projection on the part of the narrator, in the later text it is repeatedly described in real physical terms: 'They embrace and remain clasped in each other's arms, kissing silently, loving each other so much.'[33] This physical and emotional reciprocity is entirely absent in *L'amant* where Hélène functions primarily as the third term in the Durassian heterosexual triangle. In *L'amant de la Chine du Nord* lesbian love, initially at least, represents the origin of the narrator's desire as she tells Hélène: 'For me, desire, my first desire, was you.'[34] The strong affinity between the two girls is mirrored, furthermore, in several passages providing intertextual links with other significant female same-sex relationships. Thus, the section describing a lesson at school on the poet Louise Labé focuses rather unusually not on Labé's writing but on her friendship with another woman. This passage is immediately followed by a description of the narrator and Hélène dancing together in the empty corridors of the *Pension Lyautey*, a scene which is strongly reminiscent of the early friendship between Lol and Tatiana in *Le ravissement de Lol V. Stein*. These intertextual echoes lend a retrospective homoerotic dimension to the relationship between Lol and Tatiana which appears only obliquely and implicitly in Duras's 1964 novel.[35] If the brother/sister relationship in *L'amant de la Chine du Nord* provides the model for subsequent heterosexual relations, the bond between the narrator and Hélène Lagonelle is mirrored in numerous relationships between women throughout Duras's work.

However, this expression of love between the two girls is accompanied by their exchanges about the narrator's desire for her brother Paulo, the Chinese lover and their schoolfriend Alice's activities as a prostitute. Initially, this overlapping of homo- and heteroeroticism suggests a blurring of boundaries similar to that in the other texts examined here. Indeed, such boundaries might seem irrelevant in so far as homosexuality, incest, prostitution and the relationship between a white woman and a Chinese man are all forms of sexual transgression in the social context of *L'amant de la Chine du Nord*. It is worth pointing out here that, in an interview in 1980 with *Le Gai Pied*, Duras herself drew an interesting parallel between her own incestuous experience and homosexuality, since both are subject to social prohibitions which she considers to be integral to sexual desire itself.[36] Yet a closer examination of these and subsequent sections in *L'amant de la Chine du Nord* shows that the constant intervention of the heterosexual narrative serves to distance lesbian desire and to reinforce rather than challenge its construction as a hidden, unspeakable passion. Even though Hélène recognises her own duplicity in concealing the truth about their mutual passion,[37] she continues to collude with the dominant narrative by projecting her lesbian feelings on to the men desired by the narrator. Thus, when she claims, rather unconvincingly, that she is attracted first to Paulo and then to the Chinese millionaire, one suspects that this sudden desire stems from her wish to please the narrator and to ensure their continued closeness: 'It's him I desire. It's him. You know. You wanted it.'[38] It is at this point that the central female relationship in *L'amant de la Chine du Nord* becomes reintegrated into the same framework of power relations which characterises heterosexuality in so many texts by Duras. As in *L'amant*, the textual intervention of 'the lover' through the narrator's sexual fantasies re-establishes the familiar Durassian triangle, composed of one male and two female figures. It might appear at first sight that in both texts the patriarchal position of the woman-as-object has been subverted to some extent, in so far as the female narrator remains the dominant subject throughout, expressing her desire to give Hélène to the Chinese man. However, the reciprocal nature which characterises lesbian desire in earlier passages in *L'amant de la Chine du Nord* is entirely absent from the scenes staging the narrator's fantasy. Through her identification with the lover, the narrator herself comes to adopt an imaginary masculine subject position, whereas Hélène is reduced to the status of an exchange object. Indeed, the fantasized relationship between the narrator and the lover is reminiscent of Irigaray's paradigm of 'hom(m)osexual relations' where communication between men functions through the exchange of women.[39] Here the narrator's apparent 'androgyny', combining her 'femininity' vis-à-vis the Chinese lover with her 'masculinity' in relation to Hélène, is quite different from the bisexuality of earlier texts such as *Détruire dit-elle*. For whilst in the latter bisexuality stems from a lesbian deconstruction of asymmetrical gender positions, in *L'amant de la Chine du Nord* these positions are implicitly reinforced through the narrator's affirmation of her control over the other woman. Moreover, the prostitution of the reluctant Hélène[40] reintroduces a certain sadistic dimension noted by James S. Williams in his analysis of similar scenes in *L'amant*, where the narrator's homoerotic desire is allied with her wish to murder Hélène.[41] This ambivalence in Duras's representations of love between women is evident in *L'amant* and *L'amant de la Chine du Nord* and is compounded by the ultimate rejection in both texts of lesbian love in favour of heterosexuality. Indeed, Duras's overt celebrations of heterosexuality in the 1980s might be interpreted, as Williams has argued, as a 'defence against the threat of homosexual indifferentiation'.[42] I would suggest that Duras's ambivalence in this respect and her privileging of heterosexuality might also be connected to her fear of close relationships between women, stemming from the suffering she experienced as a result of maternal betrayal and rejection.[43] The co-presence of desire and fear in female relationships, although present in earlier works, is particularly poignant in *L'amant* and *L'amant de la Chine du Nord*, given the central importance of the mother/daughter relationship in both texts. It is as if the narrator needs to distance herself from the intensity of her feelings for other women, in this instance Hélène Lagonelle. Such distancing occurs either through sadomasochistic fantasies, allowing the narrator to affirm herself by her position of dominance, or through the intervention of a male figure whose presence disrupts the immediacy of the female relationship.

Despite the overt heterosexuality of Duras's texts it is possible to trace an underlying lesbian thematics and textuality. Patterns of female friendship and desire recur throughout her work from the late 1950s to the early 1990s, creating a lesbian intertextuality which links together texts like *Le ravissement de Lol V. Stein*, *Détruire dit-elle*, *La femme du Gange* and *L'amant de la Chine du Nord*. This continuity of relationships provides a certain female 'genealogy', to use Irigaray's term, and maintains a sense of kinship between women in Duras. The representation of love between women in all the texts discussed in this chapter offers a portrayal of active female desire and of women as desiring subjects. In earlier texts, such as *Détruire dit-elle*, moreover, lesbian desire was instrumental in the deconstruction of fixed gender identities, implicitly questioning the dominant status of heterosexuality and advocating instead a kind of genderless polysexuality. However, in later texts, such challenges disappear from the work of Duras as the prevalent gender models are ultimately reaffirmed in texts such as *L'amant de la Chine du Nord*. The fear of love between women, which is already implicit in *Détruire dit-elle*, becomes intensified in later works where it is expressed as Duras's desire to 'kill' her female figures, especially those to whom she felt most attached. Such metaphorical assassinations are accomplished in three ways: through sadomasochistic fantasies, the reabsorption of homoeroticism into heterosexual modalities, and the textual murder of her most important female characters. The case of Anne-Marie Stretter is exemplary in this respect and encapsulates the ambivalent conjunction of desire and aggression in Duras's representations of love between women. Duras herself commented on her feelings towards Anne-Marie Stretter in the following terms: 'I had a kind of mad passion for this woman ... and I said to myself: "She must die". That's it. Because she touched me so deeply.'[44] The gradual elimination of female same-sex desire can be seen, therefore, as a defence against the perceived threat it poses to female heterosexual identity. And yet Duras's fictional texts as well as her autobiographical statements reveal a paradoxical wish both to preserve and to destroy patriarchal concepts of gender and sexuality. The ambiguous nature of many of her female characters who fluctuate between different sexual identities confirms this paradox, and militates strongly against any unproblematic heterosexual reading of Duras.

Notes

(N.B.: All translations from the French texts are my own.)

1 Two notable exceptions in this respect are James S. Williams, *The Erotics of Passage: Pleasure, Politics, and Form in the Later Work of Marguerite Duras*, Liverpool University Press/St Martin's Press, 1997, and Emma Wilson, *Sexuality and the Reading Encounter: Identity and Desire in Proust, Duras, Tournier and Cixous*, Oxford, Clarendon Press, 1996, in particular '"Mon histoire de Lol V. Stein": Duras, Reading, and Amnesia' (pp. 163–91).

2 Adrienne Rich, 'Compulsory Heterosexuality and Lesbian Existence', *Signs*, Vol. 5, No. 4 (Summer 1980), pp. 631–60; p. 650.

3 Rich, 'Compulsory Heterosexuality', p. 648.

4 Marilyn R. Farwell, 'Heterosexual Plots and Lesbian Subtexts: Toward a Theory of Lesbian Narrative Space', in *Lesbian Texts and Contexts: Radical Revisions*, ed. K. Jay and J. Glasgow, New York University Press, 1990, pp. 91–103; p. 93.

5 See Bonnie Zimmerman, 'Lesbians Like This and That: Some Notes on Lesbian Criticism for the Nineties', in *New Lesbian Criticism*, ed. S. Munt, Harvester, 1992, pp. 1–15; p. 9.

6 Agnes Porter-Beaudry, '*Détruire dit-elle*: Destruction or Deconstruction', *International Fiction Review*, Vol. 8, No. 1 (1981), pp. 41–46; p. 44.

7 Michèle Druon, 'Le Miroir à deux faces: ambiguïtés de la figure du double dans *Détruire dit-elle* de Marguerite Duras', *Stanford French Review*, Vol. 9 (1985), pp. 223–39; p. 235.

8 Marguerite Duras, *Détruire dit-elle*, Paris, Minuit, 1969, pp. 53–54.

9 Duras, *Détruire dit-elle*, p. 61: 'Elisabeth rapproche la chaise longue d'Alissa et se rassied. Elles sont proches. Elisabeth Alione a des yeux très clairs. L'effort du regard vers Alissa est très visible. Voici: Elisabeth Alione découvre le visage d'Alissa.'

10 Duras, *Détruire dit-elle*, p. 37.

11 Duras, *Détruire dit-elle*, p. 72.

12 Zimmerman, 'Lesbians Like This and That', p. 11.

13 Duras, *Détruire dit-elle*, p. 100.

14 Marguerite Duras and Michelle Porte, *Les lieux de Marguerite Duras*, Paris, Minuit, 1977, p. 16: 'dont les hommes ont peur et qu'ils massacrent.'

15 Duras, *Détruire dit-elle*, p. 65.

16 Duras, *Détruire dit-elle*, p. 95: 'J'ai peur, dit Elisabeth Alione. J'ai peur d'Alissa. Où est elle?'

17 Marcelle Marini, *Territoires du féminin. Avec Marguerite Duras*, Paris, Minuit, 1977, p. 45: 'Culpabilité toujours inscrite dans ce retour au territoire féminin dont elle se sent exilée, culpabilité à laquelle elle souscrit toujours à un certain moment.'

18 Duras, *Détruire dit-elle*, p. 102.

19 Duras, *Détruire dit-elle*, p. 109.

20 Philippe Sollers, 'Duras "Telle Quelle"', *Le Nouvel Observateur*, 12 January 1970, p. 36.

21 Marguerite Duras and Xavière Gauthier, *Les parleuses*, Paris, Minuit, 1974, p. 22.

22 Marguerite Duras, *Nathalie Granger, suivi de La femme du Gange*, Paris, Gallimard, 1973, p. 103: 'Ce ne sont pas non plus des Voix off, dans l'acception habituelle du mot: elles ne facilitent pas le déroulement du film, au contraire, elles l'entravent, le troublent.'

23 Duras, *La femme du Gange*, p. 103.

24 Duras, *La femme du Gange*, p. 103: 'ELLES SE PARLENT. ELLES IGNORENT LA PRESENCE DU SPECTATEUR' (original capitals).

25 Duras, *La femme du Gange*, pp. 144 and 153.

26 Duras, *La femme du Gange*, p. 105: 'Les Voix: l'autre film. VOIX DE FEMMES. Très jeunes, jumelles, l'une brûlée, l'autre encore vivante. Entremêlées elles se ressemblent. Elles viennent d'un espace nocturne, comme élevé, d'un balcon au-dessus du vide, du tout. Elles sont liées par le désir. Se désirent.'

27 Sigmund Freud, *On Sexuality*, The Pelican Freud Library, Vol. 7, ed. Angela Richards, Harmondsworth, Penguin, 1977, p. 373.

28 Duras, *La femme du Gange*, p. 127: 'Voix. Elles s'inversent: Celle qui savait ne sait plus. Celle qui demandait, informe.'

29 Duras and Gauthier, *Les parleuses*, p. 69.

30 Duras and Gauthier, *Les parleuses*, p. 71.

31 Duras, *La femme du Gange*, p. 183: 'entier, mortel'.

32 Duras, *La femme du Gange*, p. 172: 'Compassion animale issue d'un état de l'amour—premier automatisme—le mouvement de se penser n'étant pas encore possible.'

33 Marguerite Duras, *L'amant de la Chine du Nord*, Paris, Gallimard, 1991, p. 57: 'Elles s'embrassent et elles restent embrassées, enlacées, à s'embrasser, à se taire, à s'aimer fort.'

34 Duras, *L'amant de la Chine du Nord*, p. 66: 'Pour moi, le désir, le premier désir, ça a été toi.'

35 See Leslie Hill, *Marguerite Duras: Apocalyptic Desires*, London and New York, Routledge, 1993, pp. 78–79.

36 Marguerite Duras, 'The Thing' (interview with Rolland Thélu), *Le Gai Pied*, No. 20 (November 1980), p. 16.

37 Duras, *L'amant de la Chine du Nord*, p. 58.

38 Duras, *L'amant de la Chine du Nord*, p. 92: 'C'est lui que je désire. C'est lui. Tu le sais. Tu le voulais.'

39 Duras, *L'amant de la Chine du Nord*, p. 183–84.

40 Duras, *L'amant de la Chine du Nord*, p. 92.

41 Williams, *The Erotics of Passage*, p. 73.

42 Williams, *The Erotics of Passage*, p. 158.

43 See, for instance, Marguerite Duras, *Le monde extérieur. Outside II*, Paris, POL, 1993, pp. 194–206.

44 Suzanne Lamy and André Roy (eds), *Marguerite Duras à Montréal*, Montreal, Editions Spirale, 1981, p. 33: 'Je vivais une sorte d'amour fou pour cette femme … et je me suis dit: "Il faut qu'elle meure". Voilà. Parce qu'elle m'a tellement atteinte.'

CHAPTER 9

Life and Death Upon the Page: Marguerite Duras and Roland Barthes

James Creech

Reviewing Edmund White's recent biography of Marcel Proust, Peter Ackroyd offers a text-book example of critical legerdemain that is lethal for gay writers. It will introduce us indirectly to the anti-homosexual tactics of Marguerite Duras:

> If there is a weakness [in this biography], it is a tendency upon White's part to assert the gay life and consciousness of Proust; it is perhaps understandable in a novelist and critic who has written extensively on gay themes, but in a subtle and unintentional way, it diminishes Proust's significance. One of the secrets of the biographical art lies in the extent to which the biographer can intuit the personal stirrings of the individual consciousness; it is not a question of admiring, or liking, the subject of the narrative. It is a question of making him, or her, live upon the page.[1]

Ackroyd's writing here is uncharacteristically murky, probably because the thinking behind it would not survive too much clarity of expression. If we dust it off and lift it up to the light, the core idea might look something like this: we readers can't tolerate too much insistence on Proust's gayness; it kills our interest in him. Edmund White 'asserts' Proust's gayness. Consequently, Proust doesn't 'live upon the page' of this biography.

It is not altogether clear why Ackroyd thinks any of this is true. One thing is clear, however: the extraneous business about 'biographical art' is like the squid's ink, as is the later suggestion that the word 'gay' is anachronistic when applied to Proust.[2] These gambits function mainly to camouflage the egregious insinuation that a gay biographer who 'asserts' Proust's 'gay life and consciousness' has failed to 'intuit the personal stirrings' of his subject, and thus, has failed to make him live upon the page. It is the other way around, of course: Edmund White asserts Proust's gayness *because* he intuits his personal stirrings so keenly. Indeed, for some of us this is a big part of what makes Proust come alive in White's biography. If indeed Proust's life or death 'upon the page' is in the balance here, Ackroyd has not claimed that the outcome is based on the truth or falsity of what White has asserted. Truth is not the issue. Proust's sexuality is not disputed. Assertion of it, however, is. And as a penalty for that assertion, Ackroyd is quite prepared to withdraw his recognition of Proust's significance.[3] Thus, it is not really the case that Proust will have died upon the page if biographers persist in asserting his gayness. Rather, the critic will have killed him off by turning away, by downgrading his importance. That is the death threat that lies behind Ackroyd's insinuations. In this sense, the apparently constative mode of his discourse actually serves to disguise a performative. In other words, lurking just beneath Ackroyd's earnest concern that we might soon notice that poor Proust is dead upon the page is a hint at the critic's power to kill him off, to declare him insignificant, unless White and his kind lay off the gay thing.

If I pause so long over this contorted little paragraph, apparently miles away from my immediate concerns here, it is not because finding the pea in a homophobic shell game is interesting or challenging in itself. Rather, I want to introduce an argument concerning the power that this kind of extortion has wielded over gay writers, readers, and critics in a variety of settings. It is a power that has often been sustained precisely by the deceptively casual linking of gayness and impotence, gayness and deadness in a constative mode, not out of malice, but in response to higher concerns such as 'biographical art', or literature itself, or psychological health. In my experience, permutations of this extortion have been most often practiced by educated people who wouldn't otherwise dream of harbouring illiberal views. This is particularly the case in France where, beyond garden-variety homophobia, the long-standing cultural imperative of universalism has often overwhelmed the perspective of non-universal, minority, or queer sexual identities as such. In an interview in 1990, the same Edmund White, fresh from living in France for a number of years, reflected on the consequences of French universalism from his distinctively non-French perspective as a self-professed gay writer:

> There is no French Jewish novel, no French Black novel—and there's not a single writer in France who would be willing to call himself a gay writer … The first European Gay Literature Conference was held in London two years

> ago [in 1988]. For that first one Yves Navarre ... Dominique Fernandez ... and Renaud Camus ... were invited. They all refused. Not one single gay or lesbian representative came from France, except for Geneviève Pastre, who had translated Sappho ... A couple of people who were invited sent angry letters, saying that they were gay and writers but not *gay writers* ... I don't want to attack the French or imply that they're all in the closet, because they're not: they think that we're reactionary because we're clinging to a gay identity that cuts us off from the mainstream of human experience ... *Le Monde* recently ran a lengthy portrait of me and just barely mentioned that my books might be of interest to gay people.[4]

And White is right. In France, homosexuality has rarely been affirmed as an interesting or valuable subject position, nor has it been easily or fully credited for its importance to literature and its production. Within the sphere of theory or philosophy beyond literary concerns, to the degree that homosexuality has been dealt with at all, counter-hegemonic thought in modern France has preferred instead to queer the universal itself. Postmodern theory has sought to discern in the universal whole a community of differences, just as identity itself has become the site of its own impossibility.[5]

In such a context, then, it is not necessarily a sign of homophobia that sexual minority in itself has rarely been acknowledged as a value worthy of literary expression, or as subjectivity with which one might be invited to identify, or as something that might bring desire and 'life' to the page. But, at the same time, French universalism can also provide a rather comfortable screen for those who are inclined to resist homosexual 'identity' for reasons that are not necessarily admirable. Marguerite Duras occupies an interesting place within this landscape because she exemplifies and renders explicit the homophobic potential that lies within these postmodern versions of French universalism. As Martin Crowley has recently written, the homosexual in Duras's writings up to the mid-1970s was an example of the many 'marginal figures whose identity is presented as in some sense fragmented, and who are celebrated on the basis of this supposed dispersal', and who are thus endowed with the potential for 'political and philosophical upheaval'.[6] Later, however, even as the concern for 'upheaval' and 'loss of self' remain the same, the homosexual's membership in the fraternity of marginals who contribute to those ends is withdrawn, and homosexuality becomes the object of a rather familiar attack.

Although she was hardly a theoretician, Duras's notion of the erotic is clearly informed by this current of French thought, and by a litany of subjacent theoretical imperatives which it has produced along the way.[7] Texts like *La maladie de la mort*, later reworked into *Les yeux bleus cheveux noirs*, suggest the influence of some of the most important theorists of the postwar period

(Lacan, Blanchot, Bataille).[8] In such an intellectual context, Duras often wrote of the blissful and excruciating conjunctions of the possible and the impossible which accompany '*différence*' in the erotic sphere. More explicitly than others, however, she insisted on the anti-homosexual corollaries that, unless one has the political will to resist them, can be developed from the theoretical discourse that defines large segments of the French intellectual ecology.[9] Against this necessary theoretical backdrop, however, I would like to propose a rather different focus in the reading of Duras that follows. I propose to look through her writing toward an inter-textual, or even extra-textual and interpersonal scene that, precisely for political reasons, we need to imagine. My perspective here is not French. Only a cross-cultural dialogue could suggest, as I intend to do, that Duras's invocations of 'difference' might have contributed, however modestly, to the virtual exclusion of explicitly homosexual speech from avant-garde theory. Such an argument is not subject to conclusive proof, of course, but a certain plausibility might be constructed if we look for a moment at the concrete example of her attitudes toward Roland Barthes. Certain aspects of this relationship will be similar to the one linking Ackroyd and Proust (and White), except that Duras participated in an extortionary logic which, as I will imagine it, must have deeply affected the life and writing of a contemporary.

Roland Barthes never came out on the page during his lifetime.[10] He was a gay man, but he never alluded to his sexuality in any personal or explicit way in his published writings.[11] One might argue that, in this respect, Barthes was hardly an exception. But that generalization doesn't hold up when we consider that Barthes's timidity about gay self-nomination, especially in one who wrote so intimately about himself, contrasts with earlier French examples of intellectual and erotic verve, fused into an unyielding self-authorization to speak *because* one is queer.[12] In contrast to, say, Gide, how pale are Barthes's remarks on the 'power of bliss of a perversion' ('pouvoir de jouissance d'une perversion'). In an ever-so-brief paragraph of *Roland Barthes par Roland Barthes* (1975), he ventured no more than this about homosexuality: 'Law, Doxa, Science don't want to understand that perversion, quite simply, *makes happy*.' But just at this point where he could have confronted that law by acknowledging 'the goddess H.' as *his* perversion, with inflections and specificities all his own—he is writing autobiography, after all—Barthes decides instead to 'further specify' ('préciser davantage') by rendering his perversion utterly imprecise. His 'gayness' is immediately dematerialized and converted into a quantitative, impersonal and textual notion of 'surplus': '[Perversion] produces a *plus*: I am more sensitive, more perceptive, more loquacious, better entertained, etc.

and in this *plus* difference comes to take up residence (and thus, the Text of life, life as text).'[13]

The best-known work to date on Barthes's reticence to speak as a gay man is D. A. Miller's *Bringing Out Roland Barthes*, in which one can read the following incisive analysis:

> Barthes's relation to the act of gay self-nomination proves nothing short of phobic. 'To proclaim yourself something [wrote Barthes] is always to speak at the behest of a vengeful Other, to enter into his discourse, to argue with him, to seek from him a scrap of identity' ... Barthes never with greater docility takes on a prescribed social identity than here in his ostensible argument against doing so. Even supposing a single individual refusal of a name could arrest the whole social process of nomination by which names are given out, it would remain the case that when the name in question is *that name*, whose most diffuse prejudicial effects depend on its *not* being pronounced—on its being restricted, quasi-catachrestically, to a system of connotation—then silence, far from guarding a subject against these effects, would leave him all the more destitute of resources for resisting them.[14]

If Barthes felt that '[t]o proclaim yourself something is always to speak at the behest of a vengeful Other', then I suggest that the 'Other' in this case is not just a spectral projection or a philosophical construct. Rather, silence seemed preferable to Barthes because real people—people like Peter Ackroyd—prescribe and extort that silence with a vengeance. Gay self-nomination, in other words, really has been perilous within the discursive world Barthes inhabited, and avant-garde French culture did little during his lifetime to make it safe to be gay upon the page.

In the fleeting passage from *Barthes par Barthes* which we just cited concerning the 'power of bliss of *a* perversion' (not 'my' perversion, not 'this' perversion), Barthes makes the oddly modest claim that perversion produces 'a *plus* ... and in this *plus* difference comes to take up residence' ('un *plus* ... et dans ce *plus* vient se loger la différence'). Thus, not only does Barthes encode his perversion as the goddess H.', not only does he reduce it to a general and impersonal economy of surplus and text, unclaimed by any embodied individual, but he takes the further step of theorizing his own perversion as a site of *différence*. Today this reads like nothing so much as a proleptic defence against the delegitimation of his 'goddess' which Barthes must have anticipated as he made so bold as to whisper its name upon the autobiographical page. In other words, his curtsy to *différence* may serve as a signpost pointing out with some precision just which avatar of the vengeful Other he sensed to be looming on the horizon. We may need to remind ourselves of the extraordinary theoretical investment in the problem of *différence* that had been made by the French intelligentsia at the time Barthes was writing his autobiography. Everyone, even the Marxists led by Althusser, sought to replace the Hegelian privilege of the whole with the revolutionary value of difference. In the sexual sphere more specifically, from Freud to Lacan, the homosexual had virtually always represented a failure to negotiate the challenge and the terror with which the male subject in particular confronted sexual difference construed as a threat of castration.

Again, it is in this context that Barthes sought to claim for homosexuality itself—under the general disguise of 'a perversion'—some of the very prestige that counter-hegemonic theory was granting notions like *différence* and surplus that escapes totalization. Barthes's effort to assimilate perversion itself to *différence* thus might begin to look like a bid for acceptance from his oppressors on their own theoretical terms, a modern avatar of nineteenth-century homosexuals who, as Foucault put it, sought recognition in the vocabulary of homosexuality, 'through the categories by which it was disqualified'.[15] For, by genuflecting at just this moment at the altar of *différence*, Barthes is surely revealing something of the price he was obliged to pay in order even to hint that perversion and its *bonheur* might be his own. Clearly, that price was desexualization and dispersal, as he will himself suggest three pages later: '*Différence*, an insistent and very vaunted word, has value above all because it dispenses with, or triumphs over, conflict. Conflict is sexual, semantic; *différence* is plural, sensual and textual; meaning and sex are principles of construction, of constitution; *différence* is the very allure of a powdery finesse [*poudroiement*], a dispersion, a shimmering.'[16]

Thus, let us turn a newly-invigorated gaze back to Marguerite Duras, Barthes's contemporary who had a few things to say about *différence*, and about Barthes. In *La maladie de la mort*, which appeared shortly after Barthes's death, it is hard to avoid the conclusion that Duras was an exemplary incarnation of the 'vengeful Other' from whom Barthes felt he would have had to beg a few scraps of identity had he chosen to speak as a gay man. Though Duras critics have not always recognized it, this text stages an encounter between a gay man and a presumably straight woman, perhaps indeed reflecting something of Duras's relationship with Yann Andréa which began in August 1980, less than two years before *La maladie de la mort* was published. The unnamed man's homosexuality is never stated outright but remains, as Martin Crowley phrased it, a matter of 'elegant innuendo', or again, 'a whispered enigma, waiting to be outed'.[17] Enigmatic though it indeed was, Duras nevertheless acknowledged later, as she contrasted the text with *Les yeux bleus cheveux noirs*, that *La maladie de la mort* was something of a 'trial' of homosexuality itself.[18] Her brief against queers was so intense, it would seem, that she violated rather blatantly the aesthetics of intransitivity which her writing heretofore had instantiated to such glorious effect.

In *La maladie de la mort*, then, a narrator tells of this present-tense encounter between homosexual man and straight woman in the typical Durassian manner, while addressing the gay man as 'vous'. The man, it seems, has hired the woman in order to experience heterosexual intercourse. His plan is 'to try' for a few days, and maybe for the rest of his life, to have heterosexual sex: 'She asks: Try what? You say: To love.'[19] Things start off rather badly, therefore, with this implication that for a gay man to achieve love his beloved must be a woman, but they proceed quickly to get a good deal worse. The man proceeds to offer explanations of his quest to experience heterosexual sex as an explicit quest to penetrate a vagina 'too'. That is, he explains, he wants now to have the experience of penetrating the vagina just as he usually penetrates the anus, in order to experience the difference: 'You say: … I would like to penetrate there too. And as violently as always. They say that it resists even more, that it's a velvet that resists even more than the void [le vide].'[20] The anal canal provides no resistance because, dixit Duras, it is empty, and thus it recapitulates the void of gay sex which the man is attempting to fill at last by penetrating the real thing. The empty vagina, however, provides a fullness through its velvety resistance which clearly figures the resistance of sexual difference itself. By seeking to penetrate 'there, too', the gay man wants at last to experience the satisfying difference that real difference makes.

But, though the homosexual in Duras's dialogue does seem at times to manage copulation, he still fails. That is, specifically, he can't see—or can't bear seeing—the woman's sexual difference, and thus remains impotent to celebrate it erotically: 'You tell her: You must be very beautiful. She says: I'm here, look, I'm in front of you. You say: I see *nothing*' (my emphasis).[21] The whole weight of the castration model of sexual difference is leveraged on this 'nothing', of course, because it is both female 'lack' which the male subject is unable to tolerate, and at the same time the erotic failure which Duras presents as the consequence of that inability. Clearly, this is the same homosexuality whose 'drama', Lacan tells us, is in 'the fact that it can find no way of becoming grounded in any satisfying action'.[22] It is the homosexuality that Freud in his essay on fetishism will infamously claim is one of the possible consequences of a pervert's inability to overcome the terror 'all men' feel at the sight of 'castrated' female genitals.[23] At first the woman cannot believe that the gay man doesn't desire women: 'You've never desired a woman? … Not one single time, not for an instant?'[24] The gay man's negative answer, his resulting denial of her, brings not the pain of rejection but the calm note of a summary judgment that is no less absolute for being bemused: 'She smiles and says: What a curious thing is a dead man

[*C'est curieux un mort*].'[25] At various moments in this dialogue both characters imagine murdering the other, although Duras disguises the heterosexual woman's violence in a questionable—perhaps even a reprehensible—way. For the man's fantasy of murdering the woman is foregrounded, and by implication connotes the rage of homosexual impotence in the face of sexual difference, or more optimistically, the urge to kill that always underlies desire in Duras. But the woman's murderous performance echoes that of Ackroyd: 'C'est curieux un mort'. Duras's narrative thus concocts an innocence for itself by seeming merely to acknowledge in the constative mode that homosexual desire is dead, 'immobile', an empty void by its very nature. But again, the constative disguises a performative: 'You are dead' in fact means 'I am killing you off'.

Proustian echoes complete more of this theoretical fiction of homosexuality as the pathological denial of difference. Again, it is the narrator who addresses the gay man:

> Surrounding this body [of the woman] is the bedroom. Perhaps it is your personal bedroom. It is inhabited by her, by a woman. You no longer recognize the room. It's emptied of life, you are absent from it, it is lacking someone like you. Only that long and supple moulding of the foreign form on the bed occupies the room now.[26]

Thus the room/self, when invaded by alterity, is no longer recognizable to the gay man. It is 'voided' ('vidée') in the sense that the presence of a woman empties it of all the sameness that the homosexual malady requires. In the Proustian topos of the bedroom—what Marcel calls 'a bedroom that I managed to fill up with my self'[27]—alterity must be banished and replaced by resemblance and sameness, with 'votre pareil', if it is to be tolerable. On and on, Duras's text is constructed on this opposition of life and death, fullness and emptiness, and it labours hard to control the distribution of the opposing terms. Hence the corollary that if the room had been occupied by a male instead of a female lover, then, like the anus itself, it would have been heterosexually—and thus truly—'empty'. And by the same token, the presence of a female lover would have magically filled the room with the same resisting difference that Duras grants to vaginal emptiness. It is only homosexual pathology which inverts the proper distribution of fullness and emptiness, and part of this text's function is clearly to police the allocation of those values. Duras's narrative serves up the 'truth' that one of these 'voids' really is empty, while the other is emptied out by the homosexuality which inevitably results in 'that blandness [*cette fadeur*] … that immobility of your sentiments',[28] qualifications that Duras began around this time to use consistently when referring to homosexuality. The narrator even attributes to the man a characteristic mode of homosexual knowing, distinct and clear, enabled by the stagnant immobility of gay 'death'. In contrast, the straight narrator wants nothing of 'this incurable monotony, the same as itself every day of your life, every night, with its lethal function of failing to love'.[29] The trick, here, is that she is again defining the monotony of homosexual knowing as nothing more than the opposite of a now-orthodox, heterosexual epistemology predicated on difference, on its concomitant mobility, and on a desire that is fuelled and renewed by each heterosexual encounter. But again, a gay-affirmative reading of this dialogue will see that the only 'death' here is the *sentence* of death pronounced by the woman herself when the man, being gay, doesn't desire her as the very instantiation of difference. Take that! *Vous êtes mort.*

In *La maladie de la mort*, however, the poor pervert is entirely acquiescent to these scraps of identity doled out so stingily and with such suppressed rage by the woman.[30] Thus defined, he becomes a supplicant for answers to essential questions to which this text seeks to allow only heterosexual responses: how is real love possible? From what does it emerge? And by extension, can I too love difference instead of loving the deathly, immobilizing, narcissistic same? Repeatedly, even as the man finds the woman completely unknowable (whereas she repeatedly presumes to have absolute knowledge of him and his sickness),[31] Duras actually stages the scene of supplication before a vengeful other for those scraps of identity that Barthes so dreaded. For the man will indeed beg the woman for an answer to this question of how to love, how to be cured, which is the question of life or death that is here folded over on to the question of being straight or gay. And it is in response to this supplication that the ventriloquist-narrator will offhandedly toss the man scraps of identity, precisely as Barthes foretold:

> You ask how the feeling of love might arise. She answers you: Perhaps from a sudden crack in the logic of the universe … You ask: Could the feeling of love arise from other things? *You beg her to say.* She says: From everything, from the flight of a night bird, from sleep … She says: Look. She opens her legs and in the hollow of her spreading legs you finally see black night.[32] (my emphasis)

And later, after the woman has disappeared, it is the voice of the narrator, no longer ventroliquized, which undertakes the litany of summary judgments that can now be addressed directly to the failed man. 'When you cried', the narrator concludes irrevocably, 'you were crying over yourself alone, and not over the admirable impossibility of joining with her across the difference that separates you'.[33] The gavel has pounded. There is no appeal.

Perhaps now, in the light of this preliminary sketch of the uses to which

Duras puts the topos of *différence*, we can begin to imagine the effect on Barthes of these set pieces of theoretical homophobia present in Duras's fiction as if by osmosis. No gay man in Barthes's position within the intellectual world of Paris could not have remained unaffected by the discursive universe which produces such enunciations. What could have been the effect on Barthes of her claim, in *La vie matérielle*, that '[*i*]*n heterosexuality*, there is no solution. Man and woman are irreconcilable and it's this impossible attempt, renewed with each new love, which makes for *its grandeur* [qui en fait *la grandeur*]' (my emphasis).[34] On the one side of this great divide of post-Lacanian French thought there is the impossible heterosexual '*relation*' whose grandeur stems from its courage to affirm—in the teeth of the impossibility of ever resolving—sexual difference. Having recycled this quasi-theological 'truth', Duras will now make explicit its omnipresent obverse by rehearsing yet again the corollary of homosexual squalor, narcissism and death. All Duras can imagine homosexuality doing, consequently, is to collapse upon itself: 'The passion of homosexuality is homosexuality. What the homosexual loves—as his lover, his fatherland, his creation, his native earth—is not his lover. It's homosexuality itself'.[35] These enormities are uttered (as are those of Ackroyd) with that particular calm which comes from the assumption that it will not be contested and that its presumed narratees will find it 'receivable'. Duras utters them with the knowledge that they resonate with the theoretical investments of an intelligentsia. In France, they could be uttered with a kind of knowledge that those in a position to protest had not done so and would not do so. And to the extent that such enormities are found acceptable, then one must ask whether there are any homophobic absurdities that can be rejected? For example, if one assumes a discursive universe in which such a proposition can be presumed receivable, is there any basis—*within* that universe—to get upset when, in *La vie matérielle*, Duras attacks Barthes by claiming that a writer who hasn't known women cannot even have a real literary career? That such a pusillanimous person can never be a master thinker (pp. 41–42)? But at the same time, in the same *La vie matérielle*, Duras condescends to toss gay men more of those 'scraps of identity' which so mortified Barthes. Here's an example. Gay men are assimilated to a kind of transvestite; they are always cute and fun, despite their mourning for the difference they cannot affirm: 'The masked transvestite—forward, always holding forth, delicious, ineffable, the darling of all social circles—bears at the centre of his being and his mind the death of the organic and fraternal antinomy between men and women, an absolute mourning for women, that second term.'[36]

Not—or perhaps not just—Duras the person, then, but the discursive potentials and norms actualized within her writing indeed seem to realize

Barthes's worst nightmare of the vengeful Other. She is only rousting more explicitly than usual the anti-gay hostility that, it would seem, sleeps rather comfortably within much recent French thought concerning *différence*—that 'insistent and very vaunted word', as Barthes called it. *La maladie de la mort* shows us that this grim dialogue of supplication which Barthes sought scrupulously to avoid through his silence was indeed there, waiting for him to assume a predetermined role within it. His posthumous *Incidents* (1987) suggests that Barthes had obviously internalized that depressive role anyway, and that speaking out would have been his only real chance to break free of it, just as D. A. Miller has argued. Perhaps it will not come as a surprise, therefore, to note in closing that Barthes's refusal to star in this role did not prevent Duras herself from casting him in the part all the same. For in the vague ramblings of *La vie matérielle* she reached the point of saying that Barthes was a man for whom she had friendship but had never been able to admire (pp. 41–42). And sure enough, once Barthes's name is mentioned, Duras then reaches back across the five years since *La maladie de la mort* for some of those earlier epithets which she will now recycle as if they were acts of thinking, rather than the tired, mnemonic devices of a homophobia remembering its lines. Thus, she proceeds to characterize *Fragments d'un discours amoureux* (1977) as jottings on love in which Barthes managed to love nothing: 'Not loving, but I mean *nothing*, it seems to me, *nothing*. Charming man, charming really, in any case. And a writer, in any case. That's it. The writer of a certain kind of writing, *immobile* and even-keeled writing' (my emphasis).[37] Here in tightly condensed form is the reiteration of the whole of her earlier *La maladie de la mort*. Only here, the indictments hurled at the nameless fictional character are now applied to the very real Roland Barthes. His fictional predecessor desired the deathly 'void' of the anus, as empty as homosexual desire itself, which resulted in a characteristic 'immobility' of gay sentiment. Now Barthes as an individual is said to have loved 'nothing', and to have produced writing that demonstrates the same immobility and the same deadly stillness that is difference denied.[38] All this is clearly associated with Duras's condescending recognition in *La vie matérielle* that Barthes was a 'charming man', reminding us once again of her judgment that gay men are always the 'darling[s] of all social circles', even though they bear within themselves 'an absolute mourning for women'.

Clearly, Duras had dug a hole for herself from which she was unable to escape. In this, she demonstrates a range of funereal and melancholy effects that can be produced from the particular avant-garde orthodoxy which so obviously informs her notions of gender, of sexuality, and of writing. It thus becomes necessary to remind ourselves, after reading such texts as these, that the extraordinary history of recent French theory does not necessarily issue in such conventionalism and such closure. Duras, in fact, may be a special case in which something potentially liberatory in postmodern thought has broken down. As Crowley has it, '[c]onfronting the sublime gap of sexual difference, Duras's writing may always, in its ambiguity, reconfirm the contingent banalities that edge it about'.[39] Thus do we need at least to remind ourselves, just for the sake of balance, that there has been a remarkable rescripting of gender and sexuality on the part of thinkers quite differently inspired by the same French thought. For the moment, however, at least in France or in French studies, it would be hard to find any recognition of the kind of problem so well formulated by Eve Kosofsky Sedgwick when she wrote:

> I know from some experience of interacting with people about this and related material how well lubricated, in contemporary critical practice … is the one-way chute from a certain specificity of discourse around gay issues and homophobia, by way of a momentarily specific pluralizing of those issues, to—with a whoosh of relief—the terminus of a magnetic almost religiously numinous insistence on a notional 'undecidability' or 'infinite plurality' of 'difference' into whose vast and shadowy spaces the machinery of heterosexist presumption and homophobic projection will already, undetected, have had ample time to creep.[40]

On the broader cultural stage, however, as represented for example by the brisk trade in gay-themed novels, we can read the following passage which I am lifting from Paul Monette's *Becoming a Man,* where the issue of sameness and difference brings with it a wholly other sensibility, one that I would suggest stems directly from a burgeoning culture of gay 'outness'. Speaking of the queer students he knew when teaching at Andover, Monette writes:

> The only thing that's the same about gay and straight people is what they do in bed. Thus what I wish for the Gay/Straight Alliance at Andover is more than a sex-positive affirmation of self, wherever they make their beds. Let them all come out, of course—bottom line. But after that I wish them the comradeship of differentness, above and beyond the carnal. Or arm in arm with it anyway, as they march down the field butched up in soccer drag and accessorized to the teeth, pearls and boas rampant. Whatever works to keep them from digging a hole. *Go team!*[41]

But elements of this sensibility are not altogether foreign to the French tradition. The time may be right now for us to seek out the buried evidence of possibilities for affirmative gay resistance to these uses and abuses of the notion of '*différence*', possibilities that have not survived into the modern era. Who knows how much French literature echoes the sentiment of Paul Monette, so little heard in France today? What are we to make, for example, of the little known novel entitled

Le prisonnier by Rachilde and André David, published in 1928, where we read that '[a]ll bodies can be electrified by rubbing, on the sole condition that the two surfaces rubbed against each other be of a different nature. But for that to occur, is it necessary that their sex be different?'[42] We could also hark back still further to a similar hypothesis in Marc-André Raffalovich who in 1895 comfortably acknowledges sexual relations between well-born young men and the servant class, 'with cast difference acting like sexual difference'.[43] Raffalovich also wrote that '[a]n invert trying out heterosexuality ... can be just as perverted as an apparently-normal individual who tries homosexuality. The passion for similarity is just as deep as is the passion for sexual contrast—and we shouldn't try to derive the one from the other'.[44] But Raffalovich's main efforts were directed at refuting the inversion model of homosexuality that saw all desire as essentially heterosexual, despite the genital similarity of the partners. It was his goal fully to accredit desire for sexual sameness per se—true *homo*-sexuality—between men who are in no way feminine:

> Some [so-called inverts] are more masculine than usual men, and are drawn to their own sex by virtue of resemblance ... Others believe that similarity is a passion comparable to the passion provoked by sexual dissimilarity. As men, they love a man; but they assert that if they were women they would love a woman. These are unisexuals *par excellence*. They are also of a superior sort, the most interesting ...[45]

It remains to be seen what will emerge if, at last, French cultural and theoretical texts come to be read unapologetically through the queered eyes of foreigners doing French studies, or by those in France who choose to reconnect with a lost tradition of gay resistance and gay-affirmative thought. Time will tell whether the French intelligentsia is amenable to change, whether queer studies has a future in French. At least some of the nineteenth century's 'inverts' found a voice in which to speak in the face of sexology, the cutting-edge theory of the day. Is it too much to hope, then, that their modern descendants might also discover, in contemporary terms, a name and a practice which will enable us to talk back to today's purveyors of a theoretical 'truth' that would also kill us 'on the page' as surely as it has killed us in the flesh.

Notes

(N.B.: All translations from the French are my own unless otherwise stated.)

1 Peter Ackroyd, 'Biography: The Short Form' (a review of Edmund White's *Marcel Proust*, New York, Viking Press, 1999), *New York Times Book Review*, 10 January 1999, p. 4.

2 The next sentence in Ackroyd's paragraph states: 'To introduce a somewhat anachronistic term such as "gay", with all its late twentieth century connotations, is to avoid making the act of personal, intimate sympathy that a great biography requires.' Are we then to presume that some other translation of Proust's lexicon of *invertis*, *homosexuels*, and *tantes* would have enhanced his significance, and White's biography? Hardly. This is an embarrassingly transparent fig leaf to cover Mr Ackroyd's more likely feeling that Proust's sexuality itself diminishes his significance, no matter what we call it. The sin is in calling it anything.

3 This sort of thing is not new, of course. In 1927, another critic, a certain Pierre Lièvre, gave evidence of similar sensibilities in an article titled 'André Gide', *Le Divan*, No. 131 (July-August 1927), republished in *Cahiers Gai-Kitsch-Camp*, No. 19 (1993), pp. 105–08. In this article, Ackroyd's predecessor lamented the publication of Gide's autobiography *Si le grain ne meurt* (1924) because his explicit avowals of homosexuality retrospectively spoiled the pleasure one used to find in reading novels like *Les nourritures terrestres*. The autobiography robbed Gide's readers of their ignorance of gay content of that novel whose attraction resided essentially in its 'manifold strangeness', the character of which one resisted trying to explain ('L'attrait du livre résidait essentiellement dans mainte étrangeté sur le caractère de quoi l'on résistait à s'expliquer'). Lièvre thus admits—in utter self-contradiction—that one could 'enjoy' homosexuality in literature so long as one is allowed to 'resist' knowing that it was homosexuality. He recognizes that Balzac's Vautrin, for example, has unambivalently homosexual passions, but claims at the same time that readers can enjoy these feelings because the text is ambiguous enough for us successfully to resist knowing their true nature. Homosexual sentiments can be enjoyed in literature only if they are accompanied by deniability: this is not a queer story, thus I can enjoy its queerness. But in saying this, Lièvre is not caught in any sort of accidental contradiction. Rather, he explicitly claims for this particular form of hypocrisy both a literary and an aesthetico-moral superiority. Seventy-nine years later Ackroyd is clearly doing something quite similar under the aegis of his concern for 'great biography', which seems to have as a requirement that the subject's 'gayness' not be asserted so insistently that we have to think about the true nature of that which moves and enlightens us in gay-authored literature.

4 *Out/Look* (Fall 1990), pp. 57–58.

5 With few exceptions, major French philosophical reflections on '*différence*' with which I am familiar have sought to approximate an economy of difference so general as to suspend *de facto* all resistance in the name of any particular

construction of identity. Emblematic of this tendency is Jean-Luc Nancy's *La communauté désoeuvrée*, Paris, Christian Bourgois, 1986.

6 Martin Crowley, '"Cest curieux un mort": Duras on Homosexuality', *Modern Language Review*, Vol. 93, No. 3 (July 1998), pp. 659–77; p. 659. This superb essay appeared after I had drafted the present remarks and offers invaluable insights into the place and function of homosexuality in Duras's entire oeuvre.

7 Chief among these imperatives, perhaps, is the psychoanalytic requirement that we assume our place within a radicalized castration model of sexual difference in which we are all castrated.

8 In his 'Hommage fait à Marguerite Duras du *Ravissement de Lol V. Stein*' (1964) Lacan wrote that 'Marguerite Duras is proved to know without me what I teach' (François Barat and Joël Farges (eds), *Marguerite Duras*, Paris, Albatros, 1975, p. 95). Mary Lydon has written, concerning this pronouncement by Lacan, that it 'sets a powerful seal on the literary critic's intuition that Duras may be interpretable with the aid of Lacan's theories, and the invitation at once to "apply" Lacan to Duras, and conversely, to use Duras to "illustrate" Lacan is so fetching as to be almost irresistible' ('*La Maladie de la mort*: Love in Marguerite Duras', in *Remains to be Seen: Essays on Marguerite Duras*, ed. Sanford S. Ames, New York, Peter Lang, 1988), p. 114). See also notes 22 and 27 below.

9 Perhaps the best succinct summary of this tradition is Michael Warner's 'Homo-Narcissism; or, Heterosexuality', in Joseph A. Boone and Michael Cadden, *Engendering Men: The Question of Male Feminist Criticism*, London, Routledge, 1990, pp. 190–206. Warner makes the astute remark that the psychoanalytically-inspired tradition of thought has assumed 'that gender is the phenomenology of difference itself'. He then traces the homophobic uses to which that assumption has been put in recent French thinking.

10 'But everybody *knew* he was gay', as a French colleague recently said to me. The following semester, however, I had two French university students in a graduate seminar, neither of whom knew that Barthes had been homosexual. In my experience, 'But everybody knew' is a frequent refrain in France and *always* implies the corollary, 'So let's not talk about it'.

11 There are coded references to queer perspectives in, for example, *L'obvie et l'obtus* (1982), but it takes a rather keen gay sensibility to discern them.

12 See, for example, the spectacular case of one Georges Hérelle cited in Philippe Lejeune, 'Autobiographie et homosexualité en France au XIXe siècle (1789–1914)', *Romantisme*, Vol. 17, No. 56 (1987), pp. 90–91.

13 Roland Barthes, *Roland Barthes par Roland Barthes*, Paris, Seuil, 1975, p. 68: '[La perversion] produit un *plus*: je suis plus sensible, plus perceptif, plus loquace, mieux distrait, etc.—et dans ce *plus* vient se loger la différence (et partant, le Texte de la vie, la vie comme texte).'

14 D. A. Miller, *Bringing Out Roland Barthes*, Berkeley, University of California Press, 1992, pp. 23–25.

15 Michel Foucault, *Histoire de la sexualité*, Vol. 1, *La volonté de savoir*, Paris, Gallimard, 1976, p. 125.

16 *Barthes par Barthes*, p. 73: 'La différence, mot insistant et très vanté, vaut surtout parce qu'elle dispense ou triomphe du conflit. Le conflit est sexuel, sémantique; la différence est plurielle, sensuelle et textuelle; le sens, le sexe sont des principes de construction, de constitution; la différence est l'allure même d'un poudroiement, d'une dispersion, d'un miroitement.'

17 Crowley, '"C'est curieux un mort"', p. 669 and p. 669, note 21, respectively.

18 Marguerite Duras, *La vie matérielle*, Paris, POL, 1987, p. 38. Duras goes on to make clear that, for her at least, sexuality is not one of the undecidables. With welcome, if unfashionable frankness, she claims that all men are either homosexual or heterosexual, even before they are plumbers, writers or taxi drivers.

19 Marguerite Duras, *La maladie de la mort*, Paris, Minuit, 1982, p. 9: 'Elle demande: Essayer quoi? Vous dites: D'aimer'.

20 Duras, *La maladie de la mort*, pp. 9–10: 'Vous dites: … je voudrais pénétrer là aussi. Et aussi violemment que j'ai l'habitude. On dit que ça résiste plus encore, que c'est un velours qui résiste plus encore que le vide.'

21 Duras, *La maladie de la mort*, pp. 21–22: 'Vous lui dites: Vous devez être très belle. Elle dit: Je suis là, regardez, je suis devant vous. Vous dites: Je ne vois rien.'

22 *The Seminar of Jacques Lacan, Book I, Freud's Papers on Technique, 1953–1954*, trans. John Forrester, ed. Jacques-Alain Miller, New York, Norton, 1991, p. 221

23 Freud, 'Fetishism', in *Standard Edition*, Vol. 21, p. 154.

24 Duras, *La maladie de la mort*, p. 34: 'Vous n'avez jamais désiré une femme? … Pas une seule fois, pas un instant?'.

25 Duras, *La maladie de la mort*, p. 35: 'Elle sourit, elle dit: C'est curieux un mort'.

26 Duras, *La maladie de la mort*, pp. 33–34: 'Autour du corps [de la femme], la chambre. Ce serait votre chambre personnelle. Elle est habitée par elle, une femme. Vous ne reconnaissez plus la chambre. Elle est vidée de vie, elle est sans vous, elle est sans votre pareil. Seule l'occupe cette coulée souple et longue de la forme étrangère sur le lit.'

27 Marcel Proust, *A la recherche du temps perdu*, Paris, Gallimard 'La Pléiade', 1954, Vol. 1, p. 10: 'chambre que j'avais fini par remplir de mon moi'. For a troubling example of how Lacanian psychoanalysis can support an analysis that is as hyperbolically homophobic as it is brilliant, see Jeffrey Mehlman's reading of Proust in his *Structural Study of Autobiography*, Ithaca, Cornell University Press, 1974, pp. 20–64.

28 Duras, *La maladie de la mort*, p. 46: 'cette fadeur … cette immobilité de votre sentiment'.

29 Duras, *La maladie de la mort*, p. 50: 'cette monotonie irrémédiable, égale à elle-même chaque jour de votre vie, chaque nuit, avec cette fonction mortelle du manque d'aimer'.

30 Although one need not refer to Duras's relationship with Andréa, it is nevertheless striking, in the light of my belief that there is suppressed rage in this text, that in 1999, during his second public interview since her death with Jean-François Kervéan in *L'Evénement*, Andréa would make the following remarks:

Andréa: She wanted my body.
L'Evénement: And you wanted hers?

Andréa: It was prohibited to pretend. I had to go at it with my body. To make love … The non-relationship of man to woman, she lived it with a passion, also with a fatigue, because she knew it was a failure …
L'Evénement: She also knew about your desire for men, which obsessed her. Between the two of you, was it all-out war?
Andréa: All the time …
L'Evénement: Did she blast you if your were negligent toward her?
Andréa: Oh, la, la, terrible. I had to be, and she had to be, the preferred one all the time.'

(Andréa: Elle voulait mon corps.
Evénement: Et vouliez-vous du sien?
Andréa: Il ne fallait pas faire semblant. Fallait y aller avec le corps. Faire l'amour … Le non-rapport homme-femme, elle le vivait avec une passion, une fatigue aussi, car elle savait que ça ratait …
L'Evénement: Elle savait aussi votre désir pour les hommes, qui l'obsédait. Entre vous, c'était la guerre?
Andréa: La guerre tout le temps …
L'Evénement: Si vous étiez négligent envers elle, elle vous foudroyait?
Andréa: Oh, là, là, terrible. Il fallait que je sois et qu'elle soit la préférée tout le temps.)

('Duras mon amour', *L'Événement*, No. 740 (7–13 January 1999), pp. 98–103; p. 102.)

31 This type of reversal of power relations has been noticed in many of Duras's writings. See, for example, Suzanne Chester, 'Writing the Subject: Exoticism/Eroticism in Marguerite Duras's *The Lover* and *The Sea Wall*', in *De/Colonizing the Subject: The Politics of Gender in Women's Autobiography*, ed. Sidonie Smith and Julia Watson, Minneapolis, University of Minnesota Press, 1992, pp. 436–57; p. 452.

32 Duras, *La maladie de la mort*, pp. 52–53: 'Vous demandez comment le sentiment d'aimer pourrait survenir. Elle vous répond: Peut-être d'une faille soudaine dans la logique de l'univers … Vous demandez: Le sentiment d'aimer pourrait-il survenir d'autres choses encore? Vous la suppliez de dire. Elle dit: De tout, d'un vol d'oiseau de nuit, d'un sommeil … Elle dit: Regardez. Elle ouvre ses jambes et dans le creux de ses jambes écartées vous voyez enfin la nuit noire.'

33 Duras, *La maladie de la mort*, p. 56: 'Quand vous avez pleuré', the narrator concludes irrevocably, 'c'était sur vous seul et non sur l'admirable impossibilité de la rejoindre à travers la différence qui vous sépare.'

34 Duras, *La vie matérielle*, p. 40: 'Dans l'hétérosexualité il n'y a pas de solution. L'homme et la femme sont irréconciliables et c'est cette tentative impossible et à chaque amour renouvelée qui en fait la grandeur.' Duras returns to—and further elaborates upon—this theme in *Le monde extérieur. Outside II* (Paris, POL, 1993). Particularly resonant is the entry for 12 June 1981 entitled 'Retake'. There, 'desire cannot take place except between the masculine and the feminine, between different sexes. The other desire is a self-desire [*auto-désir*]. For me it's like a

continuation of the masturbatory practice of men and women' (p. 13) ('le désir ne peut avoir lieu qu'entre le masculin et le féminin, entre des sexes différents. L'autre désir, c'est un auto-désir, c'est pour moi comme le prolongement de la pratique masturbatoire de l'homme et de la femme').

35 Duras, *La vie matérielle*, p. 41: 'La passion de l'homosexualité c'est l'homosexualité. Ce que l'homosexuel aime comme son amant, sa patrie, sa création, sa terre, ce n'est pas son amant, c'est l'homosexualité.'

36 Duras, *La vie matérielle*, pp. 38–39: 'Le travesti masqué envahissant, clamant, délicieux, ineffable, coqueluche de tous les milieux, porte au centre de son corps et de sa tête la mort de l'antinomie organique et fraternelle entre les hommes et les femmes, le deuil absolu de la femme, ce second terme.'

37 Duras, *La vie matérielle*, p. 42: 'n'aimant pas, mais rien, il me semble, rien, charmant homme, charmant vraiment, de toute façon. Et écrivain, de toute façon. Voilà. Ecrivain d'une certaine écriture, immobile, régulière'.

38 It is not insignificant that Blanchot, writing in the same heterosexist tradition, criticizes Proust's quest for literary immortality by using a vocabulary remarkably similar to that of Duras: 'Cette forme d'individualisme cesse bientôt d'être satisfaisante … il est vain de vouloir rester soi-même par-delà la disparition, de désirer être immobile et stable dans une oeuvre qui surplomberait le temps' ('L'oeuvre et l'espace de la mort' in *L'espace littéraire* (1955), Paris, Gallimard 'Folio', 1999, p. 116 (my emphasis)). Of course, in his reading of *La maladie de la mort* in *La communauté inavouable* (Paris, Minuit, 1983), Blanchot all but elides the possibility of the man's homosexuality and its implications. His suggestion that homosexuality is not in itself the cause of 'the sickness of death' is premissed on the blithe notion that all feelings of love and desire are universal.

39 Crowley, '"C'est curieux un mort"', p. 663.

40 Eve Kosofsky Sedgwick, *Epistemology of the Closet*, Berkeley, University of California Press, 1990, p. 247.

41 Paul Monette, *Becoming a Man*, New York, HarperCollins, 1992, p. 81.

42 Rachilde and André David, *Le prisonnier*, Paris, Editions de France, 1928, p. 44: 'Tous les corps sont électrisables par frottement, à la seule condition que les deux surfaces frottées l'une contre l'autre soient de nature différente. Mais est-il nécessaire pour cela que le sexe soit différent?' Or how many others in the French past remain to be found like Georges Hérelle who, in an 1897 letter to a sexologist, could write: 'I believe neither in your prophylaxis, nor in your treatment; I expect no cure from you; I do not consider myself sick …' (cited in Lejeune, 'Autobiographie et homosexualité', p. 90) ('Je ne crois ni à votre prophylaxie, ni à votre traitement; je n'attends pas de vous une guérison; je ne me considère pas comme un malade …').

43 Marc-André Raffalovich, 'L'Uranisme: Inversion sexuelle congénitale, Observations et Conseils', *Archives d'anthropologie criminelle*, Vol. 10, Paris and Lyons, Storck et Masson, 1895, p. 112.

44 Marc-André Raffalovich, 'L'Education des invertis', *Archives d'anthropologie criminelle*, Vol. 9, Paris and Lyons, Storck et Masson, 1894, pp. 738–49.

45 Raffalovich, 'L'Uranisme', p. 101: 'Certains sont plus masculins que les hommes habituels, et se sentent portés vers leur propre sexe en raison de la ressemblance ... D'autres croient que la similarité est une passion comparable à celle suscitée par la dissimilarité sexuelle. Hommes, ils aiment un homme; mais ils affirment que s'ils étaient femmes ils aimeraient une femme. Ce sont les unisexuels par excellence. Ce sont aussi les supérieurs, les plus intéressants, les seuls peut-être qui ne mentent pas pour le plaisir de mentir ou sans le savoir.' Raffalovich, though a problematic figure in many ways—he is elitist and utterly sexist, for example—nevertheless deserves more recognition than he has heretofore received. It is remarkable to find him, the following year, beseeching contemporary novelists to include more realistic portrayals of gay characters in their works. In some aspects, the terms of his plea still ring true today: 'Describe this passion of strong men for strong men, of Hercules types for *colossi*, for healthy flesh, as they themselves call it, for healthy flesh; show clearly that it is not only woman but the feminine that doesn't suit these virile men; part the veils of ignorance and lies, so that we no longer attribute inversion to civilization, or to twisted or overwrought minds; we must smash clichés; we must learn to see, we must will ourselves to speak out. We must think ahead to the education of our children and our grandchildren' (Marc-André Raffalovich, 'Unisexualité anglaise' (a review of Havelock Ellis), *Archives d'anthropologie criminelle*, Vol. 11, 1896, p. 431, note).

CHAPTER 10

Photography and Fetishism in *L'amant*

Alex Hughes

> That image, that unphotographed absolute image, entered into the book ... it will have been and will remain indicated; its existence, its '*retinian*' permanence will have been placed there.[1]

My purpose in the discussion that follows is to dissect the roles played by photography, photographic invention and fetishism in Marguerite Duras's *L'amant*.[2] It has already been acknowledged by critics that Duras's generically indeterminate, temporally and pronominally fluid rendition of her Indochinese childhood is inaugurated and yet unillustrated by a 'latent' photo-image that is never actually realized, but is proffered nonetheless as an object of spectatorship for the reader's gaze. This 'absolute', unmade image opens up a space of writing characterized by 'photographic' features (including a bric-à-brac organization of snapshot-like textual moments) that enhance our sense of the centrality of photography to Duras's improperly autobiographical *récit*.[3] Further, it is no less a target of the fetishizing impulse, arguably, than the 'Photographie du Jardin d'Hiver'—the photograph of his dead mother, in her childhood incarnation—that likewise features invisibly, and centrally, in Barthes's seminal treatise on photographic representation, *La chambre claire* (1980).[4] The 'presence' within *L'amant* of this absent fetish-photo offers a key to a central element in the matrix of desires revealed by Duras's self-referential tale. The nature of this desire, and the 'aberrant' nature of Duras's female photo-fetishism, will constitute my not unfetishized objects of scrutiny.

The 'image' from which the *récit* contained in *L'amant* derives its impetus is a verbalized, fantasized image, a 'fantasme de photographie'[5] that Duras's nameless, self-projective adult narrator progressively 'develops' before our eyes in the *incipit* of her story (*L'amant*, pp. 9–21; *Lover*, pp. 7–17). It exists because of—and as an *après-coup* substitute for—a photo-image that has previously failed to materialize at the point in time at which its realization became a possibility. The product of a 'photo-take' that operates, then, exclusively at the level of narrative, Duras's imaginary image 'captures' and 'stills' a scene in which her self-referential heroine journeys across the Mekong on a ferryboat, in order to return to school in Saigon after a holiday spent at home in Sadec: 'I think it was during this journey that the image became detached, removed from all the rest. It might have existed, a photograph might have been taken, just like any other, somewhere else, in other circumstances. But it wasn't … And it's to this, this failure to have been created, that the image owes its virtue: the virtue of representing, of being the creator of, an absolute' (*Lover*, pp. 13–14).[6] Incorporated into this scene is a primordial moment—that of the first look exchanged with her Chinese lover—as a result of which Duras's youthful protagonist will embark on a trajectory that breaks with the 'horror' of her family situation and impels her into the domain of (non-familial) eroticism, and, eventually, into that of writing. In her account of this centrally significant morsel of her past, and of the inexistent image within which it might have been—but missed being—embedded, Duras's adult narrator foregrounds her own, adolescent bodily appearance. Its nature and form—the essence of the phantasmatic photograph fabricated in the opening segment of Duras's story—merit precise attention.

The most striking things about the central, female, bodily entity 'snapped' by Duras's after-the-fact, narrativized photo-take are its artificial aspect and its *morcellement*, or fragmentation. Not unlike the text in which it/she features, the youthful Duras-self of *L'amant*'s phantom-photo comes across less as an homogeneous, seamless, natural being than as a kind of constructed composite, made up of a series of diverse 'pieces'. The elements out of which this composite is created are sartorial. They include a sepia-coloured silk dress with a leather belt; a pair of gold lamé high-heeled shoes; and a man's flat-brimmed felt fedora, with a wide black ribbon (*L'amant*, pp. 18–21; *Lover*, pp. 15–17). If viewed through the lens of the language of sexual fetishism, each of these vestimentary 'bits' can be read as manifesting an erotically resonant, fetishistic, phallicized/izable quality,[7] the most phallically significative of all of them—and the key source of the 'crucial ambiguity' of Duras's image—being the brownish-pink, height-enhancing 'chapeau d'homme' that contrasts strikingly with the frailty of its owner's physique. The sexually symbolic slant of the Durassian narrated photo-body represented in the incipit of *L'amant* is inescapable. It invites Duras's reader to read the broader phenomenon of her 'photographic' self-narration in the context of fetishism, and through a consideration of the fetish object itself.

In an essay entitled 'Photography and Fetish', Christian Metz has the following to say about the way in which fetishes operate:

> [W]e can state that the fetish is taken up in two chains of meaning: metonymically, it alludes to the contiguous place of the lack …; and metaphorically, according to Freud's conception, it is an equivalent of the penis, as the primordial displacement of the look aimed at replacing an absence by a presence—an object, a small object, a part object. It is remarkable that the fetish—even in the common meaning of the word, the fetish in everyday life, a re-displaced derivative of the fetish proper, the object which brings luck, the mascot, the amulet …—it is remarkable that it always combines a double and contradictory function: on the side of metaphor, an inciting and encouraging one (it is a pocket phallus); and, on the side of metonymy, an apotropaic one, that is, the averting of danger.[8]

It is my sense that Duras's narrator's phantasmatic, verbalized self-image adheres closely to the 'fetish = pocket phallus' paradigm which Metz's remarks evoke. The reasons why Duras's imaginary, unmade image of her adolescent body can be taken to be not unlike a fetish governed by the phallic-substitute function, and to be fetishized as such by Duras's self-projective narrating persona, are complex. Bearing on more than just what is figured *within* the imaginary image's imagined frame, they require careful delineation.

The fact that its focus is a scene in which Duras's heroine features as a constellation of fetishizable items—hence as a conglomerate of phallic ciphers—cannot per se be deemed to 'prove' that the narrated photo-image of Duras's text functions as a phallic fetish object, or that Duras's narrator is a/its fetishizer. On one level, this simply suggests that in the existential instant 'captured' by Duras's phantom image (or rather, envisioned in her fantasmatic elaboration of its emergence), Duras's self-referential protagonist—cast by her narrating counterpart, in Lacanian mode, as containing the site of *jouissance* (*L'amant*, p. 15; *Lover*, p. 12)—performs in a way that invokes Lacan's apprehension of femininity as a phallic masquerade: a (fake) 'being of the phallus' that 'permits the imaginary phallus which both sexes want but neither sex has, to keep functioning as a *manque à être* ("lack in being") that generates desire'.[9] It is possible nonetheless to construe Duras's phantasmatic autoportrait as resembling a fetish that, fetishized by the narrating persona of *L'amant*, works according to the 'phallic surrogate' model, and to read as at least *symptomatic* of its fetish-status the phallicity and *morcellement*[10] of the body it displays.

Fetishes of this type, Freudians contend, are made in the unconscious when the infantile gaze, faced with the spectacle of maternal Lack, fixes in fascinated distraction on substitute entities that come to replace the missing maternal phallus. Fetish objects that operate as substitutive phallic signs come into being, in other words, through a castration-anxiety averting, absence-disavowing 'stopping of the look'. As Metz suggests, a similar 'stopping of the look' occurs in the photographic act, when a 'cut inside the referent' is made and the object of the photo-take is targeted and reified, becoming at once static and separate from all of the other entities the camera lens could have picked out.[11] What is more, says Metz, the photographic still, fixed as it is by the photographic gaze in the same way that the fetish is frozen, eternally, in the psyche, shares 'many properties of the fetish (as object)'.[12]

Because the phantasmatic image that initiates *L'amant* issues out of Duras's narrator's verbal miming of the photographic gesture—a gesture that itself mimes the fixative, separating process whereby fetishization occurs—it seems reasonable to read this narrated self/photo-portrait as somehow impinging, along with the photographic artefact proper, on the space, and the nature, of the 'pocket phallus' fetish.[13] Moreover, because Duras's narrator is clearly intent on compelling a scene that failed in the 'real' either to hold the gaze or to be separated from a mass of potentially 'fixable' moments of being (*L'amant*, pp. 16–17; *Lover*, pp. 13–14) or to achieve 'retinian permanence' to do so retroactively, in the photographic realm of her *récit*, she in turn can be read as no less a fetishizing agent than the subject of photography him/herself. It is by virtue, then, of the fact that, textually and belatedly, it is made to be photographically immobile, to be 'removed from all the rest' (*Lover*, p. 13)[14] and to 'stop the look', rather than simply as a result of the phallicized, fetishizable elements which it contains, that Duras's inexistent, narrated image of her teenaged body can be conceived as being like a phallically-surrogate fetish object, the source of whose fetishization is the 'photographic' narrator of *L'amant*. This, though, poses certain problems, in that Duras's narrator's self-fetishization/phallicization—achieved via the metamorphosis of her youthful self into an invented, fetish-like photo-image that figures the female-as-masquerading-phallus/fetish[15] ('Suddenly, I see myself as another, as another would be seen, outside myself, available to all, available to all eyes, in circulation for cities, journeys, desire' (*Lover*, p. 16))[16]—is, in the context of psychoanalytic thinking at least, highly unusual.

As Naomi Schor explains in her influential essay 'Female Fetishism: the Case of George Sand', psychoanalytic theory has been loathe to recognize that women can fetishize. While individual Lacanian analysts—notably Gérard Bonnet[17]—have been willing to acknowledge that some female subjects may practice the fetishist's perversion in a 'minor' mode, it is an article of faith with Freud and Freudians, Schor reveals, that 'fetishism is the male perversion par excellence. Traditional psychoanalytic literature on the subject states over and over again that there are no female fetishists; female fetishism is, in the rhetoric of psychoanalysis, an oyxmoron'.[18] Schor is evidently not at ease with the notion that fetishism, because it derives from a castration anxiety-inspired rebuttal of maternal Lack that girl-children, always already 'castrated', have no need to effect, must be the exclusive province of men. Neither, clearly, is she wholly happy with the related contention that pseudo-fetishistic practice is only pursued by those 'viriloid' women subjects who identify intensely with the phallic masculine position and partake in the unconscious fears its occupation entails. She herself seems keen to propose that female fetishistic activity—in whose existence she is inclined to believe—stems less from male-identifiedness than from a kind of 'perverse oscillation', a refusal by (bisexual) women to be anchored on any single side of the axis of castration.[19] Ultimately, however, she cannot bring herself entirely to demasculinize female fetishism. Her reading of manifestations of fetishistic eroticization in the 'bisextual' writings of George Sand leads her finally to frame fetishism-in-the-feminine—and, we sense, feminist attempts at theorizing it as such—as a 'perversion-theft' of a predominantly male disorder, and as a form of penis envy.[20] In the light of Schor's conclusions, I want in the following section to think through the possible sources of Duras's female photo-fetishism, and to reflect on whether her narrator's fetishistic transformation of her adolescent persona into an imagined photo-entity that shares in the space of the phallicized fetish itself can be conceived as anything more than the mark of a masculinity complex. In order to do so, I shall elaborate on the kind of fetishistic function that Duras's invented photo-portrait may be taken to fulfil.

Photographs are revealed in *L'amant* to be the fief of Duras's self-projective narrator's mother. Not only does she obsessively collect snapshots of her progeniture (*L'amant*, pp. 115–17; *Lover*, pp. 99–101) but she also features prominently in the first real (hence contrapuntal) photo-image invoked by Duras's narrative (it is labelled 'la photo du désespoir' (*L'amant*, pp. 21–23, p. 41; *Lover*, pp. 17–19, p. 35)).[21] Simultaneously, however, the photographs which the mother accumulates—and which, because always taken by others, elude her control—are established as resonant with the despairing impotence ('All around her are wildernesses, wastes' (*Lover*, p. 28))[22] that is her lot. By virtue of what they do and do not represent, these objects stand as testaments to her existential dejection, her impoverished, impossible lifestyle and her fruitless struggle to transcend it. Devoid of evidence that she enjoys a valorizing role as a player in the French subjection of Indochina, and imprinted with pointers to her despondency and poverty (*L'amant*, p. 21, p. 116; *Lover*, pp. 17–18,

p. 100), they intimate the absence of mastery that, as a racially privileged yet economically powerless white female subject, she both suffers and disavows under a patriarchal colonial order that thwarts her efforts to thrive.

Viewed through a Freudian optic, the photo-images which are associated with the narrator's mother and which, in the face of others' disapprobation, she continues resolutely to show off (*L'amant*, pp. 116–17; *Lover*, pp. 100–01) can be taken to symbolize a (refused) maternal 'castration' or failed female phallicity that is certainly highly identifiable in *L'amant*. Read psychoanalytically, in other words, these images can be translated as ciphers for a maternal Lack that is evoked, allusively, each time the mother is connected with (de)privation, whether of money, authority, sanity or, most especially, *jouissance*. This, in turn, suggests several things about the self-referential narrator's own, insistent creation of a verbally 'visual' image of her adolescent self that is made fetishistic—hence semiotically/substitutionally phallic—by dint of its imaginary 'photographization'. One is that the textual existence of Duras's fetish-like phantom photo-portrait may likewise not be unrelated to the maternal phallic Lack which psychoanalysis cites as fetishism's stimulus, and which *L'amant*'s evocation of actual photographs such as the 'photo du désespoir' tacitly points up.[23] A second is that the narrator's 'photographic', fetishizing, (self-)phallicizing production of her 'absolute' self-image may mesh somehow with the classic fetishistic move whereby the maternal 'wound' is masked and castration concealed by dint of the creation/cathexis of a fantasmatic entity that stands, phallically, for what the mother has never properly possessed. This latter point can be put another way. The verbalized emergence of Duras's imaginary photo-image—an image which we can construe as (resembling) a fetish that serves as a phallic proxy and as an object whose fetish-likeness secures the fetishization/phallicization of the Durassian subject it depicts—functions within *L'amant* as a magnet for readerly attention, not to say fetishization. As readers attuned to the complexity of the desires that Duras's text bespeaks, we may opt to regard its narrative development as destined to occlude, or even compensate for, a maternal phallic 'deficiency' that is itself implied in *L'amant*'s references to despair-imbued, extant photographic artefacts and to the maternal impotence they betoken. If we choose so to do, then we need to ask ourselves to what specific end, and for whose benefit, is the photo/self-fetishism in *L'amant* staged?

By way of a response to this question, we can offer two related interpretations of the photographic, (self-)fetishizing activities inscribed in the opening segment of Duras's autobiographical novel. On the one hand, we can take them to signal that what the *incipit* of *L'amant* dramatizes are 'the symptoms of [a] fetishism [that] only develops in females in whom the illusory phallus has gained such strength as to approach the delusional'.[24] This first interpretation is broadly neo-Freudian and foregrounds the phenomenon of female male-identifiedness. It rests on the notion that if Duras's narrator elects to imagine/invent, photographically and fetishizingly, the fantasmatic, fetish-like autoportrait that *L'amant* introduces, this is because her viriloid need to allay the threat of a castration she rejects as her own portion is such that it drives her to fabricate something that replaces, however obscurely, the phallus her mother has failed to manifest and whose absence (in the (m)Other) is too anxiety-inducing to bear. Conversely, though, we can reckon with the possibility that if Duras's narrating persona photographically produces/'fetishizes' a 'visual' fetish-simulacrum that figures her adolescent body as phallicized and fetish-like, this is because she desires to fashion herself, retroactively and generously, into a consolatory surrogate for the phallus her mother did not have, and whose lack would appear to connect with the 'gothic' maternal madness that *L'amant* manifestly chronicles (*L'amant*, p. 40; *Lover*, p, 34).[25] This second reading coheres with the Lacanian stance on female fetishism, which casts the female fetishist as more concerned with being the (missing, desired) maternal phallus—hence with being a source of maternal *jouissance*—than with having or not having the penis.[26] It echoes Bonnet's argument (an argument refuting the idea of women being impervious to fetishistic desire) that if women fetishists fetishize, they do so for the mother. And it is consonant with the delight the mother in the text's diegesis displays as she witnesses her daughter's adolescent incursions into the domain of fetishistic performance: 'When my mother emerges, comes out of her despair, she sees the man's hat and the gold lamé shoes … She looks at me, is pleased, smiles … She doesn't ask if it's she who bought them, she knows she did. She knows she's capable of it' (*Lover*, p. 27).[27]

Little concrete 'evidence' supports the first of the interpretations elaborated in the preceding paragraph, save perhaps *L'amant*'s occasional hints that its heroine employs the naked body of her Chinese lover as a phallic token that offsets a lack she disavows in herself (*L'amant*, pp. 46–49; *Lover*, pp. 39–42). The second, however—which intimates that there is indeed, as Schor suggests, 'more to female fetishism than the masculinity complex'[28]—is textually endorsed. It resonates with the nexus of bonds that Duras weaves between: (i) the narrative auto-phallicization that *L'amant*'s adult daughter-narrator *retroactively* effects, by mutating her youthful persona into a fetish-like photo-object; (ii) the originary act of self-fetishization engendered by her adolescent performance as a sartorial fetish-composite; and (iii) her mother's collusion in the production of that originary act and her subsequent, vertiginous joy at it: 'My mother rattles on. She … laughs, at the scandal, the buffoonery, the [out-of-place] hat, the sublime elegance of the child who crossed the river' (*Lover*, p. 97).[29] My second interpretation spotlights, in essence, a kind of phantasmatic, reparative filial giving which, the reader senses, may relate to the human, absurd, valour-before-adversity (*Lover*, p. 101)[30] that Duras's mature narrator, for all her maternally-directed hostility and fear of maternal madness, cannot help recognizing in her mother, or seeking belatedly to gratify. I want, now, to make two further, final points in connection with it.

Firstly, the reading I am privileging here problematizes the proposition mooted in Maryse Fauvel's 'Photographie et autobiographie' that photography and (contra-)photographic writing are bound up in Duras's text with its author-narrator's antagonism towards her mother.[31] Fauvel's contention is that *L'amant* turns on a photographic evacuation that emblematizes matrophobic rejection and generates an *écriture* both obliterative of the mother and anti-photographic.[32] Working with the notion that the photo-image is the symbol par excellence of the Durassian mother's detested authority over her offspring, she argues that the unillustrated narrative space opened up by Duras's inceptive play with photographic stillbirth (*L'amant*, p. 16; *Lover*, p. 13) attests to Duras's desire to repudiate the maternal by refusing to mimic her mother's fondness for photographic display. Fauvel's exegesis is not without interest. However, her analysis ignores the way in which the photograph-free but photographically-centred discourse developed by Duras's narrator works to remedy, via the 'reparative' process of fantasmatic, photographic self-fetishization pursued, the Lack that is imbricated in the Durassian mother's manifest defects.

The second point I want to note *à propos* of my treatment of Duras's narrative photographics is that while it allows her narrator's engagement with (a form of) fetishistic activity to represent more than just a symptom of male-identifiedness, it in no way counters the phallocentric organization allotted to fetishism by psychoanalytic theory. But if its failure to do so flies in the face of feminist efforts to free female fetishism, conceptually, from the confines of the phallic paradigm,[33] it nonetheless coheres with the particular preoccupations of *L'amant*. Most notably, my reading reflects *L'amant*'s concern with a maternal 'castration' silhouetted in its narrator's summary of her mother's physical denudation, a summary that echoes and works in counterpoint to the no less sartorially-focused rendition of the contents of Duras's absent, 'compensatory' fetish-photo provided in *L'amant*'s incipit :

> My mother, my love, her incredible ungainliness, with her cotton stockings darned by Dô, in the tropics she still thinks you have to wear stockings to be a lady, a headmistress, her dreadful shapeless dresses, mended by Dô, … her shoes are down at heel, she walks awkwardly, painfully, her hair's drawn back tight into a bun like a Chinese woman's, we're ashamed of her, I'm ashamed of her … (*Lover*, pp. 26–27)[34]

In a recent overview of contemporary French autobiographical practice,[35] Michael Sheringham remarks on the increasingly significant role played in life-writing projects by photographs and other documentary artefacts stamped with visible traces of human identity. Concomitantly, he draws our attention to the current proliferation in France of innovative, mixed media autobiographical ventures predicated on an encounter between written and visual narrative objects. Duras's *L'amant* can be counted among the most modern and experimental of postwar French autobiographies. Yet it denies real photographs a space, not simply because, as Fauvel suggests, their inclusion would implicate its author in a maternal *emprise* she has fought to cast aside but rather because the activity of narrativized (self-)photographization—an activity that affords Duras the chance to manipulate her self-image as freely as she likes—allows a process of daughter-to-mother 'healing' to come belatedly into being.

Notes

1 'Cette image, cette photographie absolue non-photographiée est entrée dans le livre ... elle aura été et restera signalée, son existence, sa permanence "*rétinienne*" auront été posées là'. See Marguerite Duras, 'L'inconnue de la rue Catinat' (interview with Hervé Le Masson), *Le Nouvel Observateur*, 28 September 1984, pp. 52–54; p. 52. Duras reveals here that the original title of *L'amant* was *L'image absolue*.

2 Marguerite Duras, *L'amant*, Paris, Minuit, 1984; *The Lover*, trans. Barbara Bray, London, Flamingo, 1986.

3 On the autobiographical ambiguities of *L'amant* and on its status as 'new' or 'postmodern' autobiography, see, *inter alia*, Jacques Lecarme and Eliane-Lecarme Tabone, *L'Autobiographie*, Paris, Colin, 1997.

4 For an account of the 'photographic' nature of Duras's writing in *L'amant*, and of its similarity to the autobiographical 'écriture photographique' of Barthes, see Maryse Fauvel, 'Photographie et autobiographie: *Roland Barthes par Roland Barthes* et *L'amant* de Marguerite Duras', *Romance Notes*, Vol. 34 (1993), pp. 193–202. For Barthes's vision of photography, see *La chambre claire: Note sur la photographie*, Paris, Seuil, 1980. On the Winter Garden photo as Barthesian fetish, see Griselda Pollock, 'Gleaning in History', in *Generations and Geographies in the Visual Arts*, ed. Griselda Pollock, London and New York, Routledge, 1996, pp. 266–88; p. 284.

5 Hervé Guibert employs this term as a title for several of the *récits* contained in his essay on photography, *L'image fantôme* (Paris, Minuit, 1981). It usefully designates both the 'phantom photo' of *L'amant* and what is going on, narratively, in Duras's narrative's opening segment.

6 'C'est au cours de ce voyage que l'image se serait détachée, qu'elle aurait été enlevée à la somme. Elle aurait pu exister, une photographie aurait pu être prise, comme une autre, ailleurs, dans d'autres circonstances. Mais elle ne l'a pas été ... C'est à ce manque d'avoir été faite qu'elle doit sa vertu, celle de représenter un absolu, d'en être justement l'auteur.' (*L'amant*, p. 16)

7 For a useful account of sartorial fetishism and of the way in which objects of (female) clothing—high-heeled shoes, hats, ribbons, corsets and towering coiffures—can be presented by or function within the male imagination as fetishizable signs and as symbolic stand-ins for the (maternal) phallus, see Emily Apter, *Feminizing the Fetish*, Ithaca and London, Cornell University Press, 1991, pp. 65–98. Apter's focus is the literature and fashion of eighteenth- and nineteenth-century France.

8 See Christian Metz, 'Photography and Fetish', in *The Critical Image: Essays in Contemporary Photography*, ed. Carol Squiers, Seattle, Seattle Bay Press, 1990, pp. 155–64; p. 160.

9 See Apter, *Feminizing the Fetish*, p. 94. For Lacan's account of womanhood as phallic masquerade, see 'The Meaning of the Phallus', in *Feminine Sexuality: Jacques Lacan and the école freudienne*, ed. Juliet Mitchell and Jacqueline Rose, Basingstoke and London, 1982, pp. 74–85, as well as Jacques Lacan, *Ecrits II*, Paris, 1971, pp. 103–15. Lacan's remark here, that 'it is in order to be the phallus, that is to say, the signifier of the desire of the Other, that the woman will reject an essential part of her femininity, notably all its attributes through masquerade' (cf. 'The Meaning of the Phallus', p. 84*;* *Ecrits II*, p. 113) meshes not only with the phallicized/fetishizable appearance of Duras's heroine but also with *L'amant*'s inclusion of statements such as 'j'avais en moi la place du désir'/ 'the space existed in me for desire' (*L'amant*, p. 15; *Lover*, p. 12).

10 As Apter explains (cf. *Feminizing the Fetish*, Chapter 2), various theorists of fetishism read the fetish object as partial. The fact that the body 'revealed' in Duras's imaginary photographic image appears as a fragmented *corps morcelé* enhances our sense of the fetishistic nature of the image itself.

11 See Metz, 'Photography and Fetish', p. 158. Jérôme Beaujour also links photography and fetishization, arguing that the fetish is above all separate from what it once formed part of ('le fétiche est ce qui est définitivement séparé de ce dont il n'est que partie') and suggesting that, since photography rests on a 'fonction séparatiste', the result of the photographic act (i.e. the photograph) may be viewed as fetish-like. Interestingly, Beaujour includes these observations in an article on the role played by photography and photographs in the work of Duras. See Jérôme Beaujour, 'L'Oubli de la photographie', *Magazine Littéraire*, No. 278 (1990), pp. 49–51; p. 50.

12 See 'Photography and Fetish', p. 161. Metz does not take the non-static cinematic image to be as fetish-like as the photo-image, which is permanently 'fixed' by/in the moment the camera shutter comes down. In view of Metz's sense that 'film is much more difficult to characterize as a fetish [than the photograph]' (p. 161), it is significant that Duras chooses to create a 'photographic' rather than a 'filmic'

image in the opening section of *L'amant*; particularly since in many ways it would have been more appropriate to 'cinematize' the Mekong ferry episode.

13 Pierre Saint-Amand notes the fetish-like aspect of Duras's phantom-photo, without elaborating on it. See Pierre Saint-Amand, 'La Photographie de famille dans *L'amant*', in *Marguerite Duras: Rencontres de Cerisy*, ed. Alain Vircondelet, Paris, Ecriture, 1994, pp. 225–40 (p. 227).

14 'enlevée à la somme' (*L'amant*, p. 16).

15 In 'The Meaning of the Phallus', Lacan argues that when woman pursues that 'being of the phallus' he locates within femininity, she masquerades not only as the phallus *qua* signifier of desire but also as a fetish object. His characteristically hermetic account of this process certainly resonates with Duras's description of her heroine's 'performance' on the Mekong ferry, as does his conception of woman as the Other to, and the place of *jouissance* for, the male: 'Paradoxical as this formulation might seem, I would say that it is in order to be the phallus, that is to say, the signifier of the desire of the Other, that the woman will reject an essential part of her femininity, notably all its attributes through masquerade. It is for what she is not that she expects to be desired as well as loved. But she finds the signifier of her own desire in the body of the one to whom she addresses her demand for love. Certainly, we should not forget that the organ actually invested with this signifying function takes on the value of a fetish'. See Jacques Lacan, 'The Meaning of the Phallus', p. 84; *Ecrits II*, pp. 113–14.

16 'Soudain, je me vois comme une autre, comme une autre serait vue, au-dehors, mise à la disposition de tous, mise à la disposition de tous les regards, mise dans la circulation des villes, des regards, du désir' (*L'amant*, p. 20).

17 See Gérard Bonnet, 'Fétichisme et exhibitionnisme chez un sujet féminin', *Voir Etre vu*, Vol. 1, Paris, PUF, 1981, pp. 79–109.

18 Naomi Schor, 'Female Fetishism: the Case of George Sand', in *The Female Body in Western Culture*, ed. Susan Rubin Suleiman, Cambridge MA and London, Harvard University Press, 1985, pp. 363–72; p. 365.

19 Schor, 'Female Fetishism', pp. 368–69. In this section of her essay, Schor acknowledges her debt to Sarah Kofman's work on female fetishism.

20 Schor, 'Female Fetishism', p. 371.

21 For detail on the relationship between the real and imaginary photographs of *L'amant*, see Susan D. Cohen, 'Fiction and the Photographic Image in Duras' *The Lover*', *L'Esprit Créateur*, Vol. 30, No. 1 (Spring 1990), pp. 56–68; p. 61. For Duras's views on the 'photo du désespoir', see 'L'inconnue de la rue Catinat', p. 52.

22 'Autour d'elle, c'est les déserts' (*L'amant*, p. 33).

23 Fauvel argues that the photograph represents, for the mother of *L'amant*, (i) a substitute for happiness and power, and (ii) the sole entity she can control ('un substitut de pouvoir et de bonheur, le seul objet qu'elle est capable de dominer'). See 'Photographie et autobiographie', p. 197. While her remarks are pertinent, they obscure the way in which the actualized photo-image—emblematized by the 'photo du désespoir'—incarnates also, and above all, maternal powerlessness.

24 Juliet Hopkins, 'The Probable Role of Trauma in a Case of Foot and Shoe Fetishism: Aspects of Psychotherapy of a Six Year Old Girl', *International Review of*

Psychoanalysis, Vol. 11 (1984), pp. 79–91; p. 83, cited in Elizabeth Grosz, *space, time and perversion*, London and New York, Routledge, 1995, p. 149.

25 For an account of the mother's madness as emblematizing that of all the 'femmes folles' of Duras's creative universe, see Julia Kristeva, 'La maladie de la douleur: Duras', in *Soleil noir: dépression et mélancolie*, Paris: Gallimard, 1987, pp. 227–65; p. 249.

26 See Bonnet, *Voir Etre vu*, Vol. 1, p. 95. We need to note that while Lacanians such as Bonnet have acknowledged, albeit guardedly, the possibility of female fetishism (cf. Schor, 'Female Fetishism', p. 367), Lacan himself, although he considered woman herself to take on the role of fetish, did not see fetishism as the province of the female.

27 'Quand ma mère retrouve l'air, qu'elle sort du désespoir, elle découvre le chapeau d'homme et les lamés or ... Elle regarde, ça lui plaît, elle sourit ... Elle ne demande pas si c'est elle qui les a achetés, elle sait que c'est elle. Elle sait qu'elle en est capable' (*L'amant*, p. 32).

28 Schor, 'Female Fetishism', p. 368.

29 'La mère parle, parle. Elle ... rit, du scandale, de cette pitrerie, de ce chapeau déplacé, de cette élégance sublime de l'enfant de la traversée du fleuve' (*L'amant*, p. 113).

30 'cette vaillance de l'espèce, absurde' (*L'amant*, p. 117).

31 See Fauvel, 'Photographie et autobiographie', p. 198.

32 For the detail of Fauvel's arguments, see 'Photographie et autobiographie', pp. 197–98. Without referring to the photographic dimension of *L'amant*, Kristeva agrees that Duras's text is maternally obliterative, and relates this to Duras's fear of maternal madness. See *Soleil noir*, p. 250.

33 Apter's *Feminizing the Fetish*, for instance, seeks to challenge the Freud-inspired phallocentrism of fetish-theory.

34 'Ma mère mon amour son incroyable dégaine avec ses bas de coton reprisés par Dô, sous les Tropiques elle croit encore qu'il faut mettre des bas pour être la dame directrice de l'école, ses robes lamentables, difformes, reprisées par Dô ... ses souliers sont éculés, elle marche de travers, avec un mal de chien, ses cheveux sont tirés et serrés dans un chignon de Chinoise, elle nous fait honte, elle me fait honte ...' (*L'amant*, pp. 31–32).

35 See Michael Sheringham, 'Autobiography', in *Encylopedia of Contemporary French Culture*, ed. Alex Hughes and Keith Reader, London and New York, Routledge, 1998, pp. 38–41.

Brief Chronology of the Work of Marguerite Duras

1940 *L'empire français. Avec trois cartes* (co-authored by Philippe Roques and published under Duras's maiden name, Donnadieu)

1943 *Les impudents*

1944 *La vie tranquille*

1950 *Un barrage contre le Pacifique*

1952 *Le marin de Gibraltar*

1953 *Les petits chevaux de Tarquinia*

1954 *Des journées entières dans les arbres*

1955 *Le square*

1958 *Moderato cantabile*

1960 Script for Alain Resnais's *Hiroshima mon amour*
Dix heures et demie du soir en été
Signatory to 'Déclaration sur le droit à l'insoumission dans la guerre d'Algérie' (or 'Manifeste des 121') (banned in France)

1961 *Une aussi longue absence* (script co-authored by Gérard Jarlot)

1962 *L'après-midi de Monsieur Andesmas*

1963 *Les eaux et les forêts* (play)

1964 *Le ravissement de Lol V. Stein*

1965 *Le vice-consul*
Staging in Paris of *Des journées entières dans les arbres*, starring Madeleine Renaud.

1966 *La musica* (film), co-directed by Paul Seban, starring Delphine Seyrig.

1967 *L'amante anglaise* (text)

1968 *L'amante anglaise* (play)
Le Shaga (play)
Yes, peut-être (play)
'20 mai 1968: texte politique sur la naissance du Comité d'Action Etudiants-Ecrivains'

1969 *Détruire dit-elle* (text and film)

1970 *Abahn, Sabana, David*

1971 *L'amour*
Jaune le soleil (film)

1972 *Nathalie Granger* (film)

1973 *India Song* (texte-théâtre-film)
La femme du Gange (film)

1974 *Les parleuses* (co-authored by Xavière Gauthier)

1975 *India Song* (film)

1976 *Des journées entières dans les arbres* (film)
Son nom de Venise dans Calcutta désert (film)
May: television screening of *Les lieux de Marguerite Duras* (interview with Michelle Porte)

1977 *Le camion* (film)
Les lieux de Marguerite Duras
L'Eden cinéma (play)
Baxter, Véra Baxter (film)

1978 *Le navire Night* (film)

1979 *Césarée* (short)
Les mains négatives (short)
Aurélia Steiner (Melbourne) (short)
Aurelia Steiner (Vancouver) (short)

1980 *Véra Baxter ou les plages de l'Atlantique*
L'homme assis dans le couloir
L'été 80
'Les yeux verts' (June-July issue of *Cahiers du Cinéma*)

1981 *Agatha et les lectures illimitées* (film)
La jeune fille et l'enfant (recording)

L'homme atlantique (film)
Outside: Papiers d'un jour

1982 *L'homme atlantique* (text)
La maladie de la mort
Savannah Bay (text and play)
Dialogo di Roma (film)

1983 (*M.D.* by Yann Andréa)

1984 *L'amant* (Prix Goncourt)
Appearance on Bernard Pivot's *Apostrophes*
Oeuvres cinématographiques de Marguerite Duras: Edition Vidéographique Critique

1985 *La douleur*
'Sublime, forcément sublime Christine V.' published in *Libération* (17 July) (intervention in the 'Affaire Grégory')
La musica deuxième (text and play)
Les enfants (film) co-directed by Jean Mascolo and Jean-Marc Turine
October: 'La perte de la vérité' published in *L'Autre Journal* (intervention in Greenpeace Affair)

1986 February–May: five interviews with President François Mitterrand published in *L'Autre Journal*
La pute de la côte normande
Les yeux bleux cheveux noirs

1987 *Emily L.*
La vie matérielle
December: television screening of 'Deux ou trois choses qu'ils se sont dites' (interview with Jean-Luc Godard)

1988 June-July: television screening of 'Au-delà des pages' (interview with Luce Perrot)

1990 *La pluie d'été*

1991 *L'amant de la Chine du Nord*

1992 *Yann Andréa Steiner*

1993 *Ecrire*
Le Monde extérieur. Outside II
'Une journée à Trouville' (co-authored by Yann Andréa), November issue of *Vogue*

1995 *C'est tout*

1996 *La mer écrite* (photographs by Hélène Bamberger)

1999 (*La cuisine de Marguerite*)

1999 (*Cet amour-là*, by Yann Andréa)

Select Bibliography

(N.B.: For a complete record of both primary and secondary sources up to 1997, including interviews with Duras, see Robert Harvey and Hélène Volat, *Marguerite Duras: a bio-bibliography*, Westport CT, Greenwood Press, 1997.)

1. Works by Marguerite Duras

(a) Novels, Essays, Plays and Translations

L'empire français. Avec trois cartes (with Philippe Roques), Paris, Gallimard, 1940.

Les impudents, Paris, Plon, 1943 (republished in Folio in 1992).

La vie tranquille, Paris, Gallimard, 1944 (republished in Folio in 1982).

Un barrage contre le Pacifique, Paris, Gallimard, 1950 (republished in Folio in 1977); *The Sea Wall* [1952], trans. Herma Briffault, New York, Farrar, Straus and Giroux, 1967, with preface by Germaine Brée (also *A sea of troubles*, trans. Antonia White, London, Methuen, 1953).

Le marin de Gibraltar, Paris, Gallimard 'Folio', 1952; *The Sailor from Gibraltar*, trans. Barbara Bray, London, Calder and Boyars, 1966.

Les petits chevaux de Tarquinia, Paris, Gallimard, 1953 (republished in Folio in 1973); *The Little Horses of Tarquinia*, trans. Peter DuBerg, London, John Calder 1960.

Des journées entières dans les arbres; *Le boa; Madame Dodin; Les chantiers*, Paris, Gallimard, 1954; *Whole Days in the trees*, trans. Anita Burrows, London, John Calder, 1984.

Le square, Paris, Gallimard, 1955 (republished in Folio in 1990); *The Square*, trans. Sonia Pitt-Rivers and Irina Morduch, New York, Grove Press, 1959.

Moderato cantabile, Paris, Minuit, 1958; *Moderato Cantabile*, trans. Richard Seaver, New York, Grove Press, 1960.

Les Viaducs de la Seine-et-Oise, Paris, Gallimard, 1960.

Dix heures et demie du soir en été, Paris, Gallimard, 1960 (republished in Folio in 1985); *Ten-thirty on a summer night*, trans. Anne Borchardt, New York, Grove Press, 1962.

Hiroshima mon amour (scénario et dialogues), Paris, Gallimard 'Folio', 1960; *Hiroshima mon amour*, trans. Richard Seaver, New York, Grove Press, 1961.

Une aussi longue absence (scénario et dialogues), with Gérard Jarlot, Paris, Gallimard, 1961; *Hiroshima mon Amour and Une aussi longue absence*, trans. Richard Seaver and Barbara Wright, London, Calder and Boyars, 1966.

L'après-midi de Monsieur Andesmas, Paris, Gallimard, 1962; *The Afternoon of Mr Andesmas*, trans. Barbara Bray, in *Four novels*, New York, Grove Press, 1965, introduced by Germaine Brée.

Miracle en Alabama, Paris, L'Avant-Scène, 1963 (translation and adaptation with Gérard Jarlot of *Miracle in Alabama* by William Gibson).

Le ravissement de Lol V. Stein, Paris, Gallimard, 1964 (republished in Folio in 1976); *The Ravishing of Lol Stein*, trans. Richard Seaver, New York, Grove Press, 1966.

Théâtre I: Les eaux et forêts (1965); *Le square* (1965); *La musica* (1965), Paris, Gallimard, 1965.

Le vice-consul, Paris, Gallimard, 1965; *The Vice-Consul* (1966), trans. Eileen Ellenbogen, London, Hamish Hamilton, 1968.

L'amante anglaise (roman), Paris, Gallimard, 1967; *L'amante anglaise*, trans. Barbara Bray, New York, Grove Press, 1968.

L'amante anglaise (théâtre), Paris, Cahiers du Théâtre National Populaire, 1968.

Théâtre II: Suzanna Andler (1968); *Des journées entières dans les arbres* (1965); *Yes, peut-être* (1968); *Le Shaga* (1968); *Un homme est venu me voir* (1968), Paris, Gallimard, 1968.

Détruire dit-elle, Paris, Minuit, 1969; *Destroy, she said*, trans. Barbara Bray, New York, Grove Press, 1970 (followed by 'Destruction and language' (interview with Duras), trans. Helen Lane Cumberford).

Abahn, Sabana, David, Paris, Gallimard, 1970.

Les papiers d'Aspern, Paris, Editions Paris-Théâtre, 1970.

L'amour, Paris, Gallimard, 1971 (republished in Folio in 1992).

Ah! Ernesto, Boissy-St Léger, François Ruy-Vidal et Harlin-Quist, 1971, with illustrations by Bernard Bonhomme.

Home, Paris, Gallimard, 1973 (translation of *Home* by David Storey).

Nathalie Granger, suivi de La femme du Gange, Paris, Gallimard, 1973.

India Song (texte-théâtre-film), Paris, Gallimard, 1973; *India Song*, trans. Barbara Bray, New York, Grove Press, 1976.

Les parleuses, in collaboration with Xavière Gauthier, Paris, Minuit, 1974; *Woman to woman*, trans. Katharine A. Jensen, Lincoln, University of Nebraska Press, 1987, with afterword by Katharine A. Jensen.

Marguerite Duras, Paris, Albatros, 1975, with Maurice Blanchot, Jacques Lacan, et al, ed. Joël Farges and François Barat (republished in 1979); *DURAS by DURAS*, trans. Edith Cohen and Peter Connor, San Francisco, City Light Books, 1987.

Adoracíon, Paris, 1977 (translation of *Adoracíon* by Eduardo Chillida).

Les lieux de Marguerite Duras, with Michelle Porte, Paris, Minuit, 1977; 'The Places of Marguerite Duras', trans. Edith Cohen, *Enclitic*, Vol. 7, No. 1 (1984), pp. 54–61, and Vol. 7, No. 2 (1984), pp. 55–62.

Le camion, suivi de Entretien avec Michelle Porte, Paris, Minuit, 1977.

L'Eden cinéma, Paris, Mercure de France, 1977 (republished in Folio in 1989).

Le navire Night; Césarée; Les mains négatives; Aurélia Steiner; Aurélia Steiner; Aurélia Steiner, Paris, Mercure de France, 1979 (republished in Folio in 1989 as *Le Navire Night: et d'autres textes*).

Véra Baxter ou les plages de l'Atlantique, Paris, Albatros, 1980.

L'homme assis dans le couloir, Paris, Minuit, 1980; *The man sitting in the corridor*, trans. Barbara Bray, New York, North Star Line, 1991.

'Les yeux verts', *Cahiers du Cinéma*, Nos 312–13, June–July 1980.

L'été 80, Paris, Minuit, 1980.

Outside: Papiers d'un jour, Paris, Albin Michel, 1981 (republished by POL in 1984 and in Folio in 1995); *Outside: selected writings*, trans. Arthur Goldhammer, Boston, Beacon Press, 1986.

Agatha, Paris, Minuit, 1981; *Agatha*, trans. Howard Limoli, in *Agatha; Savannah Bay: 2 Plays*, Sausalito CA, Post-Apollo Press, 1992.

L'homme atlantique, Paris, Minuit, 1982; *The Atlantic Man*, trans. Alberto Manguel, in *Two by Duras*, Toronto, Coach House Press, 1993.

Savannah Bay, Paris, Minuit, 1982.

La maladie de la mort, Paris, Minuit, 1982; *The Malady of Death*, trans. Barbara Bray, New York, Grove Press, 1986.

Savannah Bay (nouvelle édition augmentée), Paris, Minuit, 1983; *Savannah Bay*, trans. Howard Limoli, in *Agatha; Savannah Bay: 2 Plays*, Sausalito CA, Post-Apollo Press, 1992.

Théâtre III: La Bête dans la Jungle (1962) by Henry James, adaptation by Marguerite Duras and James Lord; *Les papiers d'Aspern* (1961) by Henry James, adaptation by Marguerite Duras and Robert Antelme; *La danse de Mort* (1970) by August Strindberg, adaptation by Marguerite Duras, Paris, Gallimard, 1984.

L'amant, Paris, Minuit, 1984; *The Lover*, trans. Barbara Bray, London, Flamingo, 1986.

La douleur, Paris, POL, 1985 (republished in Folio in 1993); *La douleur*, trans. Barbara Bray, London, Collins, 1986 (also published as *The War: A Memoir*).

La musica deuxième, Paris, Gallimard, 1985. *La musica deuxième*, trans. Barbara Bray, in *Four Plays: La musica (La musica deuxième), Eden Cinéma, Savannah Bay, India Song*, London, Oberon Books, 1992.

La mouette de Tchékov, Paris, Gallimard, 1985.

Les yeux bleus cheveux noirs, Paris, Minuit, 1986; *Blue eyes, black hair*, trans. Barbara Bray, New York, Pantheon Books, 1987.

La pute de la côte normande, Paris, Minuit, 1986; *The slut of the Normandy coast*, trans. Alberto Manguel, in *Two by Duras*, Toronto, Coach House Press, 1993.

Les yeux verts (nouvelle édition augmentée), Paris, Cahiers du Cinéma, 1987 (republished by Editions de l'Etoile/Cahiers du Cinéma in 1996); *Green Eyes*, trans. Carol Barko, New York, Columbia University Press, 1990.

La vie matérielle, Paris, POL, 1987 (republished in Folio in 1994); *Practicalities: Marguerite Duras speaks to Jérôme Beaujour*, trans. Barbara Bray, London, Collins, 1990.

Emily L. (roman), Paris, Minuit, 1987; *Emily L.*, trans. Barbara Bray, London, Collins, 1989.

Eden Cinéma (nouvelle version scénique) (texte bilingue français-anglais), Paris, Actes Sud-Papiers, 1988 (translation by Barbara Bray).

La pluie d'été, Paris, POL, 1990 (republished in Folio in 1994); *Summer Rain*, trans. Barbara Bray, New York, Maxwell Macmillan International, 1992.

L'amant de la Chine du Nord, Paris, Gallimard, 1991 (republished in Folio in 1993); *The North China Lover*, trans. Leigh Hafrey, New York, The New Press, 1992.

Yann Andréa Steiner, Paris, POL, 1992; *Yann Andréa Steiner: a memoir*, trans. Barbara Bray, New York, Maxwell Macmillan International, 1993.

Ecrire, Paris, Gallimard, 1993 (republished in Folio in 1996); *Writing*, trans. Mark Polizzotti, Cambridge MA, Lumen Editions, 1998.

Le monde extérieur. Outside II, Paris, POL, 1993.

C'est tout, Paris, POL, 1995; *No More*, expanded and bilingual edition, trans. Richard Howard, New York, Seven Stories, 1998, with foreword by Paul Otchakovsky-Laurens and afterword by Christiane Blot-Labarrère.

La mer écrite, Paris, Marval, 1996, with photographs by Hélène Bamberger.

Romans, cinéma, théatre: un parcours, 1943–1993, ed. Françoise Cibiel, Paris, Gallimard 'Quarto', 1997.

(*La cuisine de Marguerite*, Paris, Benoît Jacob, 1999).

Dits à la télévision: entretiens avec Pierre Dumayet, suivi de 'La raison de Lol' par Marie-Magdeleine Lessana, Paris, EPEL, 1999.

Théâtre IV: Véra Baxter, L'éden cinéma, Le théâtre de l'amante anglaise, adaptations de *Home* (D. Storey) et *La Mouette* (A. Tchékov), Paris, Gallimard, 1999.

(b) Filmography

La musica (1966), b/w, 80′, co-dir. by Paul Seban, prod. Les Films RP, distr. Les Artistes Associés.

Détruire dit-elle (1969), b/w, 90′, prod. Ancinex, Madeleine Films, distr. SNA.

Jaune le soleil (1971), b/w, 80′, prod. Albina productions (never distributed).

Nathalie Granger (1972), b/w, 83′, prod. Luc Moullet Films et Cie, distr. Les Films Moliere.

La femme du Gange (1972–73), colour, 90′, prod. Service de la Recherche de l'ORTF and Sunchild, distr. Olympic.

India Song (1975), colour, 120′, co-prod. S. Damiani, A. Valio-Cavaglione, Sunchild, Les Films Armorial, Antenne 2, SFP, distr. Josepha Productions.

Son nom de Venise dans Calcutta désert (1976), 120′, co-prod. Cinema 9, PIPA, Editions Albatros, distr. Benoît Jacob, Cinéma 9 Ursulines.

Des journées entières dans les arbres (1976), colour, 95′, prod. Jean Baudot (Théâtre d'Orsay), distr. Gaumont.

Baxter, Véra Baxter (1976–77), colour, 90′, prod. Stella Quef (Sunchild), INA, distr. Sunschild.

Le camion (1977), colour, 80′, prod. Pierre et François Barat for Cinéma 9 and Auditel, distr. Les Films Molière.

Le navire Night (1978), b/w, 20′ (never distributed).

Le navire Night (1978), colour, 94′, prod. MK2, Gaumont, Les Films du Losange, distr. Les Films du Losange.

Césarée (1979), colour, 11′, prod. Les Films du Losange, Paris-Audiovisuel.

Les mains négatives (1979), colour, 18′, prod. Les Films du Losange, Paris-Audiovisuel.

Aurélia Steiner (Melbourne) (1979), colour, 35′, prod. Films Paris-Audiovisuel.

Aurélia Steiner (Vancouver) (1979), b/w, 48′, prod. Les Films du Losange, Paris-Audiovisuel.

Agatha et les lectures illimitées (1981), colour, 90′, prod. Les Berthemont, INA, Des Femmes Filment, distr. Hors Champ Diffusion.

L'homme atlantique (1981), colour, 42′, prod. Les Berthemont, INA, Des Femmes Filment, distr. Hors Champ Diffusion.

Dialogo di Roma (1982), colour, 62′, prod. Lunga Gittata, RAI.

Les enfants (1985), colour, 90′, co-dir. Jean Mascolo, Jean-Marc Turine, prod. Les Berthemont, distr. Films sans Frontières.

(c) Discography

Marguerite Duras parle (Alliance Française, 1964), record produced by Hughes Desalle for the series 'Français de notre temps: Hommes d'aujourd'hui'.

La jeune fille et l'enfant (1981), cassette, adaptation of *L'été 80* by Yann Andréa, prod. and distr. Editions des Femmes, 'La Bibliothèque des voix'.

Marguerite Duras ou le ravissement de la parole (INA Radio-France, 1996) (four-record set of extracts from radio interviews assembled by Jean-Marc Turine).

(d) Television, Radio and Video Work

Television:

Les lieux de Marguerite Duras, colour, 120′, dir. Michelle Porte, prod. INA, TF1, 3 and 17 May 1976.

Savannah Bay, c'est toi, colour, 66′, dir. Michelle Porte, prod. INA, Antenne 2, 2 April 1984.

'Carte blanche à une 1ère A' (discussion including Marguerite Duras), prod. Jean-Pierre Janiaud, dir. Valérie Mannel, Antenne 2, 3 September 1994.

'Marguerite Duras' (interview with Bernard Pivot), *Apostrophes*, prod. Jean Cazenave, dir. J.-L. Léridon, Antenne 2, 28 September 1984 (available on video as *Apostrophes: Bernard Pivot rencontre Marguerite Duras*, Paris, Editions du Seuil, 'Vision Seuil', 1990).

'Marguerite Duras', *The South Bank Show*, dir. Daniel Wiles, prod. Hilary Chadwick, LWT, 17 November, 1985.

'Deux ou trois choses qu'ils se sont dites' (interview with Jean-Luc Godard), *Océaniques*, prod. Colette Fellous and Pierre-André Boutang, dir. Jean-Didier Verhaeghe (recorded 2 December 1987), FR3, 28 December 1987 (partial transcription published in *Magazine littéraire*, No. 278 (June 1990), pp. 46–48).

'Au-delà des pages' (series of four interviews with Luce Perrot recorded in February–March 1988), prod. Guy Lopez, TF1, 26 June–17 July 1988.

Interview with Patrick Poivre d'Arvor, *Ex-Libris*, TF1, 15 February 1990.
Interview with Bernard Rapp, *Caractères*, Antenne 2, 5 July 1991.
Interview, *Cinéma de Poche*, FR3, 1 February 1992.
Interview with Pierre Dumayet (recorded 1992), *Lire et Ecrire*, Arte, 29 January 1993.

Radio:

'Interview de Marguerite Duras' (interview with Jacques Duchateau, Jacques Floran, and Michel Chapuis), *Le Pont des Arts*, France-Culture, 26 January 1980.
'Entretiens avec Marguerite Duras' (interviews with Jean-Pierre Ceton), *Les Nuits magnétiques*, France-Culture, 27–31 October 1980.
Quelque part ailleurs en etant là: Le bon plaisir de Marguerite Duras, prod. Marianne Alphant, with Jean Daniel, Denis Roche, Gérard Desarthe, Nicole Hiss, Catherine Sellers, France-Culture, 20 October 1984.
Interview with Pierre Assouline and others, *Inter-lire*, France-Inter, 5 July 1987.
Interview with Alain Veinstein, *Les Nuits magnétiques*, France-Culture, 25 November 1987.
'Du jour au lendemain' (interview with Alain Veinstein), France-Culture, 16 March 1990.
Interview with Patricia Martin and Gérard Courchelle, *Inter 13/14*, France Inter, 29 June 1991.
Interview with Jean-Christophe Marty, *Discothèques privées*, France-Musique, 5–9 August 1991.

Video:

Duras Filme (1981), colour, 50', dir. Jean Mascolo and Jérôme Beaujour.
Les oeuvres cinématographiques de Marguerite Duras. Edition vidéographique critique, Paris, Ministère des Relations extérieures, 1984, prod. Pascal Gallet, dir. Jean Mascolo and Jérôme Beaujour. A five-part box set of Duras's films including post-face interviews with Marguerite Duras by Dominique Noguez:
'La classe de la violence' (on *Nathalie Granger*), 48′ (with Gérard Depardieu);
'La couleur des mots' (on *India Song*), 63′ (with Delphine Seyrig, Carlos d'Alessio and Michael Lonsdale);
'Le cimetière anglais' (on *Son nom de Venise dans Calcutta désert*), 48′ (with Delphine Seyrig, Michael Lonsdale and Bruno Nuytten);
'La dame des Yvelines' (on *Le camion*), 59′ (with Dominique Auvray, Depardieu and Bruno Nuytten);
'La caverne noire' (on *Césarée*, *Les mains négatives*, *Aurélia Steiner (Melbourne)*, *Aurélia Steiner (Vancouver)*), 57′, followed by 'Work and Words' (a video Afterword by Duras).

(e) Articles, reviews and prefaces not available in published collections (*Outside. Papiers d'un jour*; *Les yeux verts (nouvelle version augmentée)*; *Le Monde extérieur. Outside II*; *Marguerite Duras (DURAS by DURAS)*)

'Détruite, Sélinonte', *L'Arc*, No. 4 (1958), pp. 63–65.

'Travailler pour le cinéma', *France-Observateur*, 31 July 1958.

'Resnais travaille comme un romancier', *Les Lettres Nouvelles*, 20 May 1959, pp. 36–38.

'Réponses à l'enquête auprès d'intellectuels français' (with a contribution by Marguerite Duras), *Le 14 Juillet*, No. 3, 18 June 1959 (republished in *Le 14 Juillet*, facsimile reprint, Paris, Lignes 1990).

'Une seule et même chose' (response to a questionnaire on 'Les écrivains et le cinéma'), *Réforme*, 23 July 1961.

'L'homme assis dans le couloir', *L'Arc*, No. 20 (October 1962), pp. 70–77.

'J'ai peur, j'ai très peur', *Les Nouvelles Littéraires*, No. 13 (August 1964).

'Pièce russe' (extrait de la dernière partie), *Cahiers Renaud-Barrault*, No. 52 (December 1965), pp. 76–90.

'Melina la superbe', *Arts*, 1–7 February, 1967.

'Le Tombeau de l'impossible', *La Quinzaine littéraire*, No. 130, 1–15 Decmeber 1971.

Le Cinéma ouvert', *Le Quotidien de Paris*, 3 June 1976.

Erika Lennard, *Les femmes, les soeurs*, Paris, Editions des Femmes, 1976, text by Elisabeth Lennard, with a post-face by Marguerite Duras.

'"Il y a en lui un doute fondamental"' (on François Mitterrand), *Le Quotidien de Paris*, 7 October 1977, p. 5.

'Le navire night' (first version), *Minuit*, No. 29, May 1978, pp. 2–14.

'Le cinéma de Lol V. Stein', *Art Press International*, No. 24, January 1979.

'*Agatha* est le premier film que j'écris sur le bonheur', *Cahiers du Cinéma*, Nos 322–24 (May 1981), pp. 4–5.

'Un Pays du Nord', *Des femmes en mouvements (hebdo)*, No. 48, 3–10 July 1981.

'*Agatha, ou les lectures illimitées*', *Des femmes en mouvement (hebdo)*, No. 57, 11–18 September 1981.

'Je n'ai rien à justifier', *Le Quotidien de Paris*, 8 October 1981.

'Les Rendez-vous manqués: après 1936 et 1956, 1981?' (petition organised by Michel Foucault and signed by Marguerite Duras and nine others), *Libération*, 15 December 1981.

'Le Château de Weatherend' (*La bête dans la jungle*), *L'Arc*, No. 89 (October 1983), pp. 100–02.

'Le monde moderne n'est pas bavard', *Rendez-vous avec le théâtre*, No. 19 (1984).

'Pourquoi écrivez-vous?': response to a questionnaire by Marguerite Duras, *Libération*, hors-série, March 1985.

'La Chair des Mots', *Autrement*, No. 70, May 1985, p. 210.

'Duras: "Les journalistes, me dit-on …"' (with Jean-Marc Turine and Jean Mascolo), *Libération*, 12 June 1985, p. 35.

'Sublime, forcément sublime Christine V.', *Libération*, 17 July 1985, pp. 4–6.

'Réponses de Marguerite Duras', *Libération*, 23 July 1985.

'Le scandale de la vérité', *Cahiers du Cinéma*, No. 374 (July–August 1985), p. 13.

'Elle a sorti la France de ses gonds' (on the death of Simone Signoret), *Le Quotidien de Paris,* 1 October 1985.

'Recevez chers amis, nos salutations mystiques et polyflores' (on Baby Doc Duvalier), (with René Depestre), *L'Autre Journal*, No. 1, 26 February–4 March 1986.

'Le Prix Ritz-Hemingway 1986 à Marguerite Duras', with a brief statement by the author, *Le Monde*, 19 April 1986.

'La pute de la côte normande', *Libération*, 14 November 1986 (reprinted in 1986 by Editions de Minuit as *La pute de la côte normande*).

'Le livre, un plaisir partagé' (a questionnaire by Pierrette Rosset and Françoise Ducout, with responses from Marguerite Duras and others), *Elle*, 23 March 1987.

'Ceux qui veulent continuer à nous lire, de gauche à droite', with a contribution by Marguerite Duras, *Le Matin*, 13–14 June 1987.

'La lecture: un bonheur sans mélange' (questionnaire by Pierrette Rosset with responses from Marguerite Duras and others), *Elle*, 31 August 1987.

'Remarques générales sur "Les Juifs" de *Jaune de Soleil* (1971) et note de tournage sur *Jaune le soleil*', *Cahiers du Cinéma*, No. 400 (October 1987), pp. 20–21.

'L'internationalisme de l'idée française', *Globe*, No. 23 (December 1987).

'Thierry Lévy, ou la littérature évitée', *Le Matin*, 17 February 1988, 'Supplément livres', p. 3.

'La Cigarette dans le couple: un mélange à trois' (a questionnaire by Christine Bravo and Patricia Gandin, with responses from Marguerite Duras and others), *Elle*, 11 July 1988.

'Denis Belloc, la nuit sociale', *Libération*, 22 September 1988, p. 8.

'Marguerite Duras, Ecrivain (et cinéaste) (Paris, 19 décembre 1984)', *L'effet-Godard*, ed. Carole Desbarats and Jean-Paul Gorce, Toulouse, Editions Milan, 1989, p. 112.

'L'année 90: Les 12 photos émotion', *France-Soir*, 29 December 1990.

'Trouville, le 10 septembre 1992', *Marguerite Duras*, Paris and Milan, Cinémathèque française and Nuove edizioni Gabriele Mazzotta, 1992.

'Une journée à Trouville' (with Yann Andréa), *Vogue*, November 1993, pp. 158–67.

Prologue to *Maisons d'Ecrivains*, ed. Francesca Premoli-Droulers, with photographs by Erica Lennard, Paris, Editions du Chêne, 1994, pp. 8–17.

2. Critical Works on Marguerite Duras

Laure Adler, *Marguerite Duras*, Paris, Gallimard, 1998.

Bernard Alazet, 'Je m'appelle Aurelia Steiner', *Didascalies*, No. 3 ('Aurélia Steiner') (April 1982), pp. 111–23.

——, 'Une écriture du soupir', in *Marguerite Duras: Rencontres de Cerisy*, ed. Vircondelet, pp. 83–96.

——, *Le Navire Night de M. Duras: écrire l'effacement*, Villeneuve-d'Ascq, Presses Universitaires de Lille, 1992.

Madeleine Alleins, *Marguerite Duras: Médium du Réel*, Paris, L'Age d'homme, 1980.

Stephanie Anderson, *Le discours féminin de Marguerite Duras: un désir pervers et ses métamorphoses*, Geneva, Droz, 1995.

Liesbeth Korthals Altes, 'L'ironie ou le savoir de l'amour et de la mort: lecture de quatre oeuvres de Marguerite Duras', *Revue des sciences humaines*, Vol. 73, No. 202 (April–June 1986), pp. 39–52.

David Amar, '"Sublime, forcément sublime": A propos d'un article paru dans *Liberation*', *Revue des sciences humaines*, Vol. 73, No. 202 (April–June 1986), pp. 153–66.

Sanford S. Ames (ed.), *Remains to be Seen: Essays on Marguerite Duras*, New York, Peter Lang, 1988.

Yann Andréa, *M.D.*, Paris, Minuit, 1983.

——, *Cet amour-là*, Paris, Pauvert, 1999.

Martine Antle, 'Panoptisme et bureaucratie coloniale dans *Un barrage contre le Pacifique*', *L'Esprit Créateur*, Vol. 34, No. 1 (Spring 1994), pp. 83–91.

L'Arc, No. 98 (1985), Special Issue: Marguerite Duras.

Aliette Armel, *Marguerite Duras et l'autobiographie*, Paris, Le Castor Astral, 1990.

——, *Marguerite Duras. Les trois lieux de l'écrit*, Paris, Christian Pirot, 1998.

Sémir Badir, '*India Song* ou le temps tragique', *Cinémas*, Vol. 5, Nos 1–2, pp. 123–34.

Jean-Claude Bacchiana et al, *Marguerite Duras*, Paris, Marval, 1997.

Ninette Bailey, 'Oublieuse Mémoire', *La Chouette*, No. 6 (January 1986), pp. 7–25.

Danielle Bajomée, *Duras ou la douleur*, Paris, Editions Universitaires, 1989.

——and Heyndels (eds), *Ecrire, dit-elle: Imaginaires de Marguerite Duras*, Brussels, Editions de l'Université de Bruxelles, 1985.

Christine Bange, *Die zurückgewiesene Faszination: Zeit, Tod und Gedactnis als Erfahrungskategorien bei Baudelaire, Benjamin and Duras*, Wienheim, Beltz, 1987.

François Barat and Joël Farges (eds), *Marguerite Duras* (1975), Paris, Albatros, 1979, with Maurice Blanchot, Marguerite Duras, Jacques Lacan, et al.; *DURAS by DURAS*, trans. Edith Cohen and Peter Connor, San Francisco, City Light Books, 1987.

Sarah Barbour, 'Where is the Woman in This Text? Marguerite Duras and *Le Navire Night*: "Histoire d'images noires"', *Journal of Durassian Studies*, No. 1 (Fall 1989), pp. 1–33.

Jean-Louis Barrault, 'Un enfant obstiné', *L'Arc*, No. 98 (1985), pp. 56–57.

Michelle Beauclair, *Albert Camus, Marguerite Duras, and the Legacy of Mourning*, Bern, Peter Lang, 'Francophone Cultures and Literatures' 21, 1998.

Pascale Bécel, '*Le Vice-Consul*: Colonial Mimicry and Partial Writing', *Cincinnati Romance Review*, No. 13 (1994), pp. 218–27.
——, 'From *The Sea Wall* to *The Lover*: Prostitution and Exotic Parody', *Studies in 20th Century Literature*, Vol. 21, No. 2 (1997), pp. 417–32.
Nicole Lise Bernheim, *Marguerite Duras tourne un film* (India Song), Paris, Albatros 'ça/Cinéma', 1979.
Victoria Best, *Critical Subjectivities: Narrative and Identity in the Work of Colette and Marguerite Duras*, Bern, Peter Lang, forthcoming.
Lia van de Biezenbos, *Fantasmes maternels dans l'oeuvre de Marguerite Duras*, Amsterdam, Rodopi, 1995.
Maurice Blanchot, *La communauté inavouable*, Paris, Minuit, 1983, pp. 50–93.
——, *Le livre à venir*, Paris, Gallimard, 1959, pp. 191–94.
Christiane Blot-Labarrère, *Marguerite Duras*, Paris, Seuil 'Les contemporains' 14, 1992.
——, *Christiane Blot-Labarrère présente* Dix heures et demie du soir en été *de Marguerite Duras*, Paris, Gallimard 'Foliothèque', 1999.
——, 'Marguerite Duras et le "Nouveau Roman"', *L'Icosathèque*, No. 16 (1999), pp. 127–53.
Béatrice Bonhomme, 'L'Ecriture de Duras ou La Récriture du Livre: *L'Amant de la Chine du Nord* ou *L'Amant Recommencé*', *Revue des Lettres Modernes (Histoire des Idées et des Littératures)* (1993), pp. 121–61.
Madeleine Borgomano, '*L'Amant*: Une hypertextualité illimitée', *Revue des Sciences Humaines*, No. 202, April–June 1986, pp. 67–77.
——, *L'écriture filmique de Marguerite Duras*, Paris, Albatros, 1985.
——, *Duras: Une lecture des fantasmes*, Brussels, Cistre 'Essais', 1985.
——, *Madeleine Borgomano présente* Le ravissement de Lol V. Stein *de Marguerite Duras*, Paris, Gallimard, 1997.
——, India Song *de Marguerite Duras*, Lyon, Collection Film, L'Interdisciplinaire, 1990.
——, Moderato Cantabile *de Marguerite Duras*, Paris, Bertrand-Lacoste, 1990.
——, 'Duras: d'une écriture politique à une écriture du politique', *L'Icosathèque*, No. 16 (1999), pp. 33–62.
Jean-Louis Bory, 'Ecrire sous la pluie', *Le Nouvel Observateur*, 11–17 January 1990, p. 75.
Germaine Brée, 'A singular adventure: The Writings of Marguerite Duras', *L'Esprit Créateur*, Vol. 30, No.1 (Spring 1990), pp. 8–14.
Peter Brooks, *Body Work: Objects of Desire in Modern Narrative*, Cambridge MA, Harvard University Press, pp. 257–86.
Jean-Pierre Brossard (ed.), *Marguerite Duras: Cinéaste, Ecrivain*, La Chaux-de-Fonds, Editions Cinédiff, 1985.
Bulletin de la Société Marguerite Duras (1997–), ed. Catherine Rodgers and Raynalle Udris.

Maurice Cagnon, 'Marguerite Duras: Willed Imagination as Release and Obstacle', *Nottingham French Studies*, Vol. 16, No. 1 (May 1977), pp. 55–64.
Cahiers de la Cinémathèque, No. 57 (October 1992), Dossier: Marguerite Duras.
Cahiers du CERF XX, No. 7 (1991), Special Issue: Marguerite Duras.

Cahiers du Cinéma, No. 501 (1996), Dossier: Marguerite Duras.

Cahiers Renaud-Barrault, Nos 52 (December 1965), 89 (October 1985), 91 (1976), 96 (1977), and 106 (September 1983), Special Issues: Marguerite Duras.

Christophe Carlier, *Marguerite Duras, Alain Resnais:* Hiroshima mon amour, Paris, PUF, 1994.

Noëlle Carruggi, *Marguerite Duras: une expérience intérieure: 'le gommage de l'être en faveur du tout'*, New York, Peter Lang, 1995.

Sue-Ellen Case, 'From Split Subject to Split Britches. The metonymically displaced subject', in *Feminine Focus: the new women playwrights*, ed. Enoch Brater, Oxford, 1989, pp. 134–41.

Claire Cerasi, *Marguerite Duras: de Lahore à Auschwitz*, Paris and Geneva, Champion-Slatkine, 1993.

——, *Du rythme au sens: Une lecture de* L'Amour *de Marguerite Duras*, Paris, Lettres Modernes, 'Archives des Lettres Modernes' 254, 1991.

Michel de Certeau, 'Marguerite Duras: On dit', in *Ecrire, dit-elle*, ed. Bajomee et Heyndels, pp. 257–65.

Jean-Pierre Ceton, *La fiction d'Emmedée*, Monaco, Rocher 'Manifeste', 1996.

Suzanne Chester, 'Writing the Subject: Exoticism/Eroticism in Marguerite Duras's *The Lover* and *The Sea Wall*', in *Decolonizing the Subject: The Politics of Gender in Women's Autobiography*, ed. Sidonie Smith and Julia Watson, Minneapolis, University of Minnesota Press, 1992, pp. 436–57.

La Chouette, No. 6 (January 1986), Special Issue: Marguerite Duras.

Hélène Cixous and Michel Foucault, 'A propos de Marguerite Duras', *Cahiers Renaud-Barrault*, No. 89 (October 1975), pp. 8–22.

Gabrielle Cody, 'Duras's Theater of Emptied Space and Impossible Performances', *Theater*, Vol. 25, No. 2 (1994), pp. 56–66.

Susan D. Cohen, 'La présence de rien', *Cahiers Renaud-Barrault*, No. 106 (1983), pp. 17–36.

——, *Women and Discourse in the Fiction of Marguerite Duras: Love, Legends, Language*, Oxford, Macmillan, 1993.

——, 'The Beast in the jungle: longing, learning, loving and luck in Marguerite Duras's "Le Boa"', in *Marguerite Duras: Lectures plurielles*, ed. Rodgers and Udris, pp. 35–55.

——, 'Fiction and the Photographic Image in Duras' *The Lover*', *L'Esprit Créateur*, Vol. 30, No. 1 (Spring 1990), pp. 56–68.

Verena Andermatt Conley, '"L'Affaire Grégory" and Duras's Textual Feminism', *L'Esprit Createur*, Vol. 30, No. 1 (Spring 1990), pp. 69–75.

——, 'Rodomontages of *Le ravissement de Lol V. Stein*', *Yale French Studies*, No. 57 (1979), pp. 23–35.

Joan Copjec, '*India Song/Son nom de Venise dans Calcutta désert*: the compulsion to repeat', *October*, No. 17 (1981), pp. 37–52.

Madeleine Cottenet-Hage and Robert P. Kolker, 'The cinema of Duras in Search of an Ideal Image', *The French Review*, Vol. 63, No. 1 (1989), pp. 87–98.

Anne Cousseau, *Poétique de l'enfance chez Marguerite Duras*, Geneva, Droz, 1999.

David Coward, *Duras,* Moderato cantabile, London, Grant and Cutler 'Critical guides to French texts', 1981.

Mechthild Cranston (ed.), *In Language and in love Marguerite Duras: The Unspeakable: essays for Marguerite Duras*, Potomac MD, Scripta Humanistica 101, 1992.

——, 'Rehearsals in Bas Relief: *Le Marin de Gibraltar* of Marguerite Duras', *Studies in 20th Century Literature*, Vol. 17, No. 2 (Summer 1993), pp. 287–307.

——, *Beyond the Book: Marguerite Duras: Infans*, Potomac MD, Scripta Humanistica 131, 1996, with a preface by Germaine Brée.

Martin Crowley, '"C'est curieux un mort": Duras on Homosexuality', *Modern Language Review,* Vol. 93, No. 3 (July 1998), pp. 659–75.

——, *Duras, Writing, and the Ethical*, Oxford, Oxford University Press, 2000.

Dalhousie French Studies, Vol. 50 (Spring 2000), Special Issue: 'Lectures de Duras: corps, voix et écriture'.

Michel David, *Marguerite Duras: une écriture de la jouissance: psychanalyse de l'écriture*, Paris, Desclée de Brouwer, 1996.

Nelcya Delanoë, 'Ascenseur pour l'échafaud', *Esprit*, No. 116 (July 1986), pp. 85–86.

Jeanne Demers, 'de la sornette à l'*Amante anglaise*: le récit au degré zéro', *Etudes Françaises*, Vol. 14, Nos 1–2 (1978), pp. 3–20.

Catherine Dhavernas, 'Colonialisme contre l'enfance, l'individualité, et l'amour: la voix de la différence chez Marguerite Duras', FRONTENAC, No. 12 (1995), pp. 90–102.

Maria DiBattista, 'The Clandestine Fictions of Marguerite Duras', in *Breaking the Sequence: Women's Experimental Fiction*, ed. Ellen G. Friedman and Ellen Fuchs, Princeton, Princeton University Press, 1989.

Michèle Druon, 'Mise en scène et catharsis de l'amour dans *Le ravissement de Lol V. Stein* de Marguerite Duras', *The French Review*, Vol. 58, No. 3 (February 1985), pp. 382–90.

Erica M. Eisinger, 'Crime and Detection in the novels of Marguerite Duras', *Contemporary Literature*, Vol. 15, No. 4 (Autumn 1974), pp. 503–20.

L'Esprit Créateur, Vol. 30, No. 1 (Spring 1990), Special Issue: Marguerite Duras.

Martha Noel Evans, 'Marguerite Duras: the Whore', in *Masks of Tradition*, Ithaca, Cornell University Press, 1987, pp. 123–56.

Wendy Everett, 'Slipping in and out of focus: words and images in the filmic discourse of Marguerite Duras', *Nottingham French Studies*, Vol. 34, No. 2 (Autumn 1995), pp. 55–66.

——, 'Destructive Directing: The Film Language of Marguerite Duras', *Quinquereme*, Vol. 13 (1990–91), pp. 71–82.

Joël Farges and François Barat (eds), *Marguerite Duras* (1975), Paris, Albatros, 1979, with Maurice Blanchot, Marguerite Duras, Jacques Lacan, et al.; *DURAS by DURAS*, trans. Edith Cohen and Peter Connor, San Francisco, City Light Books, 1987.

Maryse Fauvel, 'Photographie et autobiographie: *Roland Barthes par Roland Barthes* et *L'amant* de Marguerite Duras', *Romance Notes*, Vol. 34 (1993), pp. 193–202.

——, '*Le Marin de Gibraltar* et *Détruire dit-elle* de Duras: sous le signe de Dionysos', *French Review*, Vol. 65, No. 2 (December 1991), pp. 226–35.

Pierre Fedida, 'Entre les voix et l'image', in *Marguerite Duras*, ed. Barat and Farges, pp. 157–60.

Patricia Fedkiw, 'Marguerite Duras: Feminine Field of Hysteria', *Enclitic*, Vol. 6, No. 2 (Fall 1982), pp. 78–86.

Marie-Pierre Fernandes, *Travailler avec Duras. La Musica Deuxième*, Paris, Gallimard, 1986.

Suzanne Ferrières-Pestureau, *Une étude psychanalytique de la figure du ravissement dans l'oeuvre de M. Duras. Naissance d'une oeuvre, origine d'un style*, Paris, L'Harmattan, 1997.

Dominique Fisher, '"L'écrit", le jeu de la lecture et la mise en voix de l'écriture dans *La Vie matérielle* et dans *Les Yeux bleus cheveux noirs*', *L'Esprit Créateur*, Vol. 30, No. 1 (Spring 1990), pp. 76–85.

Jill Forbes, *The Cinema in France After the New Wave*, Bloomington and Indianapolis, Indiana University Press, 1992, pp. 94–102.

Michel Foucault and Hélène Cixous, 'A propos de Marguerite Duras', *Cahiers Renaud-Barrault*, No. 89 (October 1975), pp. 8–22.

Jérôme Game, 'The Writing of the In-Between: A Study of Marguerite Duras's *La Vie Matérielle*', *French Forum*, Vol. 23, No. 3 (September 1998), pp. 337–52.

Amelia Gamoneda Lanza, *Marguerite Duras: la textura del deseo*, Salamanca, Universidad de Salamanca, 1995.

Deborah Glassman, *Marguerite Duras: Fascinating Vision and Narrative Cure*, Cranbury NJ and London, Associated University Presses, 1991.

Yvonne Guers-Villate, *Continuité/discontinuité de l'oeuvre durassienne*, Brussels, Editions de l'Université de Bruxelles, 1985.

Daniel Gunn, *Psychoanalysis and Fiction: an exploration of literary and psychoanalytical borders*, Cambridge, Cambridge University Press, 1988, pp. 124–32.

Renate Günther, *Duras,* Le ravissement de Lol V. Stein *and* L'amant, London, Grant & Cutler 'Critical guides to French texts', 1993.

——, 'Liquid Passions: Marguerite Duras', *Romance Studies*, No. 29 (Spring 1997), pp. 21–33.

——, 'Alcoholism, melancholia and transgression: Margurite Duras' *Moderato cantabile*', *Modern and Contemporary France*, NS4, No. 2 (1996), pp. 171–81.

Marie-Paule Ha, 'Duras on the Margins', *The Romanic Review*, Vol. 83, No. 3 (1993), pp. 299–320.

——, *Figuring the East: Segalen, Malraux, Duras, and Barthes*, Albany, State University of New York Press, 2000.

——, 'Engendering French Colonial History: The Case of Indochina', *Historical Reflections/Réflexions Historiques*, Vo. 25, No. 1 (1999), pp. 95–125.

Mairéad Hanrahan, 'Je est une autre: of Rimbaud and Duras', *Modern Language Notes*, Vol. 113 (1998), pp. 915–36.

Robert Harvey and Hélène Volat, *Marguerite Duras: a bio-bibliography*, Westport CT, Greenwood Press, 1997.

Stella Harvey and Kate Ince (eds), *Duras Femme du Siècle*, Amsterdam, Rodopi, 2000.

Owen Heathcote, 'Masochism, Sadism,, and Women's Writing: The Examples of Marguerite Duras and Monique Wittig', *Nottingham French Studies*, Vol. 32, No. 2 (Autumn 1993) pp. 71–84.

——, 'Violence and Gender: Representation and Containment', *Journal of the Institute of Romance Studies*, No. 5 (1997), pp. 255–60.

Nina Hellerstein, 'Phenomenological Structures in Duras's Cinema: The Universe of *Nathalie Granger*', *Dalhousie French Studies*, No. 44 (1998), pp. 135–46.

Ralph Heyndels and Danielle Bajomée (eds), *Ecrire, dit-elle. Imaginaires de Marguerite Duras*, Brussels, Editions de l'Université de Bruxelles, 1985.

Lynn A. Higgins, *New Novel, New Wave, New Politics: Fiction and the Representation of History in Postwar France*, Lincoln NE and London, University of Nebraska Press, 1996, pp. 137–38.

Leslie Hill, 'Marguerite Duras and the limits of fiction', *Paragraph*, Vol. 12, No. 1 (March 1989), pp. 1–22.

——, 'Marguerite Duras: Sexual Difference and Tales of Apocalypse', *Modern Language Review*, No. 84 (1989), pp. 601–14.

——, 'Lacan with Duras', *Journal of the Institute of Romance Studies*, No. 1 (1992), pp. 405–24.

——, *Marguerite Duras: Apocalyptic Desires*, London and New York, Routledge, 1993.

Marianne Hirsch, *The Mother/Daughter Plot. Narrative, Psychoanalysis, Feminism*, Bloomington and Indianapolis, Indiana University Press, 1989, pp. 146–54.

——, 'Gender, Reading, and Desire in *Moderato Cantabile*', *Twentieth-Century Literature*, Vol. 28, No. 1 (Spring 1982), pp. 69–85.

Carol Hofmann, *Forgetting and Marguerite Duras*, Niwot CO, University of Colorado Press, 1991.

Diana Holmes, *French Women's Writing 1848–1994*, London, Athlone, 1996, pp. 231–45.

Christine Holmlund, 'Displacing Limits of Difference: Gender, Race, and Colonialism in Edward Said and Homi Bhabha's Theoretical Models and Marguerite Duras's Experimental Films', *Quarterly Review of Film and Video*, Vol. 13, Nos 1–3 (1991), pp. 1–22.

Kathleen Hulley, 'Contaminated Narratives: The Politics of Form and Subjectivity in Marguerite Duras's *The Lover*', *Discourse*, Vol. 15, No. 2 (Winter 1992–93), pp. 30–50.

Nancy Huston, 'Erotic Literature in Postwar France', *Raritan*, Vol. 12, No. 1 (Summer 1992), pp. 29–45.

Yvonne Y. Hsieh, 'L'évolution du discours (anti-)colonialiste dans *Un barrage contre le Pacifique*, *L'Amant* et *L'Amant de la Chine du Nord* de Marguerite Duras', *Dalhousie French Studies*, No. 35 (1996), pp. 55–65.

Kate Ince, '*L'Amour La Mort*: The Eroticism of Marguerite Duras', in *French Erotic Fiction. Women's Desiring Writing, 1880–1990*, ed. Alex Hughes and Kate Ince, Oxford, Berg, 1996, pp. 147–73.

——, 'Woman, lover, daughter, mother: female genealogies in *Le navire Night* and *Savanah Bay*', in *Duras. Lectures plurielles*, ed. Rodgers and Udris, pp. 132–49.

—— and Stella Harvey (eds), *Duras Femme du Siècle*, Amsterdam, Rodopi, 2000.

Youssef Ishaghpour, *D'une image à l'autre. La nouvelle modernité au cinéma*, Paris, Denoël-Gonthier, 1982, pp. 225–98.

——, 'La voix et le miroir', in *Ecrire, dit-elle*, ed. Bajomée and Heyndels, pp. 99–108.

Gabriel Jacobs, 'Spectres of remorse: Duras's war-time autobiography', *Romance Studies*, No. 30 (Autumn 1997), pp. 47–57.

Alice Jardine, *Gynesis, Configurations of woman and modernity*, Ithaca, Cornell University Press, 1985, pp. 159–77.

Katharine A. Jensen, Afterword to Marguerite Duras and Xavière Gauthier, *Woman to Woman*, trans. Katharine A. Jensen, Lincoln and London, University of Nebraska Press, 1987, pp. 181–95.

Thierry Jutel, 'Marguerite Duras et le cinéma de la modernité: tout [est] ce qu'il n y'a pas dans *India Song*', *French Review*, Vol. 66, No. 4 (March 1993), pp. 638–47.

E. Ann Kaplan, 'Silence as female resistance in Marguerite Duras's *Nathalie Granger* (1972)', in *Women and Film. Both Sides of the Camera*, London and New York, Routledge, 1983, pp. 91–103.

Adèle King, *French Women Novelists: defining a female style*, New York, St Martin's Press, 1989.

Bettina Knapp (ed.), *Critical Essays on Marguerite Duras*, New York, G. K. Hall, 1998.

Doris Kolesch, *Marguerite Duras*, Munich, Edition Text und Kritik, 1996.

Julia Kristeva, *Soleil noir: dépression et mélancolie*, Paris, Gallimard, 1987, pp. 227–65; *Black Sun: Depression and Melancholia*, trans. Léon Roudiez, New York, Columbia University Press, 1980, pp. 219–61.

——, 'Une étrangère', *La Nouvelle Revue Française*, No. 542 (March 1998), Special Issue: Marguerite Duras, pp. 3–9.

Jacques Lacan, 'Hommage fait à Marguerite Duras du *Ravissement de Lol V. Stein*', *Cahiers Renaud-Barrault*, No. 52 (December 1965), pp. 7–15 (reprinted in *Marguerite Duras* (1979), ed. Barat and Farges, pp. 131–37).

Suzanne Lamy and André Roy (eds), *Marguerite Duras à Montréal*, Montreal, Editions Spirale, 1981.

Nancy Lane, 'Duras and Cardinal: Writing the (M)Other', *French Forum*, Vol. 24, No. 2 (May 1999), pp. 215–32.

Frédérique Lebelley, *Duras ou le poids d'une plume*, Paris, Grasset, 1994.

Susan H. Leger, 'Marguerite Duras's Cinematic Spaces', *Women and Literature*, ed. Janet Todd, New York and London, Holmes and Meier, 1988.

Maurice Lemaître, *Marguerite Duras. Pour en finir avec cet escroc et plagiaire géneralisée*, Paris, Centre de Créativité, 1979.

Aimée Leon, 'Analyse Critique de *L'Amant*, *L'Amant de la Chine du Nord* et *La Douleur* dans un contexte socio-politique', unpublished dissertation, MA in Contemporary French Studies, London Guildhall University, June 1997.

Marie-Thérèse Ligot, *Marie-Thérèse Ligot présente* Un barrage contre le Pacifique *de Marguerite Duras*, Paris, Gallimard, 1992.

Najet Limam-Tnani, *Roman et cinéma chez Marguerite Duras. Une poétique de la spécularité*, Tunis, Faculté des Sciences humaines et sociales/Alif-Les Editions de la Méditerranée, 1986.

Mary Lydon, 'Translating Duras: *The Seated Man in the Passage*', *Contemporary Literature*, No. 24 (Summer 1983), pp. 113–26.

——, 'The Forgetfulness of Memory: Jacques Lacan, Marguerite Duras and the Text', *Comparative Literature*, No. 29 (1988), pp. 351–68.

Elisabeth Lyon, 'The Cinema of Lol. V. Stein', *camera obscura*, No. 6 (Fall 1980), pp. 9–39.

Magazine littéraire, Nos 158 (1980) and 278 (June 1990), Special Issues: Marguerite Duras.

Christiane P. Makward, 'For a stylistics of Marguerite Duras', *L'Esprit Créateur*, Vol. 30, No. 1 (Spring 1990), pp. 28–39.

Michèle Manceaux, *L'amie*, Paris, Albin Michel, 1997.

——, *Brèves: Journal*, Paris, Seuil, 1984.

Marcelle Marini, *Territoires du féminin. Avec Marguerite Duras*, Paris, Minuit, 1977.

——, 'La mort d'une érotique', *Cahiers Renaud-Barrault*, No. 106 (1983), pp. 37–57.

——, 'L'autre corps', in *Ecrire, dit-elle*, ed. Bajomée and Heyndels, pp. 21–48.

Robert Lawrence Mazzola, 'Emerging from the Shadows: Fratricidal Moves in Marguerite Duras' early Fiction', *Dalhousie French Studies*, No. 33 (Winter 1995), pp. 113–23.

Lucy Stone McNeece, *Art and Politcs in Duras's India Cycle*, Gainesville FL, University Press of Florida, 1996.

Dean McWilliams, 'Aesthetic Tripling: Marguerite Duras's *Le Navire Night*,' *Literature/Film Quarterly*, Vol. 12, No. 2 (1984), pp. 122–28.

Elizabeth A. Meese, 'Re:writing "The Other" in Marguerite Duras's *The Lover*', in *Ex(tensions): Refiguring the Other*, Urbana IL, University of Illinois Press, 1990, pp. 78–96.

Pierre Mertens, *L'agent double. Sur Duras, Gracq, Kundera etc.*, Paris, Complexe, 1989.

Vicki Mistacco, '*Plus ça change* …: The Critical Reception to *Emily L.*', *The French Review*, Vol. 66, No. 1 (October 1992), pp. 77–88.

Michèle Montrelay, *L'Ombre et le nom. Sur la feminité*, Paris, Minuit, 1977, pp. 9–23.

Janice Morgan, 'Fiction and Autobiography/Language and Silence: *L'Amant* by Duras', *French Review*, Vol. 63, No. 2 (1989), pp. 271–79.

——, 'The *caméra-stylo* of Marguerite Duras: The Translation of a Literary Aesthetic into Film', *Perspectives in Contemporary Literature*, No. 13 (1987), pp. 33–40.

George Moskos, 'Child's Play: Repetition and Death in Duras's *Savannah Bay*', *Neophilologus*, No. 77 (1993), pp. 215–21.

——, 'Odd Coupling: Duras (Reflects) on Balzac', *Contemporary Literature*, Vol. 32, No. 4 (Winter 1991), pp. 520–33.

Carol J. Murphy, *Alienation and Absence in the Novels of Marguerite Duras*, Lexington KY, French Forum Publishers, 1982.
——, 'New narrative regions: The role of desire in the films and novels of Marguerite Duras', *Literature/Film Quarterly*, Vol. 12, No. 2 (1984), pp. 122–28.
——, 'Duras's "Beast in the Jungle": Writing Fear (or Fear of Writing) in *Emily L.*', *Neophilologus*, No. 75 (1991), pp. 539–47.

Dominique Noguez, 'La gloire des mots', *L'Arc*, No. 98, 1985, pp. 25–39.
Mary Noonan, 'The Spatialization of loss in the Theatre of Marguerite Duras', *Theatre Research International*, Vol. 23, No. 3 (1998), pp. 215–24.
Panivong Norindr, '"Errances" and Memories in Duras's Colonial Cities', *differences*, Vol. 5, No. 3 (1993), pp. 52–78.
——, *Fantasmatic Indochina: French Colonial Ideology in Architecture, Cinema, and Literature*, Durham NC, Duke University Press, 1996.
La Nouvelle Revue Française, No. 542 (March 1998), Special Issue: Marguerite Duras.

John O'Brien, 'Metaphor between Lacan and Duras: Narrative Knots and the Plot of Seeing', *Forum for Modern Language Studies*, Vol. 27, No. 3 (1993), pp. 59–70.
Raylene O'Callaghan, 'The art of the (im)possible', *Australian Journal of French Studies*, No. 25 (1988), pp. 71–90.
Irène Oore, '*La Vie Matérielle* de Marguerite Duras, "aller-et-retour entre moi et moi, entre vous et moi": Réflexions sur le mouvement du texte', *Dalhousie French Studies*, No. 17 (1989), pp. 47–53.

Leopoldina Pallotta della Torre, *Marguerite Duras. La passione sospesa*, Milan, La Tartaruga, 1989.
Irène Pagès (ed.), *Marguerite Duras: dans les trous du discours*, Les Cahiers de l'Association des professeurs de français des universités et collèges canadiens, Série II, No. 1 (1987).
Liliane Papin, *L'Autre Scène: Le Théâtre de Marguerite Duras*, Saratoga, Anma Libri, 1988.
——, 'Place of Writing, Place of Love', in *Remains to be Seen*, ed. Ames, pp. 81–94.
René Payant, 'L'impossible voix', in *Duras à Montréal*, ed. Lamy and Roy, pp. 157–69.
François Peraldi, 'Waiting for the father: incidence of an interpretation on the work of Marguerite', in *Remains to be Seen*, ed. Ames, pp. 31–50.
John Phillips, 'The mathematics of meaning: Marguerite Duras's *Moderato cantabile*', *Nottingham French Studies*, Vol. 34, No. 2 (Autumn 1995), pp. 41–54.
Dennis Porter, 'Marguerite Duras: Autobiographical Acts, Celebrity Status', *Rousseau's Legacy: Emergence and Eclipse of the Writer in France*, Oxford, Oxford University Press, 1995, pp. 212–37.
Agnes Porter-Beaudry, '*Détruire dit-elle*: Destruction or Deconstruction', *International Fiction Review*, Vol. 8, No. 1 (1981), pp. 41–46.
Catherine Portuges, 'Love and Mourning in Duras's *Aurélia Steiner*', *L'Esprit Créateur*, Vol. 30, No. 1 (Spring 1990), pp. 28–39.
——, 'The Pleasures of *Nathalie Granger*', in *Remains to be Seen*, ed. Ames, pp. 219–29.

Patrick Rambaud, *Virginie Q. de Marguerite Duraille*, Paris, Balland, 1988.

Ilma Rakusa, *Marguerite Duras*, Frankfurt, Suhrkamp, 1988.

Raylene Ramsay, 'Through a Textual Glass, Darkly: The masochistic feminine self in Marguerite Duras's *Emily L.*', *Atlantis*, Vol. 17, No. 1 (1991), pp. 91–104.

——, *The French New Autobiographies: Sarraute, Duras, and Robbe-Grillet*, Gainesville FL, University Press of Florida, 1996.

Herman Rapaport, 'Durassian Extimacy', *Between the sign and the gaze*, Ithaca, Cornell University Presss, 1994, pp. 250–67.

Elena Real (ed.), *Marguerite Duras: Actes du Colloque International de Valènica*, València, Universitat de València, 1990.

James H. Reid, 'The Café Duras: Mourning Descriptive Space', *French Forum*, Vol. 19, No. 1 (January 1994), pp. 45–64.

Revue des Sciences Humaines, No. 202 (1986), Special Issue: Marguerite Duras.

Janine Ricouart, *Ecriture féminine et violence. Une étude de Marguerite Duras*, Birmingham AL, Summa Publications, 1991.

—— (ed.), *Marguerite Duras Lives On*, Lanham NY and Oxford, University Press of America, 1998.

Catherine Rodgers, '"Sublime, forcément sublime": The body in Duras's Texts', *Romance Studies*, No. 20 (Summer 1992), pp. 45–57.

——, 'Déconstruction de la masculinité dans l'oeuvre durassienne', in *Marguerite Duras: Rencontres de Cerisy*, ed. Vircondelet, pp. 47–68.

—— and Raynalle Udris (eds), *Marguerite Duras: Lectures Plurielles*, Amsterdam, Rodopi, 1998.

——, 'Lectures de la sorcière, ensorcellement de l'écriture', in *Duras. Lectures Plurielles*, ed. Rodgers and Udris, pp. 17–34.

——, '*Un homme est venu me voir* de Marguerite Duras: dédoublements, duplicités et ambiguïtés', in *Aspects of Twentieth-Century Theatre in French*, ed. M. Cardy et D. Connon, Bern, Peter Lang, 2000.

Judith Roof, 'Marguerite Duras and the Question of a Feminist Theater', in *Feminism and Psychoanalysis*, ed. Richard Feldstein and Judith Roof, Ithaca and London, Cornell University Press, 1989, pp. 323–40.

Marie-Claire Ropars-Wuilleumier, 'The Disembodied Voice: *India Song*', *Yale French Studies*, No. 60 (1980), pp. 241–68.

——, 'How history begets meaning: Alain Resnais' *Hiroshima mon amour* (1959)', in *French Film. Texts and Contexts*, ed. Susan Hayward and Ginette Vincendeau, London, Methuen, 1989, pp. 173–85.

Leon S. Roudiez, *French Fiction Revisited* (1972), Elmwood Park IL, Dalkey Archive Press, 1991, Chapter 4, 'Marguerite Duras' (pp. 68–90).

Lucie Roy, 'Marguerite Duras, scénariste exilée', *Etudes Littéraires*, Vol. 26, No. 2 (Autumn 1993), pp. 67–75.

——, 'Les réticences discursives à l'écran ou les voix négatives', in *Marguerite Duras: Recontres de Cerisy*, ed. Vircondelet, pp. 151–70.

Michelle Royer, *L'écran de la passion: une étude du cinéma de Marguerite Duras*, Mount Nebo, Queensland, Boombana Publications, 1997.

Pierre Saint-Amand, 'La Photographie de famille dans *L'Amant*', in *Marguerite Duras: Rencontres de Cerisy*, ed. Vircondelet, pp. 225–40.

Margaret Sankey, 'The Duras Phenomenon', *Australian Journal of French Studies*, Vol. 34, No. 1 (January–April 1997), pp. 60–76.

Marilyn R. Schuster, *Revisiting Duras*, New York, Twayne, 1993.

Trista Selous, 'A Triumph of the Will', *Free Associations*, No. 9 (August 1987), pp. 97–101.

——, *The Other Woman: Feminism and Femininity in the Work of Marguerite Duras*, New Haven and London, Yale University Press, 1988.

——, 'Marguerite and the Mountain', in *Contemporary French Fiction by Women*, ed. Margaret Atack and Phil Powrie, Manchester, Manchester University Press, 1990, pp. 84–95.

Jean-Luc Seylaz, *Les romans de Marguerite Duras: essai sur une thématique de la durée*, Paris, Lettres Modernes 'Archives des lettres modernes' No. 47, 1963.

Daniel Sibony, 'Repenser la déprime', *Magazine littéraire*, No. 244 (July–August 1987), Special Issue: 'Littérature et mélancolie', pp. 54–56.

Ann Smock, 'Learn to Read, She Said', *October*, No. 41 (Summer 1987), pp. 53–56.

Karen Smythe, 'The Scene of Seeing: Perception and Perversion in the *Ravishing of Lol V. Stein*', *Genders*, No. 6 (1989), pp. 49–59.

Philippe Sollers, 'Duras "Telle-Quelle"', *Le Nouvel Observateur*, 12 January 1970, p. 36.

——, 'Duras, par Sollers', *L'Evénement du Jeudi*, 3–9 September 1998, pp. 92–95.

Barbara Probst Solomon, 'Indochina mon amour', *The New Republic*, No. 3686, 9 September 1985, pp. 29–35

Sorcières, No. 1 (1976), Special Issue: Marguerite Duras.

Jean-Louis Sous, 'M. Duras ou le ravissement du réel', *Littoral*, No. 14 (1984), pp. 59–70.

H. Steinmetz-Schünemann, *Die Bedeutung der Zeit in den Romanen von Marguerite Duras*, Amsterdam, Rodopi, 1976 .

Catharine R. Stimpson, 'Marguerite Duras: A "W/Ringer's" Remarks', *L'Esprit Créateur*, Vol. 30, No. 1 (Spring 1990), pp. 15–18.

Susan Rubin Suleiman, 'Nadja, Dora, Lol V. Stein: Women, Madness, and Narrative', in *Discourse in Psychoanalysis and Literature*, ed. Sholmirh Rimmon-Kenan, New York, Methuen, 1988, pp. 124–51.

Jean-Marc Talpin, 'La fonction psychique du lecteur dans la poétique durassienne', in *Marguerite Duras: Rencontres de Cerisy*, ed. Vircondelet, pp. 117–42.

Lib Taylor, 'Soundtracks: The Soundscapes of *India Song*', *Theatre Research International*, Vol. 23, No. 3 (1998), pp. 215–14.

Charles Tesson, 'Des journées entières dans les classes', *Cahiers du Cinéma*, No. 370 (April 1985), pp. 54–56.

Chantal Théry, 'Marguerite Duras à Corps Perdu: La vie au fil de l'écriture, entre Androgynie et Anoréxie', *Etudes Litteraires*, Vol. 22, No. 2 (Autumn 1989), pp. 123–36.

Micheline Tison-Braun, *Marguerite Duras*, Amsterdam, Rodopi, 1985.

Mireille M. Truong Rootham, 'Mère/Mère patrie: Marguerite Duras et le colonialisme', *FRONTENAC*, No. 12 (1995), pp. 8–20.

Pamela Tytel, 'lacan, freud, et duras', *Magazine littéraire*, No. 158 (March 1980), pp. 14–15.

Raynalle Udris, *Welcome Unreason, A Study of 'Madness' in the Novels of Marguerite Duras*, Amsterdam, Rodopi, 1993.

—— and Catherine Rodgers (eds), *Marguerite Duras: Lectures Plurielles*, Amsterdam, Rodopi, 1998.

William F. Van Wert, 'The Cinema of Marguerite Duras: Sound and Voice in a Closed Room', *Literature/Film Quarterly*, Vol. 33, No. 1 (Fall 1979), pp. 22–29.

Alain Vircondelet, *Marguerite Duras ou le temps de détruire*, Paris, Seghers, 1972.

——, *Duras: Biographie*, Paris, François Bourin, 1991; *Duras: A biography*, trans. Thomas Buckley, Normal IL, Dalkey Archive Press, 1994.

——, (ed.), *Marguerite Duras: Rencontres de Cerisy*, Paris, Ecriture, 1994.

——, *Pour Duras*, Paris, Calmann-Lévy, 1995.

——, *Marguerite Duras: vérité et légendes*, Paris, Chêne, 1996.

—— (ed), *Duras, Dieu et l'écrit: Colloque international*, Paris, Rocher, 1998.

Hélène Volat and Robert Harvey, *Marguerite Duras: a bio-bibliography*, Westport CT, Greenwood Press, 1997.

David H. Walker, 'Consuming Passions: Marguerite Duras', Chapter 12, *Insight and Outrage: Modern French Writers and the 'Fait Divers'*, Oxford and New York, Berg, 1995.

Julia Waters, *Intersexual Rivalry: A 'Reading in Pairs' of Marguerite Duras and Alain Robbe-Grillet*, Bern, Peter Lang, 2000.

Charlotte Wardi, 'L'oubli du génocide dans le roman français de 1945 à 1970', *Les Nouveaux Cahiers*, No. 58 (Autumn 1979), pp. 4–9.

James S. Williams, *The Erotics of Passage: Pleasure, Politics, and Form in the Later Work of Marguerite Duras*, Liverpool University Press/St Martin's Press, 1997.

——, '*Le système D.*—"le malheur merveilleux": Marguerite Duras and the erotic crimes of montage in *Le camion* and *Aurélia Steiner*', *Paragraph*, No. 15 (1992), pp. 38–72.

——, 'A Beast of a Closet: the sexual differences of literary collaboration in the work of Marguerite Duras and Yann Andréa', *Modern Language Review*, Vol. 87 (July 1992), pp. 576–84.

——, 'Marguerite Duras: "La mort du jeune aviateur anglais"', in *Short French Fiction: Essays on the Short Story in France in the Twentieth Century*, ed. John Flower, Exeter, Exeter University Press, 1998, pp. 102–21.

——, 'The Point of No Return: chiastic adventures between self and other in Marguerite Duras's *Les Mains Négatives*', in *Marguerite Duras: Lectures Plurielles*, ed. Rodgers and Udris, pp. 77–94.

——, 'All Her Sons: Marguerite Duras, Anti-literature and the Outside', *Yale French Studies*, No. 90 (Winter 1996/7), pp. 47–70.

Sharon Willis, *Writing on the Body*, Urbana and Chicago, University of Illinois Press, 1986.

Emma Wilson, '"Mon histoire de Lol V. Stein": Duras, Reading, and Amnesia', *Sexuality and the Reading Encounter: Identity and Desire in Proust, Duras, Tournier and Cixous*, Oxford, Clarendon Press, 1996, pp. 163–91.

Jane Winston, 'Forever Feminine: Marguerite Duras and Her French Critics', *New Literary History*, Vol. 24, No. 2 (Spring 1993), pp. 467–82.

——, 'Marguerite Duras: Marxism, Feminism, Writing', *Theatre Journal*, No. 47 (1995) pp. 345–65.

Winifred Woodhull, 'Marguerite Duras and the question of community', *Modern Language Studies*, Vol. 17, No. 1 (Winter 1987), pp. 3–16.

Pierre Yana, 'Enonciation d'un crime', *Revue des Sciences Humaines*, No. 202 (April–June 1986), pp. 153–66.